COLLABORATIVE COMMUNITIES

Cohousing, Central Living, and Other New Forms of Housing with Shared Facilities

Dorit Fromm

 VAN NOSTRAND REINHOLD
New York

For Peter Bosselman

Every effort has been made to make the information in this book as complete and accurate as possible, but the author and publisher are not responsible for any errors or omissions, and no warranty or fitness is implied.

This book is sold with the understanding that the author and publisher are not engaged in rendering professional advice or services to the reader. Neither author nor publisher shall bear liability or responsibility to any person or entity with respect to any loss or damage arising from information contained in this book.

Copyright © 1991 by Dorit Fromm
Library of Congress Catalog Card Number 90-44673
ISBN 0-442-23785-5

Printed in the United States of America.

Van Nostrand Reinhold
115 Fifth Avenue
New York, New York 10003

Chapman and Hall
2-6 Boundary Row
London, SE1 8HN, England

Thomas Nelson Australia
102 Dodds Street
South Melbourne 3205
Victoria, Australia

Nelson Canada
1120 Birchmount Road
Scarborough, Ontario MIK 5G4, Canada

16 15 14 13 12 11 10 9 8 7 6 5 4 3 2 1

Library of Congress Cataloging-in-Publication Data
Fromm, Dorit.
    Collaborative communities: cohousing, central living, and other new forms of housing with shared facilities/Dorit Fromm.
        p.   cm.
    Includes bibliographical references and index.
    ISBN 0-442-23785-5
    1. Shared housing—Europe. 2. Shared housing—United States.
3. Community life. I. Title.
HD7287.86.E85F76 1991
363.5'8—dc20
                                                                    90-44673
                                                                    CIP

Contents

Acknowledgments

This book would not have been written without the continued support of the National Endowment for the Arts. The three sparks that started my investigation on the architecture of communities were my work in Mexicali with Christopher Alexander; the insights of John Habraken, my teacher at MIT; and the enthusiasm of Jan Gehl, Professor at the Royal Danish Academy in Copenhagen. A special thanks goes to Clare Cooper Marcus who helped this kindling to light.

During my travels many people shared their thoughts, meals, and homes with me. In Holland Robbi, B. J. Fris, the Schippers, Beatrice Kessler, and Flip Krabbendam gave me new ways to look at collaborative communities. In Sweden, Axel Ruhe, Lars Ågren, the Sundelins, Karen Palm-Lindén, Ville Herlin, Inga-Lisa Sangregorio, and Dick Urban Vestbro gave a stranger who showed up at their doors both their time and insights. In Denmark, Ole Svensson made room for me in Sættedammen, and Jan Gudmand-Høyer and Angel Colom opened the way to Skråplanet. Cara Seiderman and Liselotte Kragh helped in the cohousing research. In all three countries, numerous residents invited me to stay, and spent many hours discussing issues of collaborative living.

Todd Bresi was kind enough to read parts of the book in manuscript and offer helpful criticism, as did Suzane Chun. Brigetta Garde and Els Burger provided expert help in translations. The Ecumenical Association for Housing kindly provided a base for my research—my thanks to Mary Murtagh, Elizabeth Moody, and the knowledgeable Al Bonnett.

A thanks to the steadfast Muir Commons group whose discussions provided a clear view into many collaborative issues and whose efforts have set a standard for the communities to come. The perceptive members, especially the Ingels and Jeff Gottesman, were generous with their research and time.

I owe particular thanks to Lilian Bovinkel in Copenhagen and Thor Balkhed in Linkoping for photographs that capture "living the difference." Kevin Gilson provided photographic aid in sifting and converting my numerous slides. Brian Gotwals gave drafting assistance.

Peter Bosselmann and Paul Lukez spent many hours transforming my original scenario designs into solid architecture. Their insights and ideas helped shape the scenario chapter a great deal. I especially owe Peter an enormous debt of thanks that words cannot repay. When I stand at the periphery, he sees clear to the core.

Finally, this book could not have been completed without the help and baby-sitting support of friends—Mare, Rich, Ellen, and Aracely—and the support of my family—Leona, Anat, Leora, and Betty.

Entrance to the common house. *(Lilian Bolvinkel)*

Introduction

In the cold winter of 1985, I visited Denmark searching for a housing community that had been described to me in glowing terms. Residents planned and organized the community themselves; aside from their own private homes, they shared outdoor areas and a common house with workshops, play areas, and a dining hall. Since 1980 I have been researching, designing, and writing about housing that emphasizes community. Having firsthand experience with both the isolation of the suburban home and the impracticalities of sharing housing, long term, with several other adults, I was very interested in housing forms that balanced privacy and community. As a designer I had been taught how to create privacy, but community was, and is, a gray area in planning and architecture. The best of intentions among residents or architects does not guarantee success. I was therefore excited by what my Danish friends described, but somewhat skeptical about these communities where residents collaborate together. Were they really successful, and why?

Sættedammen, the first of over ninety of these collaborative communities, was about an hour's train ride out of Copenhagen in one of the satellite towns outside the city. But by the time I had finally located the right street, lined with suburban houses, and then the entrance to Sættedammen, a driveway flanked by covered car parking, my eagerness had decreased considerably. I glimpsed snow-covered row houses, with flat roofs and balconies, looking ludicrously Mediterranean. The common house, tucked behind a small building that turned out to house a woodworking room and furnace, seemed, to say the least, unimposing.

Hearing people talking and laughing, I walked inside the common house and turned into a large dining room. On one side was an open kitchen, and one of the residents was standing in front of a large pot, with puffs of steam rising around the lid. Loaves of freshly baked bread were cooling on the counter nearby. Children and adults sat in the wonderfully warm dining room, relaxing and talking; a few children were playing a game and the cook was chopping vegetables and stirring the steaming pot of soup. Someone told me they all had gone out on a ski trip and had just returned. I was invited to stay for dinner.

The sensation I felt on that afternoon is hard to describe. The comfort and familiarity was simultaneously exotic and rare—to be within a community that works. Neighbors had conversations with each other, children of different ages happily played together, and the food was plentiful, served and removed in a relaxed yet efficient way. After dinner, the kids disappeared into the game room while the adults lingered over coffee.

Here was something that Americans—and not just architects and planners—were talking of creating yet never seemed to get off the ground. In collaborative communities, such as Sættedammen, the residents plan and manage the housing. They maintain a balance between privacy and community through individual dwellings and a well-used common house. Although there have always been a number of intentional communities in the United States—sharing a common purpose of personal, religious, or social change—they are usually rural, and many attempt to escape from society or be self-sufficient. But Sættedammen was planned by residents who are very much a part of society—teachers, administrators, and social workers were among the original group. The autonomy of the private household was central to their planning.

From that visit, in January 1985, to this book has been a long journey of five years, and I retrace many of my steps in the three parts that follow. I quickly discovered that European collaborative housing is not tied to a specific building type or ownership. Nor is it unique to Denmark as I learned through my research in Holland and Sweden. Indeed, collaborative communities are varied in the way they are developed, in their size, and in their goals, with more radical and experimental communities found outside Denmark, often developed by nonprofit housing organizations that rent them to tenants of mixed incomes.

Part One describes an overview of Danish, Dutch, and Swedish cohousing. I describe several Danish communities, called *bofælles-skaber* or cohousing. The Dutch call them *centraal wonen,* with the first rental community, Hilversumse Meent, built in 1977, followed by an additional fifty-four communities. In Sweden, the name is *kollektivhus;* the first was a high rise, Stacken, renovated in 1980, followed by twenty-seven more collaborative communities since then. These first models set the parameters for the almost two

hundred developments that can now be found in Denmark, Holland, and Sweden.

Germany, Austria, France, Belgium, and Switzerland have a similar type of housing but do not usually include common dining. There are over a hundred of these communities in those countries, ranging from a small six-family community in Belgium to a large apartment building with more than a hundred units in Germany. The more I traveled in Europe, and the heavier my bookshelves became with French, Danish, Dutch, Swedish, and German texts, the more I began to wonder whether such communities existed in the United States.

Part Two describes the examples in the United States I found in my search. Although I uncovered many interesting leads, none in the end led to the type of collaborative housing I found in Sweden, Denmark, and the Netherlands. Instead, cousins appeared, closely resembling the European communities. Their individual stories seem to provide a preview of the kinds of issues American developments will likely face.

If collaborative housing did not exist in the United States, could the idea be transplanted? Just as Danish, Swedish, and Dutch developments differ in response to their specific cultural and economic environments, it seems likely that American communities will not be replicas of the European models. Chapter 9 presents four imaginary housing sites to model a few of the many possibilities for U.S. collaborative communities. Yet from my studies of Sættedammen and other European and American examples, I believe it is unlikely that any one of these four scenarios would function as cohousing without the participation of future residents in the planning and development, a process that seems very foreign to the way multiunit housing is designed and developed today in the United States (and, frankly, a process most architects and developers would be rather reluctant to undertake because of their unfamiliarity with the concept and the extra costs involved).

In Part Three, I give an overview of the housing development process from the time a group forms. I found two groups that had begun building cohousing-type communities on the West Coast—one near Sacramento and the other near Seattle. As I looked at their struggles and the issues the other communities I researched had faced, a composite process of development emerged that made sense in the United States. Although not every issue is discussed, this last nuts-and-bolts part covers the fundamentals from forming a core group to moving in.

Sættedammen, the first cohousing community, was considered radical when the families moved in almost twenty years ago, not knowing what to expect. Today, that community is considered conservative, a granddaddy set in its ways.

Within the next decade or two, different collaborative communities will appear in the United States, and what seems idealistic or impractical today can become a realistic option for housing ourselves.

One

European Collaborative Housing

These are my cooperative duties:

Cleaning: two hours every ninth week.
Cooking: four hours in November, February, and April.
Meeting: three hours once a month.

In exchange, there is dinner for the family twice a week at the common house. There are facilities for laundry and child care, a library, and a sewing and TV room. There is a large garden, fresh vegetables, and eggs. Together things are purchased that cannot be afforded alone. Children can play with friends by just going out the door, and the neighbors here also become friends.
Mrs. Ziebell, Æblevangen cohousing, Denmark

One- and two-story row houses and small front yards face the pedestrian street. Trudeslund cohousing, Denmark. *(Lilian Bolvinkel)*

CHAPTER 1

What Is Collaborative Housing?

The idea for collaborative housing began in the 1960s when a group of friends began talking about their living situation and realized they shared similar problems. Most were too busy working to have much time to spend with their friends, and when they came home from work, their time was taken up with cooking, cleaning, and washing. Their children spent too much time watching TV, often because no other children their age lived in the neighborhood. The kind of housing these people could afford was either isolated in suburbia or too dense and urban. They felt there had to be a better way. When they talked about the kind of place they would like to live in—good housing, lots of trees, a big playground, and many amenities all in a safe neighborhood—they realized the benefits they could gain by developing housing together.

In collaborative housing, each household has its own house or apartment and one share in the common facilities, which typically include a fully equipped kitchen, play areas, and meeting rooms. Residents share cooking, cleaning, and gardening on a rotating basis. By working together and combining their resources, collaborative housing residents can have the advantages of a private home and the convenience of shared services and amenities.

Many residents I interviewed believe that the greatest strength of this form of housing is that it creates not only a home but a small community as they actively participate in its development and management.

Sættedammen, built in 1972, was the first collaborative development. This Danish variety has row houses, with common facilities in a separate common house. Fifty-four adults, and almost as many children, were both excited and apprehensive when they moved in. "We didn't know what to expect . . . whether all our ideas and hopes would work," said one resident. Another cohousing development, Skråplanet, soon followed. Departing from the detached single-family home, the residents in these two communities pioneered new ideas of living collaboratively. Their methods influenced the many communities that have since followed.

All the elements of collaborative housing can be seen in Sættedammen:[1]

- Common facilities
- Private dwellings
- Resident-structured routines

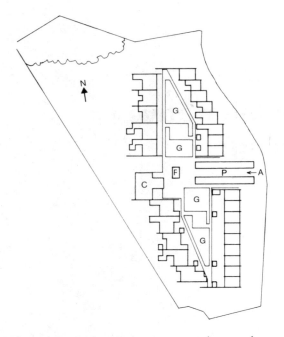

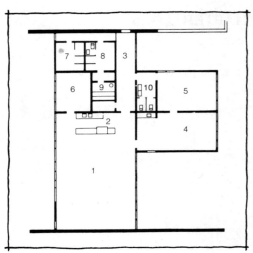

Plan of common house. *(SBI)*

1. Dining-meeting room; 2. kitchen; 3. entrance hall; 4. teen/billiard room; 5. TV room; 6. game room; 7. laundry; 8. showers; 9. sauna; 10. bathroom.

Sættedammen has twenty-seven row houses, facing inward and grouped around two common open spaces. *(SBI)*

A = access; P = parking; C = common house; G = shared green; F = workshop-central heating.

Sættedammen row house floor plan, first and second floors. *(SBI)*

1. Kitchen-dining room; 2. living room; 3. study-bedroom; 4. bathroom; 5. bedroom; 6. deck; 7. front yard; 8. back yard; 9. trellis-expansion area.

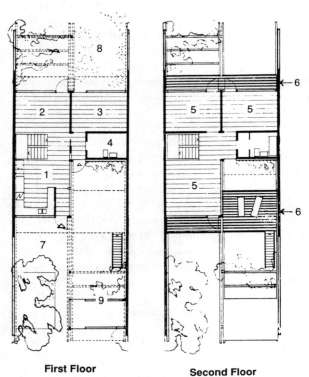

First Floor   **Second Floor**

30'/10 m

- Resident management
- Design for social contact
- Resident participation in the development process
- Pragmatic social objectives

COMMON FACILITIES

Most of the shared facilities in Sættedammen are centrally located in the common house and used daily. Here evening meals are prepared and eaten, films are shown at night, children are watched in the afternoon, and coffee is shared on Sunday mornings.

The Sættedammen residents found that possibilities arose for shared use of facilities and services among twenty-seven families— laundry room, a sauna, play areas, parking, and a central heating facility that provides heat at reduced cost.

In order to afford to build the common facilities, the floor area of each residence was reduced slightly, by 7%. The cost savings of this reduced floor area was "donated" toward the construction of the common house. "I admit we were cautious. We weren't sure how it would work out—how much we would do in common and how much would be done in the family, so we built a common house, and, just in case, houses so big we could function alone," explained a resident.

In the years since, other communities have realized that many everyday activities can be done in common, and the amount of donated floor space has averaged 10-15%, with common houses typically larger than that at Sættedammen. They include spaces that are not readily found in affordable housing today: saunas, darkrooms, soundproof music rooms, a hangout for teenagers, business rooms with computers and photocopiers, tennis courts and swimming pools, gyms, guest rooms, and cafés. By residents' pooling resources, spaces that are usually found only in the public or commercial realm are affordable and made semiprivate.

PRIVATE DWELLINGS

The private dwelling in Sættedammen reflects a new duality; it sustains the household and permits the creation of common areas. Each dwelling contains a kitchen, living-dining room, and one or more bedrooms and baths, but the layout of the home is reshuffled to reflect community priorities. The kitchen and dining areas are moved to the front of the dwelling and visually connected to the common areas. Residents can work in their kitchens and see who is passing by or keep an eye on young children playing in the commons. Bedrooms and the living room are oriented toward the back of the house for privacy.

Sættedammen's row houses rival suburban single-family houses in spaciousness, with 1,500-2,422 square feet (140-225 square meters). More recent communities, such as Andedammen, have dwellings ranging from 538 square feet to 1,313 square feet (50-122 square meters).[2] Recent cohousing dwellings are smaller than in the past because of rising housing costs and residents' preference for larger common houses. The largest space reductions have occurred in the kitchen, dining room, and living room because the common facilities have taken over some of those functions. The kitchen is shorn of large refrigerators, bulky freezers, surplus storage, and sometimes several stove burners as well. The washer and dryer, as well as storage, move out of the private and into the common sphere. The living room is smaller because common meeting space is available. The snipping away of private area continues: the workshop in the garage, the hobby room, the playroom, the den or TV room, the guest room, the library—every cohousing community has some of these rooms as part of the common amenities, and a large number have almost all of them.

The individual dwellings and the common amenities have a symbiotic relationship. So that the common spaces may exist, the dwellings give up some space and are redesigned smaller and tighter. The dwellings, in turn,

The kitchen has been reduced in size and combined with the dining area in an open floor plan: Tinggården I, Denmark. *(Vandkunsten Architects)*

The open floor plan brings light into the interior of this row house. *(Vandkunsten Architects)*

owe their increased utility to the common spaces because they are too small to function well alone.

RESIDENT-STRUCTURED ROUTINES

The essence of collaborative housing is that community is created by meeting everyday needs in a communal way. The most straightforward and utilitarian chores—cooking, watching children, sweeping the walkway—provide the opportunity to meet neighbors, talk, and develop relationships.

Preparation of shared evening meals at the common house is a routine that saves each household shopping, cooking, and cleaning for its own supper. "It's perfect, especially when you have come home from a long day of work," said one resident, "and when I don't feel like going [to the common house], I just take the food home."

The meals are inexpensive ($2-3 per adult), with a great variety of cooking styles and food. Common dining is normally voluntary, but cooking, about once a month, often a requirement. There are three basic ways

that residents organize common dining: the dinner club, where three to four households rotate dining at each other's house (say, every Sunday one family will cook and clean for two or three others); eating groups, where different groups of about six to ten households dine at the common house, with one household preparing the meal; and a residential cooking crew that prepares dinner for all the households to eat together at the common house from one to five times a week.

Sharing evening meals began as a social activity and has moved toward greater task cooperation.[3] The Sættedammen residents had intended from the beginning to share some evening meals, and they organized by dividing themselves into small eating groups. There is a Monday, a Tuesday, a Wednesday, and a Thursday eating group and a gourmet group on Sundays. Typically people sign up to eat communally once or twice a week. No money is exchanged. Some residents may be able to afford to cook fancier meals, and this is accepted. In Skråplanet, a cohousing community built in 1973, the common meal is also organized among eating groups. Each group has six families who eat together about once a week and rotate cooking among them-

Dinner at the common house. Residents choose how many meals a month they wish to eat together. Trudeslund cohousing, Denmark. *(Lilian Bolvinkel)*

Residents rotate in cooking crews that prepare dinner at the common house six days a week. Savværket cohousing, Denmark. *(Lilian Bolvinkel)*

selves. To reduce cleaning up, each family brings its own dishes to the common house and takes them back home to wash.

The following generations of cohousing have larger common houses, where the whole community can eat. In Jystrup Savværket (1985), common evening meals are available for all households six nights a week, and residents choose the days they would like to eat.[4] The food preparation is organized around cooking crews (half a dozen adults and several children per crew) that cook one week in seven. In this community, money is collected from all who eat and distributed to those who shopped.

Although some residents prefer to prepare their own meals, they can participate in the community in other ways, for example, by serving on committees that oversee maintenance, gardening, child care, or other tasks.

RESIDENT MANAGEMENT

Management responsibility is shared among the residents. The group decides on rules and policies to govern the community and criteria for new members. Although some communities have a board of directors, its decision-making power is limited to bookkeeping and organizational and secretarial tasks. All major decisions are made by the entire community of residents.

Sættedammen residents meet monthly to decide issues through a process of direct democracy and mutual agreements. Making decisions together was at first difficult; now the process is well organized:

At first we felt that everyone should discuss everything, and it took hours and hours and hours. After a while we discovered that one or two people could research it, and if they have a suggestion, we follow it. We now have another attitude toward the democracy, of having a high degree of confidence in the group.

This same sort of organization can be found in collaborative communities developed as nonprofit rentals, such as Hilver-sumse Meent in Holland. The tenants there have much more influence than is traditionally granted to renters. Their management and maintenance work (with the cooperation from the housing agency) result in cost savings for them, as well as a greater satisfaction with the housing.

Disagreements among residents usually are resolved within the community rather than by lawyer, managing company, or housing authority. Residents understand their responsibility in dealing with problems.

DESIGN FOR SOCIAL CONTACT

The emphasis on community transcends sharing common facilities and management. The layout of the development is designed to bring residents in daily contact with one another. The social contact emphasized in the design includes contact between individual residents, between residents and the cohousing community, and between the cohousing community and the public.

Residents are brought into contact with other residents in many subtle ways. Sættedammen residents must park their cars at the periphery of the site. Walking to their homes, they have a chance to stop and chat with other residents. The car-free interior area allows children to play and visit the homes of neighboring friends on their own.

The design of the housing encourages a flow from the private spaces to the semiprivate porch and front yard, These soft edges are another important design feature that allow residents a place to sit, stand, or work and still be connected to common activities going on around them (Gehl).

Residents are also brought into contact with the cohousing community through the use of the common house and outdoor areas. These common areas are centrally located so that residents can walk by and easily see what is going on. In Sættedammen, residents pass by the common areas on their way in and out of the development, which allows them to see if any events are going on without having to commit themselves or make a special trip.

Socializing and helping between residents is increased by creating soft edges (places to sit, see, and linger) between the private residence and the more public areas. In Savværket cohousing, windows face out to a covered pedestrian street, and a wide raised sidewalk is provided for small furniture, storage, and sitting. Jystrup Savværket, Denmark. *(Lilian Bolvinkel)*

A variety of meeting areas allows residents to choose the amount of social contact they wish. The front porch and yard is a semipublic area—an informal place to meet, see, and be seen.

In contrast, the back yard of each dwelling is a more intimate and private area, where friends can meet for a quiet afternoon together. Sættedammen, Denmark.

The social contact between the community and the public varies among developments. Some residents do not want the public walking freely in and out of their common areas, but neither do they want to isolate themselves from the public. Danish cohousing tends to be introverted, and many of the older communities turned their back on the neighborhood around them. Now there are developments that share a play field, parking areas, or common facilities such as child care with the surrounding community. Sættedammen does not present a public front to the street; instead the entrance to the parking lot greets passing pedestrians. The more recent cohousing community of Kilen (1989) manages both to create a tight community and orient itself toward the surrounding neighborhood. Kilen dwellings face each other along an enclosed covered street. At one end, the community shares a parking area with other housing, and the other end of the street, where the common house is located, opens out to a public plaza.

Designs that emphasize gradual transitions among private, common, and public areas increase social opportunities (McCamant and Durrett). They also make it easy to carry out tasks in private and common areas simultaneously, such as working in the kitchen and watching several children or working around the house and keeping an eye on the common areas. Although social contact is emphasized, residents can find privacy in their own dwelling and back yard.

RESIDENT PARTICIPATION IN THE DEVELOPMENT PROCESS

Groups developing a cohousing community take an active role in its design. Cohousing is never generic; each community is tailored to a specific group's requirements. The development process is often difficult and includes organizing a core group, finding land, hiring architects, and obtaining financing. Certain stages are repeated in almost every development process.

Step 1. The idea is formulated, and a core group is formed. The idea for the first cohousing community began in 1964 when architect Jan Gudmand-Høyer and a group of friends met to discuss their housing options. Unhappy with living in the city or isolated in suburban one-family houses that "destroy the landscape and the soul," they agreed it was best to live close to each other in housing designed with their needs in mind (Gudmand-Høyer). This group of friends began to meet regularly.

Interest in the idea grew, and others started to talk and write about this new possibility for community. A few years after Gudmand-Høyer's group began, author Bodil Graae's article, "Children Should Have One Hundred Parents" (1967), emphasized building community with children. More than fifty people responded to the article, and a group formed to pursue such a community.

Step 2. Goals are agreed upon. Gudmand-Høyer and his friends wanted to create a community where there would be a "big supply of friends," the possibility of child care, common parking, and common activities. The site should be near the city but provide enough open area for children to play. Graae's group focused on a community where the adults would take care of all the children and where children could move freely and be welcome at any of the homes.

Step 3. Land is obtained. Once the basic goals were decided, the search for a site began. In 1964, Gudmand-Høyer's group had purchased land in an older residential neighborhood, but strong opposition from the neighbors eventually led the group to sell out. Frustrated and disappointed, a number of families left the group.[5] In 1968, Gudmand-Høyer, Graae, and a number of interested people joined together and found a site in a small village near Copenhagen. But once the site was chosen, a falling out occurred. Ideological questions as well as site preferences caused some members to form a new group, which eventually became the Sættedammen development.

This second group of five families, influenced by Graae, located a site and advertised for participants. Specific goals were agreed upon and tasks divided among small committees: contractual issues, child care, financing, and common facilities. Meetings were held four times a month, and a newsletter, published every two weeks, kept members up to date.

Step 4. Architectural plans are completed. The two groups worked alongside each other, exchanging ideas and information. The Sættedammen group hired architects who worked with them to design the community. Architects Teo Bjerg and Palle Dyreborg attended meetings, presented sketches, budgets, and proposals, and met with individual families regarding their dwellings.

Step 5. Contractors bid on the plans, and the housing is built. In the Sættedammen group, construction bids were received for the completed plans in 1970 but were too expensive. Amid accusations and recriminations, the original design was thrown out, and a more affordable solution was sought. A small committee then researched five possibilities, and in the spring of 1971, the whole group voted on one of these projects. In October 1972, twenty-seven families moved into Sættedammen.

The group led by Gudmand-Høyer was still grappling with high construction bids. But cutbacks in the design allowed construction to begin in 1972, and a year later thirty-three families moved into Skråplanet.

Over the past fifteen years, the initiation of and participation in the development have varied. In Sættedammen, the initiative was taken by the residents who own the housing under condominium ownership. In later communities, the initiative has also been taken by nonprofit housing organizations and government housing authorities. In both scenarios, the future residents retain a high degree of control. In the process, the traditional role of the resident has expanded, with the architect's role adapting to accommodate a multi-

headed client. The result is not necessarily a new type of architecture but is a better fit.

PRAGMATIC SOCIAL OBJECTIVES

Although cohousing has been strongly influenced by the collective movement of the 1960s and 1970s when many experimentations with new ways of living together were tried, there are strong differences between the two. Members of collectives and intentional communities often see themselves as building a new society and new forms of family (McLaughlin). Cohousing residents wish to live within the existing society, with the privacy and autonomy of the household secure. Their intention is to strengthen the family by creating supportive social networks, and by sharing certain daily tasks.

Like a traditional neighborhood, Sættedammen residents may share many values but are not united by a single ideology. As they do in most other collaborative communities, residents avoid heated political and religious discussions; when they do occur, it is clear that residents have various and strong opinions.

We've had sharp political discussions, and it's absolutely obvious we don't agree. I remember three years after we moved in, someone started a committee to send humanitarian aid to the Third World. Others said, "This is rubbish; you should send machine guns. It's the only way they will improve their situation." We had quite a sharp clash.

When there are so many worthwhile causes, why does the community—having accomplished so much in developing itself—not organize to deal with more? In part, it is because their original intention remains unchanged: to create a home and community that they can control, with problems they can solve, and issues on which they can reach consensus. Without straying into religion or politics, there are many pragmatic issues on which residents do not agree: how to raise children, cleanliness, additions to the common house, and even songs sung at St. Hans Day, a Scandinavian midsummer festival.

Skråplanet, Denmark, site plan.

1. Sports field; 2. play area; 3. festival square; 4. playground square; 5. theater square; 6. common house; 7. tennis court; 8. firewood depot; 9. swimming pool; 10. private dwelling; 11. parking.

A coffee break at the common house. Collaborative communities create a social network among neighbors, where many values and viewpoints are shared without an emphasis on ideology or religion. *(Lilian Bolvinkel)*

Finding solutions with which all residents can live is the challenge and delight of cohousing. As Sættedammen resident Ole Svensson explained, "When we sit together and drink enough beer, we are all equal."

NOTES

1. There is no agreement among Denmark, Holland, and Sweden on an English term for their separate, and distinct, collective developments. Danish researchers, as well as Americans writing about *bofællesskaber,* translate the term as *cohousing* (McCamant and Durrett). The Dutch *centraal wonen* is referred to in English as simply *centraal wonen* (Backus). The Swedish *kollektivhus* has been loosely translated as *collective housing* (Woodward). The reason is that this housing type sprang up more or less independently in each country. Therefore the type of building (low rise in Denmark, towers in Sweden), the way it is developed (planned by residents in Denmark, and usually planned by local authorities in Sweden), and the ownership (mostly co-ops and home ownership in Denmark, mostly

rentals in Sweden) vary among these three countries. Since these are all essentially similar types of developments and share these seven similar elements, I refer to all of them as *collaborative housing.*

Europeans also have not agreed on the exact differences among cohousing, *centraal wonen,* and *kollektivhus.* Danish researcher Hans Skifter Andersen finds important differences between the Danish *bofællesskaber* and the Swedish *kollektivhus,* in that *kollektivhus* are planned by local authorities (Andersen). Within Sweden, *kollektivhus* is used to describe both housing developed and owned entirely by residents (such as Slottet in Lund) and that owned by housing authorities (such as Stacken in Gothenburg). The Swedes see the main difference between them and the Danes as not one of ownership but building type. The Dutch, who have developments of all these types, do not make such distinctions. The Dutch organization for *centraal wonen,* Landelijke Vereniging Centraal Wonen, considers both resident- and government-owned housing, row house and apartment, with common rooms or a separate common house, variations of one housing type (Krabbe). In truth, if a comparison were made of the cohousing development of Drejerbanken in

Denmark, the *centraal wonen* development of de Meenthe in Holland, and the *kollektivhuset* Rainbow in Sweden, few differences would be found. I am following the Dutch example of including various ownerships, location of common facilities, and densities under the umbrella of collaborative housing. To complicate matters, countries such as Germany, France, Belgium, Switzerland, and Austria (Brech, Bernfeld, Freisitzer, M.H.G.A., Reinig) also have housing that could be described as collaborative except that residents do not usually share meals. If they meet the seven criteria mentioned and have some form of common meal at least once a month, I include them in the collaborative category.

2. A typical American studio apartment is about 650 square feet and a two-bedroom house about 1,200 square feet.

3. The early communities such as Sættedammen were not built with the idea of organizing tasks efficiently. They were seen as an alternative to the isolation of single-family homes and a way of sharing amenities. As the group members became well acquainted with each other, they began to realize this new possibility. More routines have been organized to be accomplished cooperatively (Andersen).

4. Residents are required to pay a minimum of 350 kroner ($48), or the equivalent of two-thirds of the cost of the monthly meals. They can choose not to pay for eleven evening meals.

5. The first cohousing groups in Denmark had a more difficult time in development, while subsequent groups have benefitted from the insights and mistakes of the first groups and from the wider acceptance of this housing form. The evolution of cohousing can be found in the writings of Gudmand-Høyer, Kjærsdam, McCamant and Durrett, Carter, and SBI Tæt Lev.

REFERENCES

Andersen, Hans Skifter. 1985. "Danish Low-rise Housing Co-operatives (bofællesskaber) as an Example of a Local Community Organization." *Scandinavian Housing and Planning Research* **2**(May): 49–66.

Backus, H. C. S., and Beatrice Kesler. 1986. "Kollektives Wohnen—Ein Weg zu einem neuen Lebensstil? Ergebnisse einer Evaluationsstudie in einem experimentellen Wohnungsbauprojekt Centraal Wonen Hilversum." *Hauswirtschaft*, pp. 251–259.

Bernfeld, Dan, and Jean-François Mabardi. 1984. *L'Habitat Groupe Autogere au Benelux et en Europe*. Louvain-La-Neuve: Fondation Roi Baudouin—Habitat et Participation.

Brech, Joachim. 1990. *Gruppenwohnprojekte in der Bundesrepublik*. Darmstadt: Wohnbund, Verlag Für Wissenschaftliche Publikationen.

Carter, Nick. 1984. "Beyond Utopia to a More Ideal Reality, a Study of Contemporary Danish Community Housing and Its Historic Origins." Unpublished dissertation, Royal Danish Academy, Copenhagen.

Freisitzer, Kurt; Robert Koch; and Ottokar Uhl. 1987. *Mitbestimmung im Wohnbau ein Handbuch*. Vienna: Picus.

Gehl, Jan. 1987. *Life between Buildings*. New York: Van Nostrand Reinhold.

Graae, Bodil. 1967. "Born skal have 100 forældre." *Politiken*, Sept. 4.

Gudmand-Høyer, Jan. 1968. "Det manglende led mellem utopi og det forældede enfamiliehus" (The Missing Link between Utopia and the Dated One-Family House). *Information*, June 26.

Gudmand-Høyer, Jan. 1984. "Ikke kun huse for folk—ogsa huse af folk." *Information*, April 4.

Kjaersdam, Finn. 1977. *Participatory Residential Planning*. Denmark: Institute of Development and Planning, Aalborg University Center, Aalborg.

Krabbe, René, and Paul Vlug. 1986. *Centraal Wonen in beeld 1977–1986 deel 1*. Netherlands: Landelijke Vereniging Centraal Wonen.

McCamant, Kathryn, and Charles Durrett. 1988. *Cohousing*. Berkeley: Ten Speed Press.

McLaughlin, Corinne, and Gordon Davidson. 1986. *Builders of the Dawn, Community Lifestyles in a Changing World*. Shutesbury, Mass.: Sirius Publishing.

Mouvement de L'Habitat Groupé Autogéré (MHGA). 1989. *Habitats Autogeres*. Paris: Editions Alternatives.

Reinig, Joachim. 1989. *Wohn Projekte in Hamburg von 1980–1989*. Darmstadt: Wohnbund, Verlag Für Wissenschaftliche Publikationen.

SBI. 1972 and 1976. Tæt Lev. Statens Byggeforskningsinstitut Rapport 82 and 83 (in Danish).

Woodward, A. 1987. "Public Housing Communes: Swedish Response to Post-material Demands." In *Housing and Neighborhoods*, ed. W. van Vliet et al., pp. 215–238. Westport, Conn.: Greenwood Press.

CHAPTER 2

Danish Cohousing:
A Housing Alternative

Danish *bofællesskaber* "to live together" is entering its third decade of development. Known as cohousing, ninety communities have been built, housing 6,000 residents (Andersen). The first communities were developed privately. Yet the people who gathered to discuss such a housing possibility came from a culture that well understands social organization and participation.

When a general rethinking of life-styles and community began in the 1960s, the American ideal was a rural back-to-the-land commune. In contrast, the Danish collective movement grew in towns and cities, and thousands of urban collectives formed. These influenced many people who faced the problems of juggling their jobs, households, and children. Inflation, the demands of both parents' working, the high rate of divorce, and growing isolation made today's wage earners, unlike their parents, eager to try alternatives. The motivation behind the first cohousing developments was to create a strong social network for the nuclear family; "few had thought in advance about the practical advantage" of cohousing (Andersen).

The cohousing form was influenced by traditional Danish low-density housing arrangements. The Danish government has a long history of concern for housing, not only providing capital but supporting new and innovative solutions to housing needs.

In the 1960s, as a reaction against the tall apartment towers that were then being constructed, tenants demanded more participation in the design of housing. The result was a new housing type, designed of densely built low-rise units. At that time, new attitudes toward design placed residents in a position of responsibility concerning their housing. The Danish Building Research Institute declared, "Dwellings and cities must be administrated by the people who live in them. Decisions in connection with programming, projecting, daily functioning, and reshaping must, to the widest possible extent, be made by the inhabitants themselves."

The result was housing on a more human scale, with outdoor spaces that emphasized contact among residents. Between 1965 and 1976, housing designs evolved toward smaller and better planned units, a greater choice of units, and more common space and common facilities. Four well-known housing communities, developed by the same cooperative housing society—Albertslund, Galgebakken, Gadekæret, and Hyldespjælet—show an evolution toward common spaces, meeting areas between buildings, and resident participation in the design process (Agger).

Danish cohousing combines a way of living with this specific dense and low form.[1] The dwellings were built as traditional owner-oc-

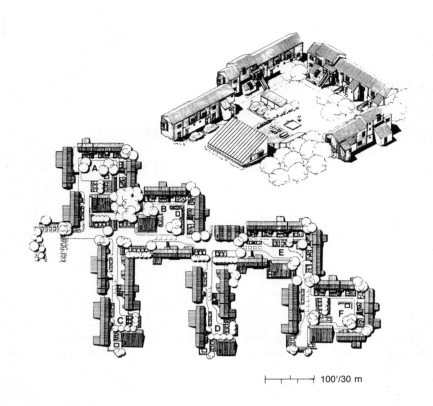

├──┬──┬──┬──┤ 100'/30 m

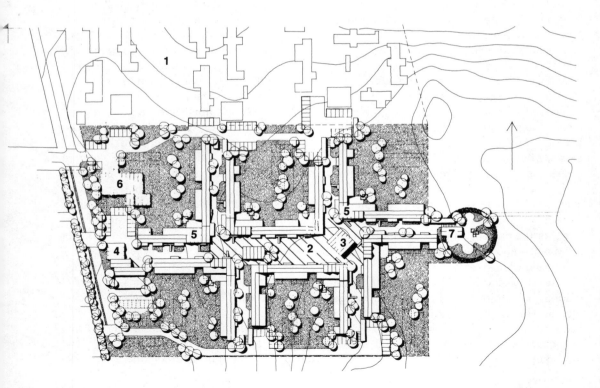

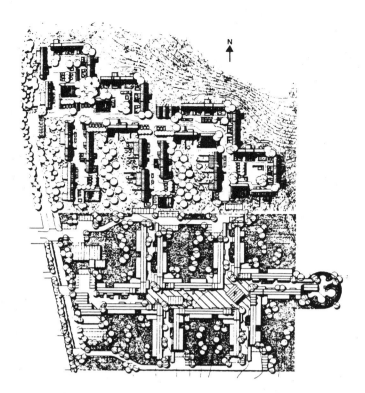

Tinggården and Tinggården 2

Tinggården (1977-1979), located south of Copenhagen, was the first public cohousing development in Denmark. Tenants are divided into six housing clusters (A-F, top left drawing, with enlarged cluster axio) of about fifteen households each, organized around an outdoore square and a small common house. Tinggården 2 (1983-1984), the second phase of the development, is more urban, with an emphasis on streets and squares (lower left drawing); 1. Tinggården 1; 2. community square; 3. common house; 4. workshops; 5. common meeting hall; 6. central heating building (straw-burning furnace); 7. children's house. *(Both drawings at left; Vandkunsten)*

cupied housing, with shared facilities in a separate common house. Since then, two other forms of tenure, aside from the privately owned, have been developed: rentals and cooperatives.

The first rental cohousing, Tinggården, a seventy-nine-unit development, was initiated by government and housing organizations.[2] In 1978, tenants moved into six family groups, with ten to fifteen households in each group. Drejerbanken, where half the units are owned by the residents and half by a cooperative housing association, was also completed that year. Cooperative housing associations (independent nonprofit organizations supervised by municipalities) were developed to

manage this subsidized rental housing with resident participation. The four rental cohousing developments in Denmark total 240 units.

In 1982, Denmark passed a law that makes low-income housing easier to finance through cooperative ownership.[3] This housing is subsidized by the state, with strict budgets and limits on dwelling size, making limited equity cohousing affordable to a wider range of people. Cohousing is now divided among the three types of ownership: 60% under cooperative ownership, 32% owner occupied, and 8% rentals. See Table 2.1 for detailed information on thirty-three cohousing communities. Cohousing averages twenty-four households in a development, with

Table 2.1   Data for Danish Collaborative Housing

Project	Owner-ship[a]	No. of Residents	No. of Units	Site Size Square Meters	Site Size Acres	Build-ing %[b]	No. of Units per Hectare[c]	No. of Units per Acre	Land Pur-chased
Andedammen	Co-op	51	18	6,400	1.59	32	28	11.33	1983
Askebakken	Co-op	44	17	4,820	1.19	35	35	14.16	1983
Bakken	Owner	88	28	22,000	5.44	17	12	4.86	1976
Blåhøjen	Co-op	74	25	10,000	2.47	25	25	10.12	1983
Bofælleden	Co-op	31	8	9,500	2.35	14	8	3.24	1980
Bofællesskabet I Gug	Owner	66	22	17,000	4.20	16	13	5.26	1979
Drejerbanken	Own/rent	50	20	15,000	3.71	15	13	5.26	1976
Drivhuset	Co-op	51	18	10,600	2.62	20	17	6.88	1983
Fladengrund	Owner	45	12	12,300	3.04	14	10	4.05	1979
Frugthaven	Owner	45	12	14,000	3.46	14	9	3.64	1977
Gyldenmuld	Owner	49	12	15,000	3.71	12	8	3.24	1975
Gyndbjerg	Owner	54	14	11,100	2.74	22	13	5.26	1976
Håndværkerparken	Rental	55	32	7,599	1.88	33	42	17.00	
Ibsgården	Co-op	53	21	6,040	1.49	33	35	14.16	1982
Jerngården	Owner	28	8	2,300	0.57	44	35	14.16	1976
Jernstøberiet	Owner	53	21	8,150	2.01	29	26	10.52	1980
Jystrup Savværket	Co-op	70	21	12,500	3.09	17	17	7.00	1981
Kolbøtten	Owner	26	6	6,960	1.72	14	9	3.64	1980
Leerbjerg Lod	Owner	104	30	28,000	6.92	14	11	4.45	1977
Mejdal	Owner	48	12	13,900	3.43	14	9	3.64	1977
Nonbo Hede	Owner	54	16	22,000	5.44	11	7	2.83	1973
Nørgårds Plantage	Co-op	56	24	15,150	3.74	16	16	6.48	1981
Overdrevet	Owner	93	25	28,000	6.92	13	9	3.64	1979
Skråplanet	Owner	138	33	24,750	6.12	21	13	5.26	1968
Sol og Vind	Owner	96	30	20,000	4.94	17	15	6.07	1979
Stavnsbåndet	Owner	96	26	13,000	3.21	31	20	8.09	1977
Sættedammen	Owner	100	27	20,000	4.94	28	14	5.67	1969
Tinggården	Rental	218	79	25,600	6.33	32	31	12.55	1975
Tinggården 2	Rental	162	76	25,000	6.18	33	30	12.14	1982
Tornevangsgården	Owner	25	6	4,400	1.09	21	14	5.67	1977
Trudeslund	Owner	115	33	18,000	4.45	22	18	7.28	1979
Uldalen	Co-op	57	18	5,050	1.25	35	35	14.16	1982
Vejgård Bymidte	Owner	75	40	4,720	1.17	70	85	34.40	1981

Source: STATENS BYGGEFORSKNINGSINSTITUT (SBI Rapport 187).
[a]Owner: Similar to condominium ownership, where the resident owns the dwelling and has an ownership share in the common areas.
  Co-op: Government financed where the resale value is restricted.
  Rental: Owned by private nonprofit housing associations.
[b]The building percentage is the percentage of the site that has been built up.
[c]A hectare is a metric unit of area equal to 2.5 acres.
[d]Range = range of unit sizes. For square footages, multiply the square meters by 10.76 square feet.

about a 14% reduction in the size of the private dwelling area that is donated to the common spaces.

Although cohousing strives for a mix of ages and backgrounds, and there are residents from infants to eighty years old, the majority of residents are in their thirties and forties, with backgrounds in social work, education, and similar white-collar fields. Resi-dents have been aging with the communities, and some are entering their retirement years. A sampling of cohousing built in the 1970s shows that residents were primarily professional couples with good incomes. The dwellings were spacious, averaging 1,054-1,668 square feet (98-155 square meters).[4] A sampling of cohousing communities built in the 1980s shows that the creation of cooperative

| Con- struction Started | Con- struction Completed | Units | | | | Common House | | | | | |
		Range[d] of sizes (sq. m)	Built Area[e] (sq. m)	Total (sq. m)	Base- ment (sq. m)	New (N) or Ren- ovated (R)	Built Area (sq. m)	Total Area (sq. m)	Base- ment (sq. m)	Meters per Unit[f]	% per Unit[g]
1984	1984	50-122	1100	1901	0	R	128	128	200	7	7
1983	1984	63-110	774	1548	0	N	130	158	103	9	10
1979	1979	100-154	2100	3400	0	N	303	375	190	15	11
1984	1985	70-110	2000	2225	0	N	265	265	265	11	12
1980	1980	95-110		840	16	R		147	130	18	18
1980	1980	90-140	1260	2500	0	N	140	330	195	15	13
1977	1978	74-129	1552	1950	0	N	236	236	236	12	12
1983	1984	57-119	1000	1588	0	N	99	133	360	7	8
1980	1980	108-148	1577	1577	0	N	185	185	175	15	12
1979	1979	131	944	1574	0	N	220	320	0	27	20
1976	1976	116-142	1140	1470	0	N+R	302	302	40	25	21
1976	1976	55-210	1360	2520	95	R	350	350	10	25	14
1984	1985	52- 85		1975	0	N		527	0	16	27
1982	1983	56- 95	845	1678	0	R	155	287	60	14	17
1976	1977	95-150	451	896	240	R	67	114	73	14	13
1980	1981	38-127	1366	1754	0	N	135	265	225	13	15
1983	1984	63- 98		1780	0	N		404	0	19	22
1981	1981	118-134	451	756	0	N	109	190	45	32	25
1978	1979	110-148	2154	3720	0	N	240	600	240	20	16
1978	1979	120-150	1530	1708	0	N	180	242	36	20	14
1974	1974	105-142	1530	1946	0	N	269	422	0	26	22
1983	1983	95	2309	2309	0	N	113	113	64	5	5
1979	1980	60- 90	1360	2350	0	N+R	380	620	154	25	26
1971	1973	150	3300	4950	0	N	225	350	0	11	7
1980	1980	78-130	1800	2810	0	N	462	550	23	18	20
1979	1979	116-173	2396	3774	0	N	165	298	257	11	8
1971	1972	140-225	3600	5200	0	N	300	300	0	11	6
1977	1979	49-147	3996	6428	0	N	894	954	0	12	15
1983	1984	44- 99	3262	5460	0	N	885	914	0	12	17
1977	1978	123	480	744	0	R	120	190	0	32	26
1980	1981	90-138	2986	3605	300	N	288	407	225	12	11
1982	1983	62-130	820	1640	0	N	150	150	60	8	9
1981	1982	44-116	1971	3211	50	R		125	90	3	4

[e]The building footprint. One-story buildings have the same total area as the built area. Buildings of several stories have a larger total floor area than built area.

[f]Meters per Unit = total common house floorage per private unit. The common house floor area divided by the number of units gives the amount of floorage each unit contributes to the common house.

[g]% per Unit = total common house floorage as a percentage of unit floorage. The common house floor area per unit divided by the unit's floor area gives % per Unit, the percentage of floor area each unit contributes to the common house.

ownership has had an influence on the appearance of cohousing. Dwellings are smaller, with a one-bedroom unit averaging about 700 square feet and a three-bedroom unit about 1,250 square feet (65-116 square meters).[5] Under cooperative law, there is a limit to the amount of reduction in private square footage to create common areas, and this has reduced the amount of common space. The strict limits on size under cooperative ownership have made the housing more affordable, and residents now include a number of singles and single parents.[6]

Another change, mirroring the change in architecture styles, has been an evolution from housing loosely placed around a shared area to housing ordered around streets, squares, and plazas. The community of

A renovated farmhouse serves as the common house and faces a shared court formed by the surrounding twenty-two new residences. Ibsgården, Denmark. *(Lilian Bolvinkel)*

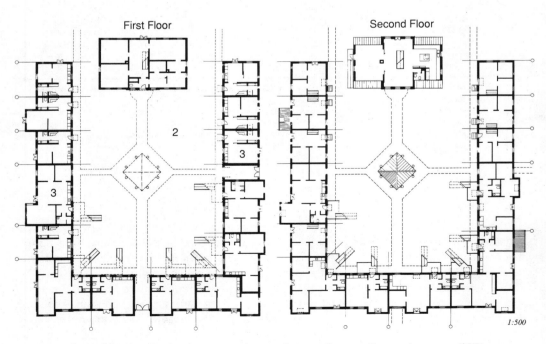

Ibsgården: 1. renovated common house, 2. central court, 3. new housing. *(SBI)*

Trudeslund reflects this change, with the housing ordered along two streets rising up to a central common house.

There is a strong preference for new construction where the private units and the common house can be built to residents' specifications. Only five developments are in renovated buildings.[7] In Ibsgården, an old farmhouse has been restored as the common house, with new housing built to create an interior court. This development took advantage of the co-operative law. The tight budget resulted in long, simple buildings. Wooden bays project off their brick facade where extra space was needed so that units could be individualized. The bedrooms face small, private gardens to the back, and the kitchen and living rooms are oriented to the more public court.

Using renewable resources has been the goal of a few cohousing developments, including Sol og Vind (Sun and Wind) and Overdrevet (created by part of the original Sun

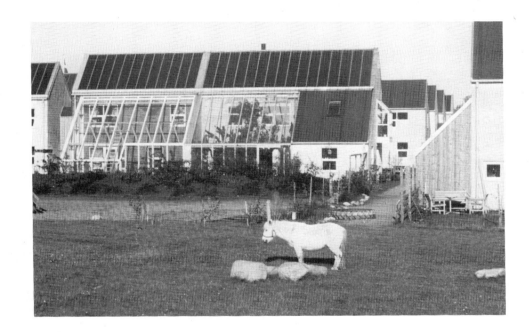

Sun and Wind (*photo*) and Overdrevet (*drawing*) are reminiscent of older Danish village designs, yet both have solar panels and a windmill to provide part of their community's energy. (*Arkitektur*)

and Wind group). Both of these communities, completed in 1980, have a similar architectural style, reminiscent of rural Danish villages. In Overdrevet, the houses are built around a shared green, with a solar collector and windmill providing 60% of the energy used. In Sun and Wind, the housing is organized along pedestrian streets and squares. The houses are built with roof pitches designed to maximize the solar gain to the roof-

top collectors. A windmill located on a nearby hill provides electrical power. The high cost and the difficulties encountered with this relatively new technology have encouraged other developments to take a passive solar energy approach.

The desire to get the most use out of common spaces year round and to save energy has led to the creation of cohousing under one roof. Ten years after the prototype design

1. Parking
2. Hobby room
3. Semiprivate areas
4. Community rooms
5. Kindergarten
6. Swimming pool
7. Playground

Evolution of cohousing under one roof: 1970, the Farum project. Forty-four houses and the common spaces are connected under a glass-covered arcade in the Farum scheme by architect Jan Gudmand-Høyer. The residences, either 1,180 or 2,270 square feet (110 or 210 square meters), donated about 25% of their private area so that the common house could be built. (*Gudmand-Høyer*)

of the Farum project (1970), architect Jan Gudmand-Høyer designed Jernstøberiet, a renovated iron foundry with wings of housing on both sides. This concrete and brick foundry has two rows of shed-roofed housing connected by a large hall that serves as a recreational area. Located at one end of this hall is the common area, with cooking and dining facilities. Three other covered-street communities have been built, including Håndvær-

kerparken, a small rental development. Residents are particularly happy with covered passageways, especially in the cold Danish winter. Maria, a working mother, feels "it's a paradise for children."

In many ways, the greatest strengths of cohousing have also been its drawbacks. The dwellings are clustered to create a shared central area, which results in housing invariably turned inward. The car-free zone results in

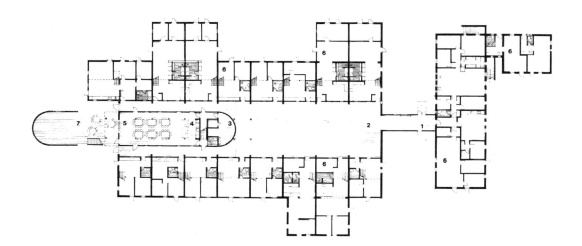

Evolution of cohousing under one roof: 1981, Jernstøberiet. Also designed by Gudmand-Høyer, this renovated iron foundry has a covered hall that connects the housing and common house. The privately owned residences range in size from 410 to 1,370 square feet (38-127 square meters), with 15% of the area given over to create the common areas. (*Gudmand-Høyer*)

1. Entrance; 2. central common space; 3. storage; 4. kitchen; 5. common dining; 6. private residence; 7. outdoor deck.

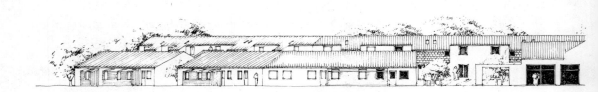

Evolution of cohousing under one roof: 1985, Håndværkerparken. This rental cohousing development has thirty-five residences grouped along a covered street. The residences range from 280 to 825 square feet (26–77 square meters), with 20% of their area given to create the common areas. (*Arkitektgruppen I Aarhus*)

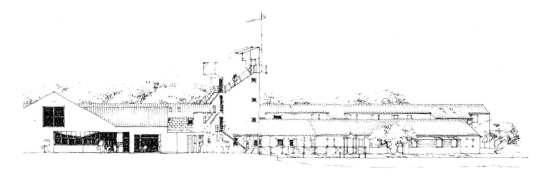

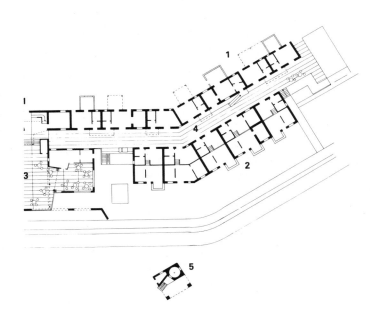

1. Two-story apartments
2. One-and-a-half-story apartments
3. Common house
4. Covered street
5. Tower

parking located nearest the road and does not add much to the street or neighborhood. The sense of an enclave heightens a feeling of community within but not necessarily for the larger neighborhood. The residents organize many activities together, creating greater intimacy as well as conflict.

Following are two cohousing examples that illustrate these strengths and weaknesses. The first, Jystrup Savværket, is the best known of the covered street developments with a design that emphasizes the self-contained community. The second example previews the new wave of cohousing developments and their integration into the neighborhood.

JYSTRUP SAVVÆRKET: A GLASS STREET

Jystrup, Denmark
Units: 21
Ownership: Cooperative
Site: Suburban, 2.7 acres
Began/Moved in: 1979/1984
Architect: Vandkunsten

Of all the cohousing projects, surely Savværket must be one of the most radical, with 40% of the floor area allocated to common use. The plan is a simple one, with twenty-one row houses on each side of a glass-covered pedestrian street. The street is bent to form an L, with the common house placed at the junction.

Jens Arnfred of Vandkunsten Architects used ordinary inexpensive materials of sheetrock, stained plywood, cement siding, and marine-blue paint to create the most extraordinary of interiors. The use of light and shadow interweaves common and semiprivate areas, erasing the silhouette of doorways and tracing new borderlines on the street. Plants, shoes, clothes, small tables and chairs, and an occasional painting have slipped out from private doors to decorate the corridor.

The street is the most successful and inviting of spaces, with year-round use. In the cold of the Danish winter, children play in the sandboxes along the path, and families chat together at picnic tables under a canopy of green leaves. Along the street are also common facilities: two workshops, the laundry room, and two supplementary spaces used at various times as an office or guest rooms.

Walking down this main artery, with the private entrances recessed slightly into walls of glass, the passerby has an aquarium view into the dwellings. A few blinds and curtains are drawn across the glass for privacy or adjusted in increments of sociability.

To American eyes, the dwellings are tiny: a one bedroom the size of a studio (680 square feet) and a three bedroom less than twice that size (1,050 square feet). The open floor plan, opening out to a private back yard terrace, allows light into the dwelling and increases the apparent size. Still, it is difficult to imagine a couple and child living comfortably in the smallest unit, as some do. Residents obtain bigger or smaller units by exchanging apartments, since only one wall can be moved within the dwelling. "The small space forces people to use the common rooms, and I think that's good. You wouldn't like to live here otherwise," says resident Birte Sorenson.

The extensive common space includes a 4,000-square-foot common house where the two pedestrian streets converge. A glass wall separates the common house from the street to reduce noise and heat loss, but visually the common areas float together seamlessly. The common house is constructed in a series of levels, with the dining area opening to a wide terrace. The whole dining area has a high ceiling, with a mezzanine halfway leading to the children's playrooms, a room for teenagers, and storage. A few steps down from the dining area, in a corner, is a subterranean kitchen, professionally equipped. (The space, dug into the hill, is considered too dark by residents.)

In the center of the common house is a coffee table, wedged like a triangle, red as a heart. Residents at this command post, littered with pillows, newspapers, and coffee mugs, can view a whole vista of common areas from different angles: the kitchen, the outdoor common green, and down the length of the buildings.

Playing along the covered street. Jystrup Savværket, Denmark. (*Lilian Bolvinkel*)

Sitting in the *alrum,* a combination kitchen-dining area inside the private dwelling. The residents have a clear view out to the covered street through the glass facade. (*Seiderman & Kragh*)

The Two Communities

Savværket is located in Jystrup, a storybook village with winding roads and snug brick and plaster homes, an hour and a half's ride from Copenhagen. The simplicity, leisurely pace, and green meadows and hills attracted the group of families to this area in 1979. Intent on building a cohousing community, the small group of families grew through friends and through advertising in the newspaper *Information.* By 1980, a site was found on a small hill in Jystrup, and three architectural firms were asked to prepare sketches. Vandkunsten architects was chosen.

The villagers viewed the idea of families' living together under one roof with suspicion. To add to their discomfort, the housing was designed to sit on top of the hill, while the rest of the village homes were between the hills. The villagers banded together, afraid not only of the housing location but of the kind of people who would move in. A petition was signed, a town meeting held, and like a witch banished, the group had to choose another plot (on the site of an old sawmill), down off the hill. The village's opposition had delayed the project, and the group did not move in until July 1984, a year after construction began.

Perhaps it came as no surprise to the villagers that the new community of Savværket ("sawmill") deviates in every aspect from the surrounding homes. The large, dark, angular building turns its back on the street. The siding and most of the roofing are black corrugated asbestos cement, with towers and dormers of black-stained plywood. The houses, described by one outsider as "claws," are staggered in relationship to each other, their entrances facing inward, creating the internal street.

Although the neighboring farmers and merchants are not enamored of the style, architects throughout Europe have been drawn to the innovative design of this development. The villagers tolerate the architecture, and relations have improved somewhat between the bigger community and the little community. But they still ask the group, When are you going to paint those houses a different color?

A Housing Experiment

Savværket is a success both architecturally and as a cohousing community, albeit for certain types of people. Many residents say that the quality of their lives is substantially better, that their children are happier, and that they have no intention of moving back to a single-family home. But there are critics who are not comfortable with this particular kind of cohousing community or with the level of participation required. A few of those critics are past residents of the community.

In the summer of 1989, four families decided to move out of Savværket into private homes. Two of the families felt that not enough was done in common. They were concerned with environmental issues and felt the group should be more careful with its resources, for example, by using less electricity. The other two couples, more career minded, thought there was too much in common. One resident summed it up: "Those on the extreme, either right or left, leave, and those in the middle remain."

Some residents feel that it is difficult to live in Savværket without being a couple and without having children because the majority of the households are families. Of the twenty-one households, nineteen are couples and

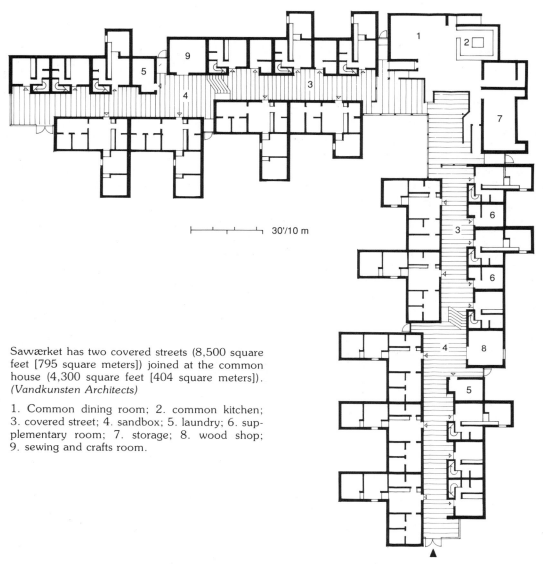

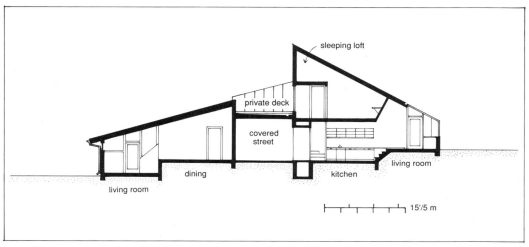

Savværket has two covered streets (8,500 square feet [795 square meters]) joined at the common house (4,300 square feet [404 square meters]). *(Vandkunsten Architects)*

1. Common dining room; 2. common kitchen; 3. covered street; 4. sandbox; 5. laundry; 6. supplementary room; 7. storage; 8. wood shop; 9. sewing and crafts room.

30'/10 m

sleeping loft

private deck

covered street

dining

kitchen

living room

living room

15'/5 m

The massing, color, and materials of Savværket contrast with the neighboring homes.
(Vandkunsten Architects)

two are single parents (three households have no children). In addition, the price of a dwelling can be too expensive for a single income, and the rooms are too small to rent out.[8] A turnover rate that averages 8% a year in part reflects the fact that couples who divorce cannot afford to stay.[9]

Small communities with a covered street are particularly intimate since the common "room" is just outside each front door. A minority of Danish cohousing communities have chosen to reduce their private square footage to the minimum in order to afford a common covered street. Not only is there an increase in socializing and children's play during the winter months, but there is also an increase in the overall level of community intimacy. Savværket is an experiment, a new vehicle for community. Like a submarine, some find it claustrophobic; others see the means toward a new, deep, and almost unexplored region.

THE URBAN NEIGHBORHOOD: MIXING COHOUSING, SCHOOLS, AND BUSINESSES

The urban neighborhood is a way to tie cohousing to the larger community, enhancing both. The idea is to integrate housing, businesses, and commercial services in an old-fashioned market town. The kinds of neighborhoods that people used to live in were very much an inspiration for cohousing, and the urban neighborhood attempts to recreate a similar concept on a larger scale. The first phases of the residences have been completed in two ambitious developments near Copenhagen.

A competition was held in 1985 for the planning and building of two urban neighborhoods—at Egebjerggård and Østerhøj, both in Ballerup. The competition sponsors were

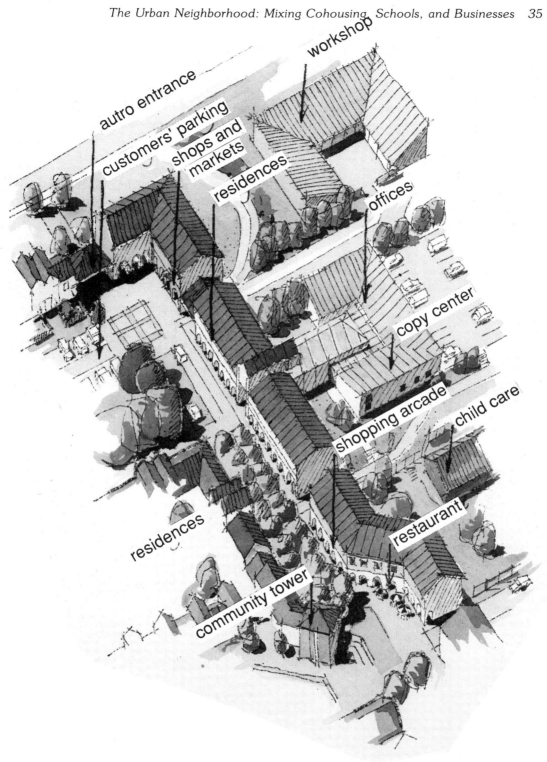

autro entrance

workshop

customers' parking

shops and markets

residences

offices

copy center

shopping arcade

child care

residences

restaurant

community tower

The urban neighborhood combines housing, local shops, day care, and small businesses located along pedestrian streets, with parking at the periphery. (*Ballerup Council*)

seeking alternatives to suburban housing and planning.[10] The town of Ballerup already had its share of suburban sprawl, requiring a car to go shopping and isolating residents from services and amenities.

Some of the ideas that came out of the competition sound like a pedestrian's dream:

- Schools, local shops, and small businesses should not be isolated but combined with housing along a pedestrian street, which would open into public squares and parks. Children could use the main square as their playground.
- Housing would not all look the same, but would appear in a variety of types and ownerships—multistory and detached houses and a mix of rentals, cooperatives, and privately owned units. The elderly and the handicapped would live among the other households rather than separately.
- The housing should not be built in endless rows; instead the units should be divided into small enclaves of twenty to fifty households, sited around open green areas, each with a common house. Artists could decorate the houses and the streets.
- The residents should have the opportunity to open up shops in their homes and walk down the block to the grocery store or hairdresser's. Child care should be a short walk away.
- Through traffic should occur at the periphery of the neighborhood (an emphasis on pedestrian streets), with housing density and activity concentrated on the central streets.

A second competition for detailed site plans for the two areas was held in 1986. An urban neighborhood catalog was put together by the Ballerup council with two town planners and two members of the Danish Building Research Institute (Ballerup Kommune 1986). The catalog contains descriptions of the various elements that should make up the urban neighborhood. (The source of most of the material was the ideas competition.)

The winners of both competitions were architects Angels Colom and Jan Gudmand-Høyer (the initiator of the cohousing movement), who are now designing the first of four phases for the two areas in Ballerup. Their vision for the two new quarters is to have up to forty clustered communities, all tied to a pedestrian street with the existing school as the center. Depending on the type of ownership, the communities follow several different development processes. The architect's office has been moved into one of the classrooms at the school in Egebjerggård, the center of the building site, to coordinate this massive undertaking.

On the site, two large lakes have been dug, one geometrical and the other designed to appear natural. Parks, plazas, and pedestrian pathways combine with housing clusters. The various housing enclaves include a variety of amenities, ownerships, and degrees of participation by the future residents. Each is located along a public path, with a large gateway as the entrance to all the units, both for surveillance by the neighbors and for the residents to meet each other when walking to their own houses.

The urban neighborhood is an experiment on a grand scale.[11] A closer look at the housing of the new quarters follows. Two types of developments are described: rental developments in Egebjerggård and cooperatives on Østerhøj. Although the architects of these developments have described each as cohousing, their descriptions show that the difference is in the degree of cooperation—both before and after residents move in.

Two Cooperative Developments

Two cooperatives, Kilen and Østerhøj I, sit side by side, sharing a parking lot between them. They are part of the first stage of development at Østerhøj.[12] Although both have been built with resident participation (with the same architects), both have common houses, both the same number of households (twenty), and

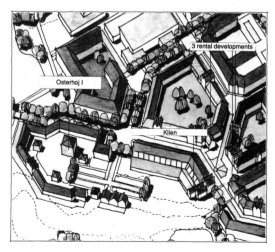

Plan of Østerhøj, located in the town of Ballerup, just west of Copenhagen. The darkened buildings are shops, schools, and businesses; the lighter buildings are housing. *(Ballerup Council)*

both the same form of ownership, they are extraordinarily different.[13] Østerhøj is in reality not a strong collaborative community, whereas Kilen is. The difference is one of social and participatory degrees, and not necessarily architecture, ownership, or size.

In the development of Østerhøj 1, a board of directors, chosen by the future residents, worked with the architects on the design. (The head of the board is Eric Holm, the conservative representative on the Ballerup city council.)[14] "Holm didn't like the idea of cohousing, but the community had decided that each development should have a space for a common house. By designing through participation, they got together and talked, became more friendly, and decided to have less borders between each other," explains Gudmand-Høyer. The planning process took three years, and most of the decisions were made by the board.

Østerhøj 1 has twenty dwellings around a grassy outdoor area. The architect has made an effort to distinguish the appearance of the dwellings from each other, and they do not appear as though they are all from the same development. Each has a private entrance and a mailbox next to its door. About 5% of the private area was "taken" to create the common house, which has a dining room, a kitchen, and a library. The laundry area is separated from the common house, and several residents mentioned they would have preferred the two combined.

Management relies on the board of directors to make many decisions, although there are meetings of all the residents to discuss policies. Residents do not decide on new members together but take the lowest number on a waiting list held by the housing authority, a list that now has a hundred names. The residents share tasks concerning the common outdoor areas but not much more; they cut the grass, remove snow, and use the community washing machines. Evening meals are not shared, although there are occasional parties in the common house. Some residents would like a more active community. One resident had this to say about Østerhøj 1:

The common house, instead of being a place where you have all talked about it, is only a house for parties. At the first meeting we had, they said we shouldn't each have our own key for the common house, and we voted not to have our own key. But things are changing. People have gotten dissatisfied. No one uses the common house; no one goes there.

Østerhøj 1 is popular among older people, who enjoy the cost savings of cooperatives and the community atmosphere. The residents—four singles, two single parents, four couples with children, and ten couples (for a total of thirty-four adults and five children)—moved in in August 1989.

In Kilen, just across the way, the residents participated 110%. Planning started in August 1984 with five families from Ballerup and six from Copenhagen. Through advertisements, they attracted two hundred people to a large meeting. Of those, fifty-five were very interested, and each paid about $20 to create a group. Lengthy discussions were held as to how the group would like to live and how much to have in common. In 1987, the Ballerup city council approved the site but only for twenty households. The rest of the group were placed on a waiting list, and the twenty households each paid about $700, plus a certain amount per month, to become an association.* Five of the twenty households dropped out (most of them because they could not qualify for a loan), so the group chose new members through a long interviewing process. Throughout the five years, the group met at least once a month and during the design process several times a week.

Architects Colom and Gudmand-Høyer have been working with the group for almost all of the five years. The architecture reflects their ideals of creating a close community

---

*Danish kroner, Dutch guilders, and Swedish crowns have been converted to U.S. dollars at the exchange rate for the year(s) when the costs occurred. From 1984 to 1990, the exchange rate has fluctuated for Danish crowns from 10.3 to 6.7 for the dollar, Dutch guilders from 8.6 to 6.1 for the dollar, and Swedish crowns from 3.2 to 1.9 for the dollar (International Financial Statistics).

The facade of two row houses (*top*) in Østerhøj 1, designed to look like single-family homes. The future residents, through their board of directors, had some influence on the design and rejected an earlier version (*bottom*) by the architect. (*Ballerup Council*)

(eating together six nights a week). Kilen has two rows of housing on each side of a glass-covered street. The dwellings are small, with 15% of their area "taken" to provide for the common street and house.[15] Entrances to all the dwellings are through the common street, with mailboxes grouped together at several entrances. While the dwellings themselves are plain, the common house is distinct and colorful. The residents saved their money to pay for an artist, who painted a unique interior.

The common house includes a kitchen, dining room, workshops, guest rooms, two rooms for teenagers, large freezers in the basement, and a laundry. The residents have organized themselves to meet once a month, and common meals are available every weeknight.

The group moved in in May 1989, with thirteen couples, five single parents, and two single households, for a total of thirty adults and thirty children. The week they moved in,

Moving-in day, looking down the covered street of Kilen, Denmark.

Plan of Kilen. *(Gudmand-Høyer)*

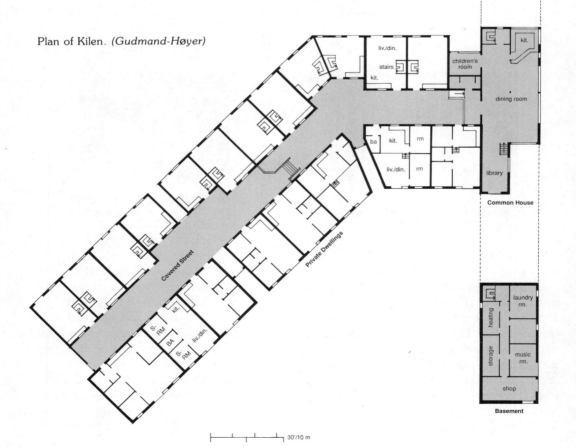

30'/10 m

the entire glass-covered street was lined with boxes, suitcases, toys, chairs, tables, and bundles of clothes. Weary residents sat together on a makeshift table, a beer glass in front of each. Jens Jensen, a teacher and one of the main organizers of Kilen said, "It's hard to believe we've finally managed to see it realized. Now it really begins."

Four Rental Cohousing Developments

In Egebjerggård, four rental developments have been built one next to the other as part of the urban neighborhood. Egebjerghave I, II, III, and IV each has the basic common facilities of kitchen and dining area. In addition, each has a special amenity that can be used by all the tenants in the four developments. One has facilities for the elderly, another a laundry (centrally located), a third has child care, and the fourth has workshops. The common facilities can be used more effectively, with less duplication.

In these developments, elderly and handicapped units are intermixed with other housing units. There are also a few group homes—studio bedrooms for four persons with a shared kitchen that can be used by young people as a step from moving out of their parents' home. They can also be used by frail elderly, sharing one caretaker. The state provides some funding support for this type of housing.

Some of the regular dwellings can be altered into mixed use, with both housing and a business. These dwellings are located on the side along the pedestrian street. The residents can turn part of their home into a small shop and enlarge the pedestrian walk to their back door (covering their small private garden). With not much effort, they can create a small shop facing the street. Tenants who move into these developments agree beforehand that such shops should be a possibility.

Another new amenity is the inclusion of an artist's live-work space within the rental development. The artist is chosen by the tenants to live in their community for one year and is under an obligation to add art to their environment. After one year, a new artist is chosen. The rent for the studio becomes part of the cost for common amenities.

Most of these special characteristics have not been tried and are possible because the housing will be owned by the nonprofit housing association, not the residents. The association has the funds for this kind of experimentation, can oversee the management, and can step in if there is a dispute. People who own cohousing generally prefer smaller communities and may not have extra funding for housing experiments.

The rental developments, owned by nonprofit organizations, are designed with less involvement by future residents than the ownership developments. A certain number of interested people on the waiting list for nonprofit rental cohousing are asked to participate in the design process. (Not all the future tenants can be chosen since a certain percentage of those with low incomes are selected at the end of the construction.) No money is required as a down payment, allowing people with varied incomes to participate but also resulting in less commitment to move in through a long development process. These future tenants have no legal influence over the development process; their involvement is one of interest, not capital. Also, there are greater restrictions in what can be built in public housing. According to architect Jan Gudmand-Høyer, "Here it is much more our [the architect's] decision in the design. We show them our ideas and other alternatives, and they say what they like. And maybe we change it and maybe not."

Aside from the different level of participation in programming, the number of dwellings is almost twice as many as cooperative or private ownership cohousing—about forty-five households. The reason, says Gudmand-Høyer, is that in rentals, only about half the households can be counted on to participate. Also less floor area is donated for common facilities, and so more units are needed.

Although there are more restrictions in rental cohousing and less participation, ten-

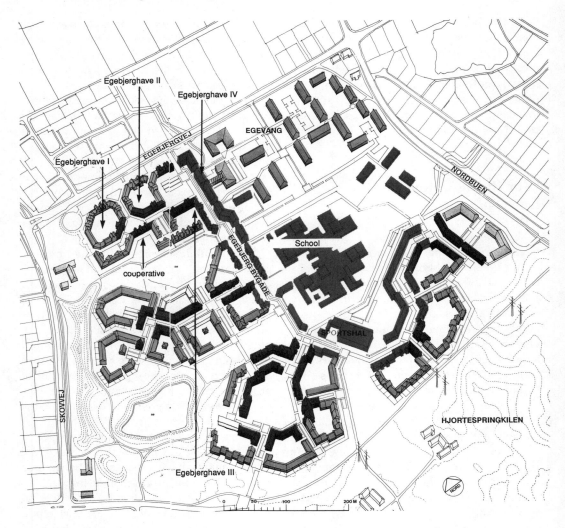

Plan of Egebjerggård developments, also in Ballerup. Each of the four rental cohousing projects is distinct, with its own common house. The four also share some common amenities. (*Ballerup Council*)

ants are happy to have this kind of alternative and find living in these communities more satisfying than traditional rentals. They have the benefits of the cohousing form: a central shared outdoor area, common facilities, and a design that emphasizes a sense of identity and mutual security. Since working together helps shape households into a community, the common house, play areas, and common garden are left unfinished and funds set aside

for residents to complete the projects as they wish.

The Egebjerghave rental developments will house about the same number of people as the first rental cohousing, Tinggården (1978). The difference is that Tinggården divided the tenants into small groups. "On a psychological viewpoint, small groups are not safe because there is only one inner circle," believes Gudmand-Høyer. If one in the circle becomes unfriendly, there is conflict. With thirty or forty households, you cannot be intimate with everyone. If you don't fit into one circle, you'll find a place to fit in another." (Residents of Tinggården who live in successful small groups say they are happy with them, while those in clusters not as neighborly believe that a larger cluster group might be better.)

NOTES

1. While architectural styles vary, cohousing shares a consistent residential form. The architectural evolution of cohousing can be found in Blod By 13 and 31, *Arkitektur* 1984, Fromm, Vedel-Peterson, and in the reports of Byggeriets Udviklingsrad (BUR) covering specific projects such as Jystrup Savværk, Sol og Vind, and Handværkerparken.
2. Danish nonprofit rental housing (*lejeboliger*) is built by independent state-supported nonprofit housing companies. The tenants directly participate in the approval of economic and other matters at general meetings (Cronberg). Tenants of all incomes can move into nonprofit rentals, although low-income households pay substantially less because of individual government subsidies. The government finances the construction through index-linked loans of up to 80% from private mortgage credit institutions, with the remaining portion usually paid by local government loans. Almost half of all rental housing units are built by nonprofit housing companies. Renting is an accepted form of long-term housing for the middle class.
3. In Danish cooperative ownership (*andelsboliger*), the government loans up to 90% of the construction costs, which is financed by issuing bonds. Residents, through forming a housing association, pay the remaining 10% down payment. (The housing association can borrow 8% from state and local authorities.) The Ministry of Housing sets strict guidelines for construction costs and unit sizes. The government loan is paid back by residents over a number of years, interest free, creating inexpensive housing, the reason that cooperatives are a popular type of ownership. (The cooperative law has been amended; by 1993 residents will be required to pay back 25% of the total interest for the loan.) The government financing requires a limit on members' equity and, therefore, unit resale value is restricted.
4. The sample was from fourteen cohousing communities built from 1972 to 1979. They averaged twenty-three units on four acres (16,000 square meters) of land. The density is similar to that of an older American suburb (about six units per acre.)
5. Jernstøberiet, a renovated iron factory, has units as small as 400 square feet (38 square meters).
6. The sampling was of nineteen communities built between 1980 and 1985. The density is about ten units to the acre.
7. Jerngården, Århus (renovated row houses); Vejgård, Ålborg (renovated factory): Toustrup Mark, Århus; Bofælleden, Beder (renovated school building); and Jernstøberiet, Roskilde (renovated iron factory).
8. The one-bedroom units cost $287 (2,095 kroner) a month, and the three-bedroom units cost $467 (3,414 kroner) a month. The total project cost was $1,745,876 (18.5 million kroner). (The accounting of construction costs has not yet been completely resolved.) The costs of the project were partially subsidized by the Danish government through cooperative financing. The project also received a subsidy from the Danish Building Research Institute and indirectly by the architects, who donated part of their time.
9. In the first five years (1982-1989), eight households moved.
10. The competition sponsors included the Ballerup council, the Danish Building Research Institute (SBI), and the Federation of Danish Architects. The sponsors of the two developments included the Ballerup council (providing infrastructure such as roads, sewers, and utilities), the Ministry of Housing (providing funds for construction), SBI (supervising the development and researching design solutions), the Federation of Danish Architects (supporting the master plan by providing technical information), and the Ministry of Culture (providing funds for artists working for the Ballerup council).
11. In this first phase, each neighborhood will have 170 houses (50 privately owned, 20 cooperatively owned, 25 for teens and young adults, and 75 rentals owned by nonprofit housing organizations). Business will be integrated into the housing (hairdressers, accountants, photographers, etc.) along main streets (shops, bicycle repair, bookbinders, copy shop, etc.) and in workshop areas (plumbing, electrician, car repair). The business premises will total about 30,000 square feet (3,000 square meters), also integrated into the neighborhood (Ballerup Kommune 1988).

12. Three rental clusters are being developed by a nonprofit housing association next to Østerhøj 1 and Kilen.
13. Both are limited-equity cooperatives (where the resale value is limited by law) and have been subsidized by the government. A 1,020-square-foot unit (95 square meters) costs $130,000 (950,000 kroner), but the owner pays only about 10-20% of that cost initially.
14. The residents of Østerhøj I met in a meeting announced by the Ballerup city council for people interested in cooperative housing. Forty people came and chose four members among themselves as a board of directors. The rest of the people put their names in a hat; the first sixteen (and the four on the board) chosen would move in; the rest placed on a waiting list.
15. Dwelling sizes: nine are 1,023 square feet (95 square meters), and four are 915 square feet (85 square meters), two are 807 square feet (75 square meters), and five are 700 square feet (65 square meters).

REFERENCES

Agger, Erik. 1976. "Malet er det menneskelige faellesskab." [The goal is human fellowship.] *Arkitekten* (November).

Andersen, Hans Skifter. 1989. "Housing Communities in Denmark." In *Neue Wohnformen in Europa, Berichte des vierten Internationalen Wohnbund—Kongresses in Hamburg*, ed. Joachim Brech, pp. 251-260. Darmstadt: Wohnbund, Verlag Für Wissenschaftliche Publikationen (in English and German).

Arkitektur DK. 1985. Nos. 5-6, special issue on Tegnestuen Vandkunsten architects (with English summaries).

Arkitektur DK. 1984. No. 6, special issue on cohousing (with English summaries).

Ballerup Kommune. 1989. *Bykvarterkatalog, Østerhøj og Egebjerggård*.

Ballerup Kommune. 1986. *Indbudt Konkurrence I Ballerup Kommune*.

Blød By. 1984. No. 31, special issue on users' influence in housing developments.

Blød By. 1981. No. 13, special issue on bofællesskaber.

Byggeriets Udviklingsråd. 1987a. *Andelsboligfællesskaber*. Copenhagen: BUR.

Byggeriets Udviklingsråd. 1987b. *Bofællesskabet Jystrup Savværk*. Copenhagen: BUR.

Byggeriets Udviklingsråd. 1983. *Veje til Bofællesskab*. Copenhagen: BUR.

Cronberg, Tarja. 1986. "Tenants' Involvement in the Management of Social Housing in the Nordic Countries," *Scandinavian Housing and Planning Research* **3**:65-87.

Fromm, Dorit. 1985. "Living-Together Housing." *Architectural Review* (April):62-71.

Vedel-Petersen, Finn; Erik B. Jantzen; and Karen Ranten. 1988. *Bofællesskaber*. Hørsholm: Danish Building Research Institute SBI Rapport 187 (in Danish with four-page English summary; includes statistics, floor plans, and explanations of thirty-one cohousing developments; available through SBI, Postboks 119, 2970 Hørsholm, Denmark).

CHAPTER 3

Dutch Collaborative Housing

HILVERSUMSE MEENT: URBAN CLUSTERS

Hilversum, Holland
Units: 50
Tenure: Rental
Site: Urban, 4.5 acres

Began/Moved in: 1970/1977
Architects: Leo de Jonge and Pieter Weeda

Hilversumse Meent (Hilversum Commons), the first Dutch collaborative housing (built in 1977), proclaims itself boldly to the public.

A housing cluster seen from the pedestrian street. Roofs differentiate private from common: barrel-vaulted roofs cover the residences, and a flat roof deck covers the common kitchen-dining area. *(Jonge)*

The arched roof, the red-lipstick-colored facade, and the common spaces protruding along the pedestrian path are hard to ignore. The public front is only one indication of this different, more urban type of cohousing. Within, a mixed population has been housed under rental ownership (twenty-four singles, eleven single parents, six couples, and thirteen couples with children, with 15% unemployed). Walking along the public paths, pedestrians can glimpse into the windows of a number of smaller common houses and begin to get a sense of the levels of community created through the architecture.

This rental community, located in Hilversum, between Utrecht and Amsterdam, is moving successfully into its second decade. It was the first collaborative housing built in Holland and had to tackle the issues involved in rental development, management, and organization.[1]

The future residents envisioned a community where they would live in less isolation; their goals—for themselves and their children—were to develop new friendships. Neither relief from chores nor greater efficiency in completing tasks were major expectations (Backus and Kesler). Their strong participation in the development process resulted in an architecture that reflects these goals and has influenced many of the communities built since.

The future residents faced the question of how to create an intimate community with large numbers of people.[2] Of the several possibilities available—a large central dining hall, dividing into two projects, or dividing into small subgroups—they chose to divide into ten subgroups, called clusters. B. J. Fris, a founding member, explains:

At a certain moment, a decision had to be made on how we would take our meals together. Separate or common? Only one person opted for separate meals, and two wanted a restaurant arrangement. All the rest wanted smaller groups and intimacy. It's the most direct neighborship. We could go to a restaurant-type meal a few times a week, and have a looser connection among ourselves. But our concept was a more intensive cooperation.

Once the decision was made to create common kitchens for restricted numbers of people, the housing was placed around the common kitchens. The group wanted to dine with seven or eight households together, and the architect reduced that number to five. Daily management and maintenance naturally followed this organizational division, to be done by five households together.

The architecture therefore divides the housing into clusters of four or five, and small versions of common kitchen and dining facilities are attached to each cluster. The cluster kitchen is used exclusively by the surrounding four or five households.[3] (Four households chose not to live in clusters but rather as independent houses, and an additional two houses for young people also do not belong to a cluster.) A wider social level is created through sharing of certain amenities by all fifty households: a meeting room, hobby shop, sauna, bar, three guest rooms, and a common garden.[4]

The clusters are not the most efficient way of organizing the daily tasks and common facilities. Inherent in them is some redundancy in common facilities. In Hilversumse Meent, there are ten kitchens, and two different kinds of meeting areas are required—one for the clusters and one for all the residents. In addition, the design has not been planned for completing chores in a cooperative manner. Kitchen-dining areas and laundries are far from each other, and small children cannot be supervised easily from the various common facilities.

The emphasis is on completing chores within this smaller group of cluster households, creating a sort of community-family. With 65% of the residents in this community single or single parents, clustering is an effective way of socially organizing them (Van Rooijen and Veldkamp).

The households are not isolated from other clusters or from the public. The design has also taken great care in not appearing isolated from the surrounding neighborhood. The clusters are located along two pedestrian streets, open to the neighborhood, which cross to form a square in the center of the site.

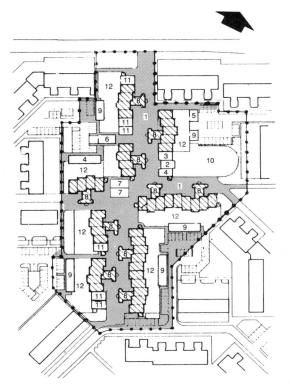

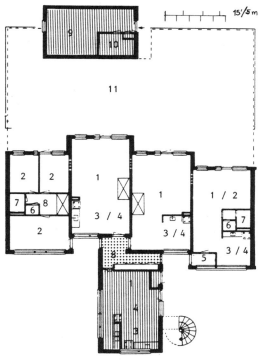

Hilversumse Meent has ten clusters, each with a common kitchen-dining room. *(Jonge).*

1. Public pedestrian walkway; 2. library; 3. meeting room; 4. bar-café; 5. sauna; 6. workshop; 7. studio (formerly teen room); 8. cluster kitchen-dining room; 9. cluster laundry and storage; 10. common garden; 11. dwellings not sharing cluster kitchen; 12. private or cluster garden.

Each cluster consists of five complete living units, each with its own kitchen, bedrooms, and bathroom, plus a shared kitchen-dining area in front. There are sixteen different combinations of units, with bedrooms and kitchens on either the first or second floor. *(Jonge)*

1. Living room; 2. bedroom; 3. kitchen; 4. dining room; 5. entrance; 6. toilet; 7. shower; 8. hall; 9. cluster storage; 10. cluster laundry; 11. private or cluster garden.

The neighbors, suspicious at first, have accepted the community.[5]

Working with Nonprofit Sponsors

The start of Dutch *centraal wonen* ("central living") began in 1969 when Lies van Dooremaal, a mother overwhelmed by the combination of work, housekeeping, and tending to the children, published an ad in the newspaper, making a plea for housing with common amenities to break the cycle of the isolated and overworked mother. She reasoned that other mothers shared her problems, and that instead of living in isolation, they could help each other.

The ad sparked an enthusiastic response in much the same way as the similar articles had in Denmark a few years before, but there was a distinct difference between the groups that formed. While the Danish articles attracted married couples, the Dutch group grew to include not only couples but singles, single parents, and elderly. Their motivations were also similar to the Danes as far as sharing amenities and management and creating a community with more social contact. Much more strongly than the Danes, however, the Dutch viewed collaborative housing as a tool to reform society, or as the National Association of Centraal Wonen (LVCW), created in 1971 as an umbrella organization for the new collective housing, would also proclaim, "for the emancipation of man, women and child" (Krabbe). In a sense, the Dutch groups questioned not only the isolation of the one-family home but also the isolation brought about by the nuclear family structure.

In 1970, a group of thirty to thirty-five people (twenty-five households) organized with the intention of building collaborative housing, in Hilversum. Although central living is similar in concept to cohousing, it grew independently of the Danish efforts. Danish cohousing was originally a home ownership alternative. Dutch central living was originally conceived as a rental alternative. Realizing collaborative housing as rentals was more difficult and time-consuming because the future residents were not the only ones who had to be convinced that this form of housing was a good idea. The group wanted to reach all levels of society through affordable housing.

In Holland social (subsidized) housing has traditionally been built by local nonprofit housing associations with government funding. Since the beginning of this century, such housing sponsors have been the channel for government subsidies to build rental housing. Many nonprofit sponsors were not willing to take the risk of sponsoring this new type of housing since common facilities were not defined in the government's affordable-housing legislation.

The group enlisted the aid of architects Leo de Jonge and Pieter Weeda from Rotterdam to prepare a few sketches. (The architects agreed to work without being paid until sponsorship was acquired.) The first nonprofit organization the group approached rejected the idea, but the second, Stichting Woningcorporaties, agreed to take on this experiment.

Because they were working with a nonprofit organization, the Hilversum group could not see many of their wishes realized. In addition, Stichting Woningcorporaties required an alternative floor plan showing how the dwellings could be converted back to "normal" housing. The plans allowed such a transformation into small units for the elderly with a minimum of alteration.

The advantages of not having to pay or sign anything during the long development process meant that many people, with different backgrounds and financial means, could participate and eventually be housed. The disadvantage was that working with a nonprofit organization required dealing with bureaucracy, which takes time. People who have not had to commit themselves monetarily drop out more easily.[6]

The group formed an association that leases all the buildings from the nonprofit housing society, rents out the housing to members, and is responsible for collecting rent. A second association made up of all the residents, the membership association, makes decisions and manages the community.

Construction began in 1976, and a year later eighty-eight adults and fifty-four children moved into the community of Hilversumse Meent. To allow for a diversity of households, the dwellings come in four sizes, ranging from 441 square feet to 1,152 square feet (41–107 meters). The layout allows many combinations by locating the stairs and bathroom in the center and freeing the rooms on each end to become the living room, the kitchen, or bedrooms. The families participated in the design of their own units, resulting in about thirty variations.

The Clusters

The ten clusters have different levels of participation. Three years after Hilversumse Meent started, researcher Beatrice Kesler noted that in three clusters, the tenants share dinner five or six nights a week, in three clusters meals are shared at least twice a week, and in four clusters residents share evening meals once or twice a week. In all clusters, there had been serious conflicts, but solutions to most problems had been found. (A small number of households stopped participating in cluster activities or moved out.) Kesler concludes that the cluster is an "extremely successful social construction" and that "in all ten clusters there are social activities, 40 out of 44 households have cluster contacts . . . with an average time-investment of 10 hours a week" (Kesler).[7]

In its fourteen years of operation, Hilversumse Meent has been a stable community. Nineteen of the fifty original households remain (one-third of all the adults but only a few of the children, who are now teenagers). The resident composition has remained about the same.[8]

Most residents would say the clusters have proved to be a success. Each cluster has its own administration concerning cooking and cleaning. Common meals are cooked up to five times a week in some clusters. At the end of the week, each cook receives a set amount of money—around 4 guilders ($2)—from each person who has eaten. In B. J. Fris's cluster, the cook for the day does his or her own shopping. "If I cook for only myself, it takes me 10 minutes. I do my best for these ten to thirteen people, and I cook for hours, but I enjoy it more," says one resident. Others might choose not to spend the extra time or money. A mother with three boys, says: "When I have to cook, it takes me 2 hours, and this way I only have to spend the time once a week." Another cluster buys groceries and basic household goods in common to receive bulk prices.

Two clusters no longer cook or eat together. One of them has turned the common space into a cluster living room.[9] The other eight clusters share common meals from one to five times a week. Yet all the tenants participate in the community to some extent by attending meetings, gardening, or working behind the bar for the evening.

Some problems have occurred within clusters but not between them. All clusters have experienced some conflicts among residents over selecting new members, concerning divorce, handling children, and carrying out tasks. Some households have solved these issues better than others; a few have retreated socially, if not physically. The clusters have become a kind of extended family; like families, they can be more sensitive and nurturing to individuals or more disappointing than a larger group.

DUTCH CENTRAL LIVING: LEVELS OF COMMUNITY

In the Netherlands, there are fifty-five *centraal wonen* developments; almost 2,000 dwellings and fifteen more communities are being developed. Dutch collaborative housing is typically larger and more urban than Danish cohousing.[10] About 93% of the dwellings are rentals, owned by large, independent, nonprofit organizations funded by the government. The remaining are resident owned, and their small number places them on the sidelines of the Dutch collaborative movement.[11]

Rentals raise issues that are less common in private ownership: a large size due to economic considerations, greater turnover, and fewer membership selection criteria (since public housing needs to be made available to the public). While Danish cohousing is typically rowhouses with a shared kitchen in the common house, the diversity of Dutch developments makes generalizations difficult. The Dutch projects have a wide range of households, housing types, number of common kitchens and amount of common space, as shown in Table 3.1 (pages 52-53). Almost half the tenants are single (Table 3.2, page 53) and a third are single parents. (In contrast, Danish cohousing is almost two-thirds traditional families.) There are children in half the households.[12] Typically turnover is 6-10% per year in the Dutch developments, compared to 3-5% a year in the Danish developments (but lower than in other types of Dutch rental housing).[13] One reason is that the Danish residents are home owners. Another is that singles and single parents between 20 and 50 years of age are often in transition. "We have need for experiences, for changing situations. We are in development," explained an ex-member, a divorced man who moved out after he remarried.

In collaborative housing, the residents are

Members of a cluster share chores, rotate meal preparation, and dine together. The small number of households creates a more intimate family feeling within the larger collaborative community.

subdivided into groups to accomplish tasks, but these divisions are social (not part of a physical structure). In about 50% of the Dutch developments with over forty households, the architecture physically divides the households into clusters, as does the first collaborative development in Hilversum.[14]

The Dutch physically create levels of socializing between the private dwelling and the collaborating community through smaller common areas for the exclusive use of a specific cluster of households. Hilversumse Meent contains the private level of the dwelling, the semiprivate area of shared backyards, the semicommon level of the cluster kitchen, the common level of shared workshops and pub, and the public level of the pedestrian paths in front of the homes.

Dividing the larger households into smaller groups fosters a greater sense of intimacy. Many decisions about organization can be tailored more closely to the individual clusters. On the flip side, small groups of twelve

households or fewer have more small-scale social problems because of their intimacy. In addition, there is no clear division between the jurisdiction of the community as a whole and that of the cluster. For example, should the cluster or the whole community decide on a new member?[15]

When the kitchen-dining area is no longer central but scattered among the clusters, the sense of community is altered. Providing a common kitchen is substantially different from providing other kinds of common areas for specific groups of dwellings. Cooking and eating together is one of the fundamental ways that individual households retain a sense of community. A strong social grouping is created, similar to a family clan. One reason for its popularity is that the majority of households are single or single parents (75 percent). The strength of these clusters or clans of households has a bearing on the strength of the community.[16]

Architecture can reinforce these social

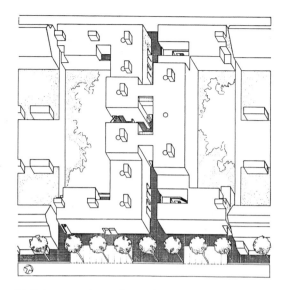

Hallehuis, in Amersfoort, has a pedestrian street created by the two housing blocks, whose wings continue the scale and form of the surrounding houses and create two open spaces used as common gardens. *(Dolf Floors)*

Hallehuis has three types of living spaces: thirty-one basic units (living room, bedroom, and kitchenette), twenty-two rooms, and twenty individual units for one or two persons who choose not to be in the group (located at the ends of the building). *(Dolf Floors)*

A. Individual unit for two persons; B. individual unit for one or two persons; BU. basic units. 1. Room; 2. common kitchen-dining area; 3. café; 4. laundry; 5. storage.

Table 3.1   Data for Dutch Collaborative Housing

Project	Owner-ship[a]	No. of Residents	No. of Units	Site Size	No. of Units per Hectare[b]	Built Area (foot-print) (sq. m)	Percentage of Built Area	Gross Built Area	Date of First Initiative or Land Purchase
Arnhem	Rental	57	30	4,125	73	775	0.19		1979
Banier	Rental	89	51	2,520	202	2,000	0.79	5,800	1975
Beuk	Owner	11	10	900	111	138	0.15	450	1977
Bijvanck	Rental	93	50	6,000	83	1,804	0.30	6,300	1979
Cayenne	Owner	17	5	600	83	400	0.67	612	1978
Delft	Rental	130	80	6,500	123	2,170	0.33	6,900	1975
Drielandenhuis	Rental	66	39	3,000	130	1,168	0.39	3,560	1984
Emmen	Rental	118	51	9,100	56	3,250	0.36	4,500	1980
Gerestraat	Rental	70	37	3,600	103	1,288	0.36	3,582	1984
Heerd	Rental	76	49	8,400	58	1,200	0.14	4,159	1979
Het Hallehuis	Rental	47	31	3,500	89	2,000	0.57	2,970	1976
Het Punt	Rental	124	43	4,575	94	1,872	0.41	4,057	1980
Het Woonschap	Rental	44	26	3,648	71	1,402	0.38	2,900	1984
Hilversumse	Rental	116	54	18,110	30	2,381	0.13	6,930	1973
Hofstede	Owner	28	12	1,400	86	340	0.24	1,040	1980
Lelystad	Rental	67	32	7,500	43	1,658	0.22	3,718	1982
Lismortel	Rental	112	67	13,750	49	3,340	0.24		1979
Meenthe	Mixed	63	20	10,000	20	2,500	0.25	2,514	1976
Mienskiplik Wenjen	Rental	16	8	1,521	53	336	0.22	990	1979
Nieuwegein	Rental	205	167	12,100	154	3,670	0.30	11,900	1979
Purmerend	Mixed	154	71	8,400	85	2,550	0.30		1982
Regenbog	Rental	76	40	5,250	76	2,321	0.44	4,266	1981
Rensumaheerd	Rental	55	27	2,700	100	1,120	0.41	2,945	1980
Rups	Rental	24	9	1,250	72	420	0.34		1981
Spijkenisse	Rental	71	60	9,500	63	2,145	0.23	6,312	1979
't Houtwijk	Rental	92	49	4,482	109	1,034	0.23	5,219	1981
't Oud Armenhuis	Owner	14	4	780	51	275	0.35		1980
't Vierschaar	Rental	62	25	6,000	42	1,012	0.17		1980
Utrecht	Rental	118	80	12,000	67	1,518	0.13	4,895	1982
Vught	Mixed	62	29	5,000	58	1,626	0.33		1984
Wierden	Rental	38	20	2,720	74	1,208	0.44	1,970	1982
Winihoes	Owner	16	5	1,200	42	400	0.33	764	1983
Zaandam	Rental	14	11	1,000	110	648	0.65		1983
Zevenkamp	Rental	127	60	10,500	57	3,135	0.30	6,935	1979
Zwartehandspoort	Mixed	12	11	835	132	403	0.48	924	1983
Zwolle	Rental	78	35	4,500	78	1,383	0.31	3,633	1983

[a] Owner: Similar to condominium ownership, where the resident owns the dwelling and has an ownership share in the common areas.
Rental: Owned by private nonprofit housing associations.
Mixed: Combination of rental and owner housing.
[b] A hectare is a metric unit of area equal to 2.5 acres.
[c] Closed cluster, indicating housing connected to a specific cluster kitchen.
[d] Also twenty-two independent houses that share a common-house kitchen, and three group houses each with a shared kitchen.
[e] Groups, indicating many units do not have private kitchens but share them with another unit.

groupings by connecting the housing to a specific cluster kitchen, as in Hilversum. In Hilversum, some residents felt locked into their particular cluster. Unlike the Danish example, there is little opportunity to mix or eat with a larger group. New communities allow for more flexible architecture so that clusters are open to various social groupings. Two differ-ent types of clusters now occur in large projects: the closed cluster of Hilversumse Meent, where the cluster rooms are physically tied to the dwellings, and the open cluster, where common facilities are not connected to a particular group of dwellings.

In Het Hallehuis (the Hall House, built in Amersfoort in 1984), six cluster kitchens are

		Private Units		Common Spaces					
Construction Started	Move-In Date	Range of Sizes (sq. m)	Total Area (sq. m)	Total Area (sq. m)	Meters per Unit	Percentage of Meters per Unit	Housing Type	No. of Common Kitchens	No. of Clusters
1979	1980	40-58	2,039	310	10	0.15	Row houses	0	0
1978	1980	88-118	4,100	790	15	0.19	Midrise	8	0
1977	1977	26-47	260	131	13	0.50	Renovated bldg.	1	0
1981	1982	45-90	3,945	1,038	21	0.26	2 Buildings	6	6
1979	1979	88-90	415	156	31	0.38	Houses	1	0
1980	1981	30-60	4,700	1,300	16	0.28	5 Buildings	12	4C^c
1985	1986	45-95	2,047	478	12	0.23	Midrise	3	3
1984	1985	45-83	3,600	450	9	0.13	Row houses	3	0
1985	1986	57-113	2,480	622	17	0.25	Midrise	7	7
1981	1982	12-90	3,316	790	16	0.24	2 Buildings	7	6-10
1983	1984	42-50	1,303	755	24	0.58	2 Buildings	6	6
1984	1985	45-90	3,630	427	10	0.12	Mixed^d	7	3
1985	1985	53-102	2,161	400	15	0.19	Row buildings	1	0
1976	1977	36-100	4,270	1,740	32	0.41	Low Rise	10	10C^c
1981	1981	45-90	850	132	11	0.16	Houses	1	0
1985	1986	40-118	3,437	260	8	0.08	Row houses	1	0
1982	1983	40-100	3,891	630	9	0.16	Row buildings	10	10
1980	1981	120	1,908	308	15	0.16	Row houses	1	0
1980	1982	78-124	897	60	8	0.07	Row buildings	1	0
1981	1982	20-38	9,000	2,400	14	0.27	9 Buildings	31	G^e
1984	1985	66-95	4,900	927	13	0.19	Row buildings	10	10C^c
1985	1985	50-85	2,405	555	14	0.23	Row houses	6	6
1981	1982	40-90	1,964	643	24	0.33	Renovated	1	0
1983	1983	35-70	810	70	8	0.09	Row buildings	1	0
1981	1981	50-100	5,502	810	14	0.15	10 Buildings	7	10C^c
1983	1984	50-108	2,898	966	20	0.33	Midrise	1	0
1981	1981	70	469	39	10	0.08	Houses	0	0
1983	1984	72-125	2,533	300	12	0.12	Row buildings	2	0
1983	1984	12-50	3,567	1,328	17	0.37	12 Towers	21	12C^c
1984	1985	67-130	3,564	136	5	0.04	Row buildings	0	0
1984	1984	64-98	1,732	200	10	0.12	Row houses	1	0
1984	1985	100	580	164	33	0.28	Row houses	1	0
1985	1985	44-64	600	180	16	0.30	Midrise	2	2G^e
1981	1982	55-116	4,105	819	14	0.20	7 Apt buildings	0	6
1985	1985	67-120	744	45	4	0.06	Renovated	1	0
1984	1985	35-100	2,385	585	17	0.25	Row buildings	6	6

Table 3.2   Average Household Composition in Centraal Wonen (from 36 projects)

Singles	47.4%
Single parents	28.2%
Couples	6.8%
Couples w/children	16.0%
3 or more person household	0.5%
3 or more person w/children	0.6%
Unknown	0.5%

Source: Van Rooijen and Veldkamp, 1989.

located along interior hallways. The tenants are divided among six groups (corresponding to the number of kitchens), but the division was intended to be social, not architectural. To outward appearances, the separate groups are indistinguishable. Nevertheless, each of the six groups is tightly organized; members view themselves as a household, deciding how and when to share meals. Each shared kitchen has a distinct character. Residents do not walk into or use the kitchen of another group or enter another group's rooms (although the doors are unlocked).

Eight of the thirty-one units are designed to provide an option of belonging to more than one kitchen. If there is disharmony in the cluster, a resident can join another kitchen.[17] In addition, twenty separate units, located at the end of each building, do not belong to a cluster.

The open cluster has the advantage of allowing residents some socializing choices, but those living in a closed cluster argue otherwise. A resident of Hilversumse believes that a closed cluster "forces the people to cooperate or leave." In an open cluster, people can drop out of one group, and not get around to joining another, basically not participating or seeing the necessity to do so.

Stretching the concept of open or increased options, the dwellings in some collab-

44

basic units and rooms
individual units for persons not connected with group

private accomodation:
first floor plan

second floor plan

third floor plan

45

group rooms
common facilities
toilets / bathrooms
deck

common facility accommodation:
first floor plan

second floor plan

third floor plan
1-6, division of housing clusters for one group

Each household *(top)* has one basic unit and, if desired, one or more rooms. The number of households in a cluster varies because of the possibilities of interchanging units and rooms among residents and with adjacent housing clusters. Cluster rooms contain a kitchen-dining area, bathroom, and storage. Common facilities *(bottom)* for all members include a meeting hall, guest room, laundry, café, and garden. Hallways allow internal access to all units. *(LVCW)*

orative developments have the ability to be readjusted. The majority of residents in Hallehuis are nontraditional families—61% single households, 36% single parents, and only 2% couples with children.[18] (Some of the single households are couples who have chosen to live in separate units.) The unique requirements of the households resulted in the design of two different unit types: thirty-one studios (33 square meters) and twenty-six rooms (7–11 square meters). Small bathrooms (5 square meters) are located next to the studios. Several types of spaces can be created—one large studio with a kitchenette, a separate room with its own entrance, or a small room with a toilet and sink. With the closing of a hall door, these separate rooms can also be one complete dwelling, up to 540 square feet (50 square meters).[19] As new partnerships are made or dissolved, as children visit or leave, as jobs are accomplished at home or the workplace, the dwelling can change. Sixteen of the single rooms are located on the second floor for children and teenagers. As children

grow older, they have the choice of moving upstairs into their own wing of the building.

The tenants at Hallehuis appreciate their unique apartment designs. The disadvantage of such flexibility is that the line between private and common becomes blurred. Dwellings can turn into shared units or other interesting combinations, and this may bother more traditional households. Also, there may be more conflicts when less privacy is available (for example, over the issue of cleaning in sharing a toilet).

Communities in Delft, Nieuwegein, and Utrecht do not have completely independent units. In these group dwellings, several residents share bathrooms and kitchens, similar to shared housing (see Appendix A). There is also a cluster kitchen and dining area shared by a group of seven to thirteen residents. A number of residents want more privacy; they are particularly unhappy about sharing bathrooms. Almost all recent Dutch collaborative developments have independent dwellings.

Het Punt (The Point, Wageningen 1985)

Unusual for collaborative developments, this cluster kitchen *(right)*, one of six, is not a supplementary space. The private units have kitchenettes *(above)* for making coffee or warming up food but are too small for making daily meals. *(Ans Melse)*

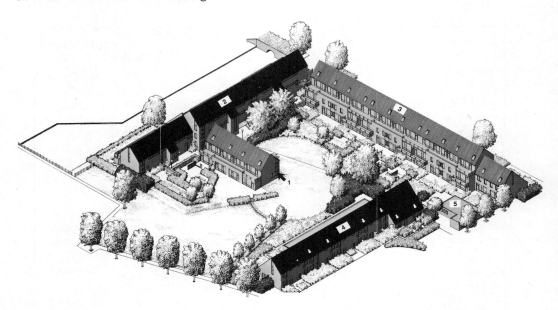

Het Punt, Wageningen, has three clusters, three group residences, and twenty-one independent residences with four rooms in the common house for troubled teenagers. *(René Siemens)*

1. Common house; 2. independent apartments; 3. closed cluster apartments; 4. row houses; 5. bicycle storage.

tries to combine the best of all worlds with its three types of living arrangements: three closed clusters, twenty-two independent dwellings, and three group dwellings.[20] In addition, there is a separate common house, with four of the upstairs rooms rented to troubled teenagers. (A special committee oversees the teenagers and receives a stipend from the city.) The closed clusters are located in an apartment building. Each cluster, which contains six households, has its own stairway and ground-level kitchen-dining area. The households are predominantly single and single parents and eat together five nights a week. The independent dwellings—both apartments and row houses—make primary use of the common house through eating groups. The group dwellings contain two five-bedroom row houses (one altered for a handicapped person) and one apartment; each member of the group has a private bedroom but shares the kitchen and living room.

Het Punt also has flexible apartments; in effect, they have two front doors and between them is a room (or sometimes several). By us-

ing the second front door as the entrance to the apartment, the room in front can be used as a studio, office, or separate bedroom. (One wall within the apartment can also be moved.)

These various levels of community involvement have worked out well for the tenants. One couple eager to move into a cluster was rejected as incompatible by the other cluster-mates, and they now happily live in one of the row houses. Tenants can and do move within the community, a housing rich with choices.

Another level of choice has been tried in four developments, where renters are mixed with owners. In Zwartehandspoort, Leiden, eight of the eleven dwellings are under home ownership, and three are nonprofit rentals. All the households belong to one association of residents.

Zwartehandspoort is located around an old courtyard in the heart of Leiden, and the housing has been carefully renovated. New housing has been constructed between the existing dwellings, financed by a public hous-

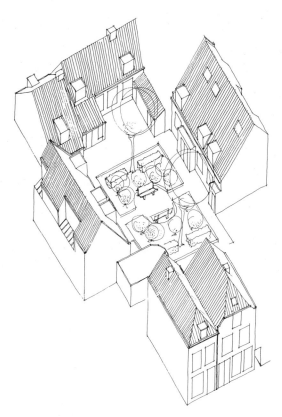

Zwartehandspoort, Leiden, has eight renovated houses owned by the residents and three rentals, constructed in 1985. One of the renovated buildings houses the common house. *(LVCW)*

ing company. One of the old homes has been renovated into a common house. Four other renovations of older buildings now house collaborative communities.

Of the fifty-five developments, six are owned entirely by the residents. These residents have higher incomes than the renters, and the number of households is much smaller. The smaller, richer communities appear to function very smoothly, as do the higher-income rentals. The large lowest-income rental developments have more problems in organization and among residents because of financial difficulties and turnover.

The forty-nine rental developments (including four with mixed ownerships) have proved to be fairly successful.[21] The amount of collaboration is high, although it decreases

when there are more than fifty households. Then there is less interest in attending meetings, due in part to the stronger role of the cluster and in part to some apathy that seems to occur more in a large group. Communities that are divided into clusters, including those under fifty households, generally have one or two clusters that do not share common meals.

A very different viewpoint can be taken: that stability over time is not important in this way of living. Resident Jaap Schippers, of Hallehuis in Amersfoort believes these communities satisfy a different kind of need: "You do not move here to stop changes. You come here to be more alive, to develop yourself. You need changing people around you who play the role of different mirrors, all playing back different facets of yourself to you. It's natural and good that things are not always smooth and that there are turnovers in the group. The group is not a purpose in itself but the medium, the driving force."

PURMEREND: FINANCING EXPERIMENTS

Purmerend, Holland
Units: 71
Tenure: Rental
Site: Urban, 8,400 square meters
Began/Moved in: 1982/1985
Architects: Verhoeven Architects

Computers, good child care, a large common house, a small store—tenants have a list of wishes and needs for their communities. But financing rental collaborative housing is a growing issue. In Holland, the rental subsidies that most of the developments depend on are not keeping pace with inflation. In addition, how can the communities afford the extra facilities that make this a new way of living? An average of 17% of the private floor area is given over to common facilities, and as costs rise, the amount will decrease.

Woon Kollektief Purmerend completed in 1985, tackled the problem of financing by mixing owners with renters, distributing costs

Three-story housing encircles the common garden in Purmerend, Holland.

Plan of Purmerend. Dark gray indicates the common house and common passageways; light gray, cluster kitchen-dining rooms. *(Verhoeven)*

A. Common house; B. central hallway; C. cluster kitchen; D. shared garden.

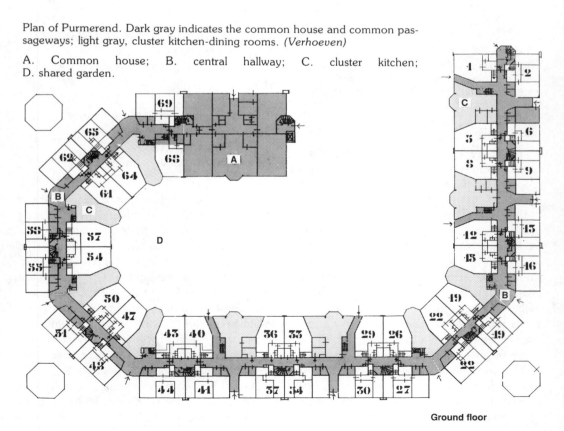

Ground floor

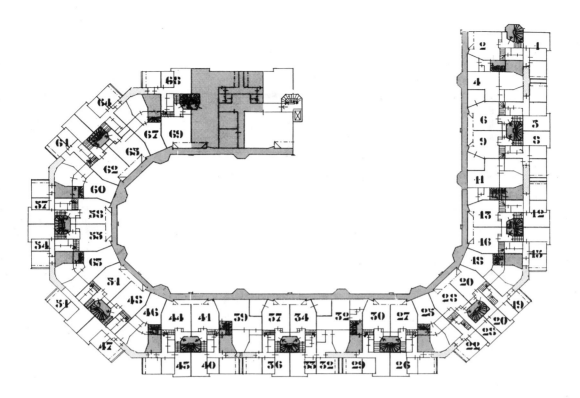

Second floor

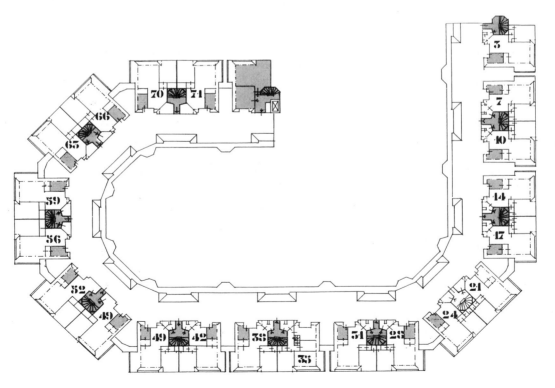

Third floor

59

Plan of the common house. *(Verhoeven)*

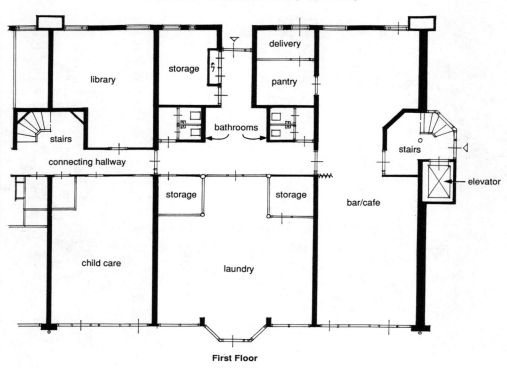

First Floor

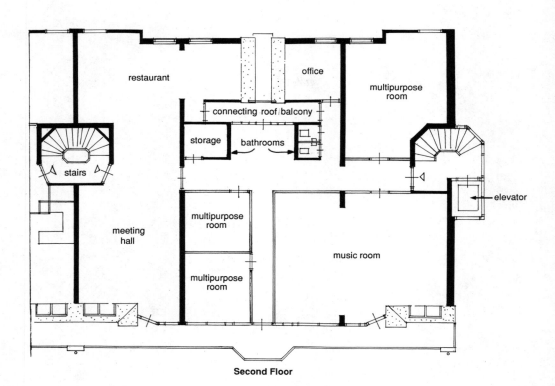

Second Floor

equitably among all the tenants, providing common facilities to be used and paid for by the surrounding neighborhood, sweat equity, and creative financing.

Purmerend is located in a newly built extension of the town of Purmerend, about a half-hour's commute from Amsterdam. The seventy-one households have been divided into ten clusters, each with a cluster kitchen. Each cluster is a three-story "house" with its own staircase and seven individual apartments. These "houses" are strung together, giving the appearance of oversized row houses. An interior corridor, like a street, runs through the ground level from one end to the other, connecting all the clusters and the common house. The "houses" curve around a garden but remain open at one end to the neighborhood.

The common house is located at the open end, closest to the neighborhood. Inside are a pub, a kitchen, meeting rooms, a day care center, a laundromat, office spaces, and a manager's unit. Purmerend is an architectur-

ally interesting project, with much of its construction in wood, unusual for Holland. The architect, Jan Verhoeven, used detailing and colors to emphasize differences between the cluster levels. The soft contours, with right angles consciously avoided, and the warm colors and materials create a cozy type of housing for the 160 residents.

Purmerend today contains seventy-one households. Of them, 35% are couples with children, 35% are singles, 26% are single parents, and 4% are couples. Twenty percent have monthly income levels under $485, 46% range from $486 to $690, 10% range from $691 to $920, 7% range from $921 to $1,150, and 17% earn over $1,150 (van Rooijen and Veldkamp).

Innovative Ideas

Purmerend was begun by a group of fifteen to twenty people in 1980. The most farsighted of the members, Henk van Schaijk

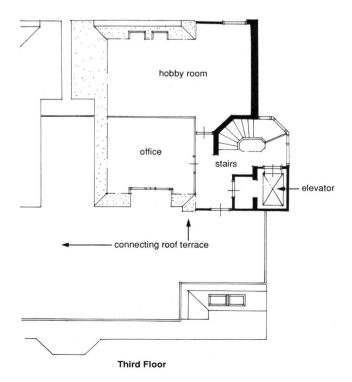

Third Floor

(pronounced "schank"), combined a number of innovative financing ideas; in theory they were sound, but they became difficult to execute.

Mixing Owners with Renters

Of the four Dutch developments that mix rentals with owners, Purmerend is the largest.[22] Forty-two households rent, and twenty-nine are owners. There are several advantages of mixing ownership: owners can afford more amenities and receive tax benefits, renters can receive government subsidies, and in combination more money is available to the community. Owners have also been found to be more responsible than renters, with a positive effect on managing the development.

In Purmerend, funding regulations required a clear distinction between the location of housing for renters and for owners. The architects' solution was to create "half-houses" placed on either side of common kitchens. By connecting two half-houses, renters' and owners' units didn't appear to be in separate buildings but could still share the cluster kitchen.

Renters and owners together make decisions on management and maintenance.[23] The association chooses the new buyers for the housing. In effect, the buyers receive user rights but not full property rights. The selling price for the owned units is also set by the association.

On the whole, there is little difference between the renters and owners as far as management and maintenance. One difference is the typical one that owners are personally liable for their house payments and renters are not. Normally this difference is not felt, but if the development faces economic problems, as Purmerend does, the difference becomes important. Financial meeting are heavily attended by owners; renters do not feel as responsible. Albert Ringer, an owner, points out, "The renters don't feel the importance of solving financial problems, but the owners feel it's very important. When someone rents a place like this, he can just leave, but owners have obligations."

Equitable Distribution of Costs

Purmerend is one of the very few developments where the central living association not the nonprofit housing corporation, collects the rent. The residents sign their housing contracts with the collaborative association, made up of all the residents. The reason is that the residents have decided to calculate housing expenses according to their own formula, which takes into account household income, dwelling size, and household size. Although this establishes an equitable system in dividing expenses, its administration is difficult, and not everyone agrees to it. There is now talk of changes to this system.

One reason is that the association has to evict tenants who do not pay. The residents find it very hard to throw their neighbor out, and evictions of nonpaying residents can take over six months to a year. Resident Lucy van Rooy, an ex-board member, explains the difficulty:

You know almost everyone that lives here. And there are people that you like, or personally you respect them, and then when you're on the board and you get letters about the same nice people— that they don't want to pay or that they don't want to work or are making problems—and it's so hard—you just can't imagine those people doing things like that. You can't have a businesslike relationship with people.

Providing Common Facilities to the Neighborhood

Purmerend has a three-story common house and a number of amenities. The pub, child care, laundry, rentable spaces, and restaurant were built with the idea that the surrounding neighborhood would use them and thus offset the costs. Although the reason that each of these amenities has not been a financial success varies, they seem to point to the difficulty of mixing business with housing.

The pub was a popular meeting place for residents and neighborhood people. It contained a bar, with drinks and snacks served most evenings; often live music by local musicians; and a billiard table. But running the bar with resident volunteers proved to be time-consuming and not a financial success. Eventually the bar was sold to outsiders and turned into a private enterprise—a combination restaurant and bar—with prices too high for most residents. A separate restaurant started by several residents as a collaborative housing enterprise was closed when the resident cook moved out of Purmerend and has not reopened.

The laundry has commercial-size washers and dryers in a large, attractive room. Residents took turns overseeing the laundry and providing detergent. Unfortunately, the neighborhood has not made enough use of these machines to offset the expense of the equipment cost. Some residents claim that the idea was not a good one and that most neighbors use their own machines at home. Another opinion was voiced by several residents: "There were many complaints by the neighbors because of the service. If you start your own business, you need to be a workaholic. It's not something you do part time."

The child care is one of the most successful of the Purmerend enterprises, with twenty-five children (twenty from the neighborhood and five from Purmerend) between $1\frac{1}{2}$ and 4 years old. At first the child care was run as a cooperative but became too difficult to organize. Now there is a team of five volunteers who run the day care from 8:00 A.M. to 5:30 P.M. and receive a small stipend. Child care has not proved to be a money-making operation; if the workers received a normal salary, the cost for the care would be too high for the neighborhood.

The idea of business's subsidizing the housing has not worked in Purmerend. Residents believe there is not enough time and energy to run these businesses or the dedication and business mentality required to get the businesses off the ground.[24]

Sweat Equity

The intention was to save about $70,000 (150,000–200,000 guilders) on construction through residents' contributing labor (each prospective resident contributed 80 hours of work). In the end, more money was spent than hoped to be saved. One reason was the difficulty in motivating people to complete the work and another was the level of skill required. They were not professionals and went through a good deal of expensive finishing material without the best results. Then professionals were hired to finish the job at a higher rate than the job would have cost if it had been part of the total construction costs.

Creative Financing

By claiming all the shared amenities as a commercial enterprise, the association hoped to receive a tax break. Initially they did, but then the tax authorities reversed their stand and held that many of the common spaces had nothing to do with businesses and taxes would have to be paid. The tax money, unfortunately, had already been reinvested in the project.

Another source of money was to have been the various businesses started in the common house. These businesses required start-up money to furnish the spaces and buy equipment.[25] When the loan could not be paid off because the businesses had faltered, the common house was legally split from the rest of the housing. The spaces in the common house were rented out to small business enterprises, but the administration and upkeep of these rented spaces was considered too bothersome by many of the Purmerend residents. Eventually the common house was sold to pay for the taxes and the loans.

Purmerend Today

Purmerend is still experiencing financial difficulties; its back taxes and business start-up loans have not been paid off.[26] The financial problems have been difficult for this central living community. The complicated nature of the financing is beyond the comprehension of most of the residents, and many find this frus-

The common house, in back, is no longer part of the development. The downstairs bar is now a private restaurant, and the upstairs meeting hall is rented out for community events. Residents still retain other common spaces, such as the cluster kitchens, gardens, and play areas.

trating. Part of the original group has moved out in altercations over the financing. Nevertheless, the community continues to manage and maintain itself. Common meals, child care, social events, and daily shared tasks have not stopped, nor has the community changed its goals or objectives. Of the ten clusters, seven function well, and three do not

have meals on a regular basis. There is a great deal of contact between the clusters.

Purmerend is not typical of Dutch central living. Most of the other communities are conventionally financed and make no attempt to mix housing with other sources of revenue. Purmerend is an exception, intended to show a flip side to the housing experiments. (Denmark and Sweden also have a few developments with social or financial difficulties.) The skepticism that such results elicit need to be measured—if one can measure such things—against the large number of successful projects.

NOTES

1. Tinggården (1978), a rental cohousing development, divides residents into clusters similar to Hilversumse Meent.
2. The large number of households was required to offset the cost of development for the non-profit organization, to provide enough room for the common amenities, and to allow a range of amenities, such as rooms for child care.
3. Each household has its own complete dwelling, with kitchen, bathrooms, and private back yard (40–100 square meters).
4. Originally there was a kindergarten and a club for teenagers. The kindergarten closed after a number of years because of too few children. (A tapestry artist is now renting the space.) The club was sacrificed because a resident with an invalid child needed an addition to his house.
5. Although one older man in the neighborhood, questioned about the pedestrian paths that admit the public, remarked, "A harlot is open to the neighborhood, but that does not mean she fits in."
6. By 1973, the design work began in earnest—and a slow process it was. The housing program was discussed and rediscussed with the architects. At the same time, the group began a major lobbying effort for extensive common areas, which had never previously been included in rental housing designs. The non-profit representatives met with the group, and many differences arose about the day-to-day running of the buildings, including management.
7. The long time that residents worked together before the project was realized, the high rents charged, and the relatively high incomes of residents (33% of the tenants making over 2,500 guilders a month) help make this a successful development. The larger and poorer developments, such as De Klopvaart in Utrecht, with eighty tenants (58% unemployed), or Spijkenisse, with sixty households (44% unemployed), experience more problems in the clusters.
8. In 1977, 135 people moved in (79 adults and 54 children): 16 singles, 9 couples, 13 single parents, and 16 couples with children. In 1990, there are 116 people (78 adults, 38 children and teenagers: 24 singles, 6 couples, 11 single parents, and 13 couples with children. There are fewer children, as would be expected over time.
9. Two other common space alterations have occurred. The kindergarten was closed when the number of young children become too few, and the room for teenagers has been converted into a private office space.
10. The Netherlands is one of the most densely populated countries in the world (with 426 people per square kilometer).
11. The owner-occupied projects make up about 10% of the total projects built, but their small size (an average of seven units) in comparison to rental projects (an average of forty-three units) makes the total dwelling percentage quite small. In addition, 14% of the projects mix rentals and owners.
12. Children are under 18 years of age. The data have been compiled by Landelijke Vereniging Centraal Wonen (the national Dutch collaborative housing organization) from thirty-six projects built from 1977 to 1986. Children under 12 make up 25% of all residents, and a third of all the residents are children under 18 years of age (Van Rooijen and Veldkamp.)
13. In comparison, American renters move two to three times as often.

    Two developments in Holland have a 20% turnover a year, in one case because of many student residents and in another because of the general poverty of the residents and surrounding area. In Dutch collaborative housing, revenue loss from vacancy is usually paid for by the public housing company for the first few months. After that time, the residents must pay. If the unit remains vacant for a long time, the housing company takes over the payments for that unit, as well as the tenant selection process. On the other hand, if the vacancy rate is very low, the residents can receive the reserve set aside in the rent for vacancies.
14. One notable exception is Emmen, where the fifty-one households are not subdivided into clusters but instead share two common kitchen-dining rooms among all the tenants (and when necessary also use the kitchen-dining facilities of the café).
15. In Purmerend cluster tenants choose new members. But each cluster is connected to the next, so that one's neighbor is often from a different cluster, and this has caused some problems. At times, clusters argue among themselves, such as when one cluster feels entitled to more garden space.

16. An example is the Utrecht development (1984), which has twelve four-story towers, each with its own kitchen-dining area. The organization of all the tenants is much weaker than the organization of the individual towers, and there are problems in trying to coordinate these separate groups.
17. In reality this architectural flexibility is fixed by social concerns because each of the kitchen groups is reluctant to "give up" an apartment to another group. Fewer units mean fewer members' cooking and participating in tasks.
18. Women make up over 70% of the tenants, and 25% of the tenants are unemployed.
19. The flexibility of this arrangement is clear. Some tenants use the separate room as an office or as a bedroom for their children, or they rent it out as another unit (with a shared bathroom). Another unique feature is that *older children* (over 10 years old) have the option of living in their own separate wing with small individual bedrooms and a shared play area. The smaller children look forward to "graduating" to this wing.
20. There are forty houses (both row houses and apartments), fifteen rooms (three group houses with five rooms each), and four youth rooms, for a total of fifty-six units. But tenant Beatrice Kesler explains that the tenants count forty-three "front doors." There are 124 tenants (about a third are children): 21% singles, 28% single parents, and 37% couples with children. Of the adults, 26% are unemployed. (Van Roijen and Veldkamp).
21. In 1989, Mienskiplik Wenjen (in Sneek, Holland) was abolished. Growing turnover made the group of steady residents feel very uneasy. The group asked the nonprofit housing corporation to "take back" the dwellings and common house. Three collaborative developments have financial difficulties. The remaining forty-six rental developments have not run into serious problems.
22. Zwartehandspoort: eleven households, 73% owners; De Meenthe: twenty households, 60% owners; Vught: twenty-nine households, 17% owners; Purmerend: seventy-one households, 41% owners (Van Rooijen and Veldkamp). Of these, Vught has been experiencing problems between owners and renters.
23. Zwartehandspoort, another mixed rental and ownership development, has an association of all residents, as well as an association of owners, where maintenance and management agreements are made. Renters have an agreement with the nonprofit housing association that owns their units. Each owner is responsible for selling his or her house. If two-thirds of the cohousing association members object to the buyer, the association has the option of finding a new buyer within two months, for the same selling price.
24. In contrast, some of the newer Danish experiments to allow residents to set up a private business in their dwelling may prove more successful.
25. Part of the loan to build Purmerend—350,000 guilders—was used to build the common house (and the residents built smaller dwellings with the remaining money); 150,000 more guilders were added for furnishings and machinery. Altogether, a loan of 500,000 guilders was due (about $200,000).
26. The two other Dutch developments experiencing financial difficulties are Het Woonschap (some financial problems, although they are not serious) and Spijkenisse (serious financial problems caused by a 25% rate of unrented units).

REFERENCES

Backus, H. C. S., and Beatrice Kesler. 1986. "Kollektives Wohnen—Ein Weg zu einem neuen Lebensstil? Ergebnisse einer Evaluationsstudie in einem experimentellen Wohnungsbauprojekt Centraal Wonen Hilversum." *Hauswirtschaft,* pp. 251-259.

Kesler, B. E. TH. A. "Communal Housing Conditions: A Way towards a New Life Style." Unpublished.

Kesler, Beatrice; René Siemens; and Maarten van der Vlist. 1988. *EEn Tuin Belicht.* Utrecht/Wageningen: Landelijke Vereninging Centraal Wonen.

Krabbe, René, and Paul Vlug. 1986. *Centraal Wonen in beeld 1977-1986 deel 1.* Utrecht: Landelijke Vereninging Centraal Wonen.

Van Rooijen, Herman, and Freerk Veldkamp. 1989. *Centraal Wonen in beeld deel 2.* Utrecht: Landelijke Vereninging Centraal Wonen.

CHAPTER 4

Swedish Collaborative Housing

STACKEN: A RENTAL TOWER

Units: 33
Ownership: Rental
Site: Suburban
Began/Moved in: 1979/1980
Architect: Lars Ågren, SAR

Because of an overly ambitious building program enacted by the Swedish government in the late 1960s and early 1970s, the housing authority of Gothenburg found itself with over 2,000 units for which no renters could be found. Particularly hard to rent were the high-rise towers in the outlying area of the city, such as those along Telescope Street.[1] Ten identical towers, eight stories high and erected one behind the other, run the length of Telescope Street. All have identical three-room apartments, five to a floor, laid out in a star plan. They were designed in the late 1950s by architect Lars Ågren. The odd configuration resulted from pressing the building regulations to the maximum requested by the builder)—as tall as possible and still be reached by a fire ladder and as many apartments as possible around one open staircase and elevator core. Rows of buildings were constructed to defray the prefabrication costs. But tenants could not be found to move into

the high rises because of the distant location, the poor reputation of the neighborhood, and the unappealing architecture. Those problems spurred the public housing company, Göteborgshem, to consider alternatives.[2] When architect Ågren suggested that Sweden's new type of collaborative housing be carried out in one of the towers, the housing authority was willing to take the chance, motivated largely by economics (it had little to lose), and suggested the tower on 2 Telescope Street (Caldenby and Wallden).

On September 5, 1979, the first meeting over renovating the tower took place. Drawn by newspaper advertisements, referrals from the public housing agency, and by word of mouth, a hundred people arrived. Some sought a better way of living or a good environment for children, some had social and political goals, and some were just curious. They talked about the theory and their possibility to shape it into reality and then met in small groups to specify their wishes and aspirations. They also divided into six committees: dining room, laundry, workshop, child care, the association (administrative agreement), and ideology (goals and apprehensions). A newspaper reported the next day, humorously, that the building had stood empty for ten years, and now there was a waiting list. At

Stacken, Sweden. *(Matts Pettersson)*

the next meeting, people began talking and planning in earnest. The Chalmers Institute of Technology, where Ågren taught, made it a research project, and the housing authority agreed to pay the consultants and the renovation costs.

Each household could design its own unit, taking out all the interior walls or putting in more walls.[3] Ågren explains the design process:

Some asked me, Do you think it would be wise to take out this wall? And I said, Well, try it if you think it's correct. Once the walls were all gone, they had to decide on the configuration that they wanted. Some of them told me that was the first time they felt like grown-up human beings, and some said that is the best that has happened to them at any time—no one coming and telling them how to do it.

The location of the common areas was considered for several floors before settling on the fifth. The ground floor (convenient), the fourth floor (midway) and the eighth floor (great view) were discussed but discarded. The fifth floor, altered previously, would be easiest to convert into the common spaces.[4] (To meet the Fire Department's requirement for two exits from that floor, an exterior spiral staircase was added.) "A lot of the solutions were very poor from an architectural point of view, but they were intelligent and very clever from a social point of view," recalls the archi-

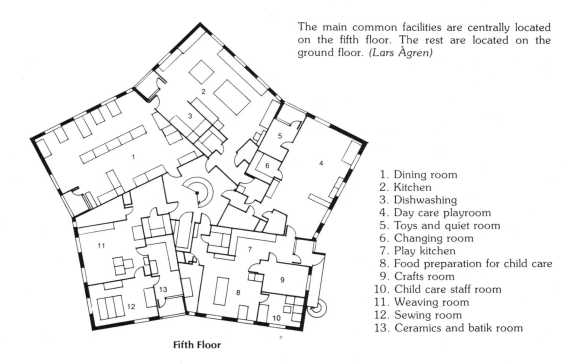

The main common facilities are centrally located on the fifth floor. The rest are located on the ground floor. *(Lars Ågren)*

1. Dining room
2. Kitchen
3. Dishwashing
4. Day care playroom
5. Toys and quiet room
6. Changing room
7. Play kitchen
8. Food preparation for child care
9. Crafts room
10. Child care staff room
11. Weaving room
12. Sewing room
13. Ceramics and batik room

Fifth Floor

30'/10 m

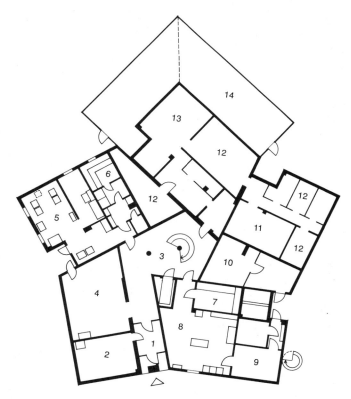

Ground Floor

1. Entry
2. Baby carriage storage
3. Main staircase
4. Teen room (formerly café)
5. Laundry
6. Sauna
7. Photo lab
8. Wood shop
9. Building maintenance shop
10. Garbage room
11. Music room
12. Storage
13. Table tennis/game room
14. Bicycle storage shed

69

tect. "Our dining room was a poor interior architecturally, but we succeeded in deciding to have it in such a way."

The committee trying to negotiate the contract with Göteborgshem (the public housing company) found itself busy with lawyers and the tenants' association.[5] The group's request for self-management, with clauses to prevent the closing of common facilities, resulted in conflicts with Göteborgshem, which was used to dealing with more traditional tenant relationships. In the final contract, the housing authority agreed to be responsible for the capital costs and utilities (heat, gas, and water). It leases the building to the tenants' association, which is responsible for collecting rent, management, and maintenance.

In the summer of 1980, fifty-five adults and twenty-five children moved into the tower named Stacken (*Stacken*, is a red ants' hill built by stacking up pine needles).[6] The residents—families, singles, and couples—were not (and still are not) typical public housing tenants. In some ways they can be characterized as the "new" working class of a service economy—teachers and social workers who have a higher education but do not hold more professional jobs or managerial positions. Their work ends after 8 hours, and there is a clear separation between work and home—a choice often made consciously. Their values are different from those of the traditional public housing tenant, including interest in alternative life-styles, relationships, and concern about the environment.[7]

Of the twenty-five households from the first meeting the year before, ten had left and been replaced. Ågren also moved into Stacken: "I was not quite clear from the beginning if I should move in. I decided it quite late. I was not organizing it for myself, but I thought, if I don't move in, how will I find out if it works?"

Living in Stacken

Creating collaborative housing in a high-density renovated building, instead of small houses around an open green space, was a challenge. A number of people, including housing officials, believed the experiment would last a year or maybe two, and that certainly in five years it would be all over. But many of the people moving into Stacken had a totally different viewpoint—that one big sustaining family was about to be created.

Once the residents had moved in, group activities began. Meetings were held, and to some, they were wonderful, with many problems solved. To others—often less verbal residents—they were "impossible meetings where nothing had been done and no real problems raised." The residents decided to divide into small groups to talk about problems, so that everyone had a chance to be involved. They found that a handful of people could not be in charge, and that for the community to work well, responsibility had to be shared. "Spreading responsibility is a kind of insurance," said Jens, "that ensures there will always be someone new to take the place of another and keep the community functioning."

Although Stacken did not turn into the tight community some residents had envisioned, a strong sense of community began to grow. The parents with children connected immediately. One early member comments: "On our floor, there were five couples, and four had children. Our doors were always open. The children ran from me to my neighbor, and the next neighbor, and back to me. One couple had no children, so they become second parents to ours. When Marie cried on the stairs, she didn't come to me; she went to them. And there were always baby-sitters, and the older children took care of the younger ones."

Twenty-five children were now living in Stacken, and organized child care began. A parent cooperative called Myran ("The Ant"), located on the fifth floor, provided all-day child care. An enormous amount of work was required to get the child care functioning. The first year, each family spent about 150 hours on various day care tasks. In addition, "There were many disputes and difficulties," recalls Jonas, the current day care teacher. Now, four hired teachers run the child care, with one volunteer parent each day. Parents who participate are required to work ten 8-hour days a year. Participating parents are enthusiastic about the benefits: "We can make our own decisions on the kind of care we want; the kids are used to having friends all around instead of just in school; it's an easier transition, and they're more relaxed because they all know each other; and there's more time in the morning because I don't have to dress him and take him somewhere else." A few members chose not to participate. Former Stacken member Karin Jershed said, "I didn't want to have my child there. I think my children should meet other children, outside Stacken. And they change parents every day, and I don't think that's good for the children. Besides, I don't have the time. I want to take my vacation together with my husband and not spend it working."

These differences of opinions were not confined to child care; they appeared in every other area of the community—from cooking to cleaning. The first year was bumpy; some residents moved out. No one had known what to expect, and some had hoped for more and others less community. By the second and third years, the residents had worked out many of their problems, and the community had settled down to a less intense but quieter life.

Lars Ågren considers Stacken to be a success: "Looking back, for me it was a fantastic life. I had been living alone. When I moved into Stacken, I found such a difference—a better living on a higher social level. I was sitting next to interesting, open-minded people, talking about everything, about nothing. My evening was some cups of tea here, and talking there, and a meeting, kids coming in there—and suddenly it was time to sleep. What I found was people, and I did not find them before I came to this house."

Stacken Today

Children run in and out from the playground outside. Adults sit on the benches in the front of the entrance watching toddlers play, talking to each other or waiting for the nearby washing machines to finish their cycles. The common areas upstairs, on the ground level, and on the landings create a shared path from the entrance to the very highest dwelling.

The central staircase, from the basement to the eighth floor, is like a vertical street enclosed by a green spiral railing. Well used, it echoes with steps, whistled songs, and snatches of conversations. Spiraling down and around, like a carousel, whoever climbs the stairs can glimpse from one floor down to the next passing doors taped with pictures and postcards, shoes lined up against the walls, posters, paintings, and maps of Sweden. The elevator, though painted green with four black ants crawling up the side, is very blank, very quiet inside, and used less often.

The central location of the common rooms encourages the use of the stairs, and a large bulletin board full of notices and the dinner menu invites lingering.[8] Originally designed for five 775-square-feet (72-square-meter) apartments, the converted common rooms do not work as well as those designed specifically for common living. The kitchen is too big and institutional in appearance; it takes up what would have been one full apartment. The shape of the dining room is awkward, the children's area is a bit small, and the sewing room is too big. Nevertheless, the common rooms are well used. (In retrospect, several multipurpose rooms with storage shelves would have been most useful.)

The maintenance and management continue to be run by the residents, and dinner is served five nights a week in the common dining room. Although the number of members who dine communally has decreased to about 30% of all the households, those who eat in the dining room praise it highly. Birgitta Sundelin, a regular with her husband and children, says: "I don't have to cook dinner every day, and I love that. I love it!" Those who eat in their own home do so for several reasons: they eat their big meal at lunch, feel the food is too expensive (at about $3 [17 crowns] a meal for adults, larger families feel they can eat more cheaply at home), or do not feel socially inclined.

The professional restaurant kitchen installed at Stacken is too large and shiny, not a cozy place to cook.

After almost ten years, only six of the thirty-four original households remain. Residents in Stacken move, on the average, about every three years. Although this is about the same rate of turnover that residents have had before they move into Stacken (Caldenby and Wallden), the rate is higher than for collaborative housing built after Stacken. One reason may be that residents were idealistic in this first community and expected too much.

The mobility of tenants works against a close sense of community. An ex-member recalls why her family moved:

We were very close on our floor; we had many parties and teas and picnics. We were very much together, almost every weekend. We had so much fun, we wanted it to be that way forever. Then one couple moved because of a job, and another came in. Then another couple moved, and another one came in. And it wasn't the same; we couldn't get close to them. The doors were closed. Many of our friends moved. And we moved.

A few original residents, as well as some ex-residents, believe that the attitudes in Stacken have changed from the more ideological to the more practical. The new residents, they say, are more interested in rules and cleanliness. Since residents share hallways, stairs, and other interior spaces, there are some disagreements as to what is considered clean enough. Childrens' behavior has also caused some tension because parents have different values about what is and is not permissible.

Stacken is a different place than it was ten years ago. The number of adults has decreased (because the number of single parents has increased from about one in eight residents to about one in two), and the number of children has increased from twenty-five to fifty-one (which includes eleven children who rotate between parents.) Part of the problems Stacken is experiencing can be attributed to the high density of children, a number now teenagers, and the difficulty single parents experience in juggling their time and energy.

Stacken is a different kind of success than many of the Danish models. There is a wider range of participation among residents. Rosa Larsén, 70 years old, does not participate in common dining but enjoys many other aspects of Stacken: "It's a living house, never silence. A good kind of living."

Tenants in Gothenburg have shown an interest in renovating more high-rise buildings to emulate Stacken, but the public housing companies have not responded with much eagerness. The original impetus to create Stacken—as a way to fill otherwise empty apartments—is no longer a compelling rationale. By the mid-1980s, most of the empty apartments in Gothenburg had been filled. Telescope Street has itself undergone a transformation. The government gave the non-profit housing company owned by the trade unionists, Riksbyggen, an enticing offer to buy all ten buildings and turn them into condominiums. Riksbyggen was not aware that Stacken was occupied and that the tenants could not be moved. The relationship between the two has yet to be smoothed out. These strains have increased the reluctance of other groups to renovate buildings.

In the ten years since the Stacken experiment began, many other collaborative developments have appeared, but only one other high-rise building, named Trädet ("the tree that grows in the forest"), has been renovated in Gothenburg. Trädet is an older building that was difficult to rent and was renovated into collaborative housing in 1985. The renovation was overseen by architect Siv Carlsson, who had assisted Lars Ågren on Stacken. "There is still a suspicion of these types of organizations among the housing companies," she says. "It's extra work to inform people and make a new project. If the apartments don't work well the other way, then they'll do it."

Trädet improves on Stacken's design with a smaller and less institutional kitchen and a way of serving residents over the counter. The common spaces are connected to the outside with a roomy deck, and there is a popular café. The turnover in Trädet is very low. Carlsson speculates the reason is that Trädet residents' expectations were not too high and that they are not as idealistic as those living in Stacken. As in Stacken, common meals are available every evening, and there is also full-time child care. Carlsson adds, "Other housing companies come to look, and they think it's very interesting. They say they like the experiment, and they want one. But not now, later. Not here, but somewhere."

SWEDISH KOLLEKTIVHUS: A PUBLIC ALTERNATIVE

Twenty-seven collaborative housing developments have been built since Stacken (about 1,100 units of housing), and another ten are expected to be completed within the next two years. Called *kollektivhus* ("collective housing") in Sweden, these developments are typically in apartment buildings with common spaces located on one or two floors. More than 85% are owned by public (nonprofit) housing associations and are rented to collaborative housing groups.[9] Collaborative housing is developed with the group and is managed and maintained by them with the cooperation of the housing association. Fifteen percent are stock cooperatives that are developed and managed entirely by the residents.[10]

Sweden's long history of collective living was motivated by practical requirements. At the turn of the century, apartment houses raised issues of collective living that had not been considered for detached homes, but creating community was not one of them. An apartment building with central kitchen and a paid staff first appeared in 1907 in response to a shortage of servants. Hemgarden provided residents with three meals a day, in addition to cleaning and laundry services (Vestbro).

The first collective service house, built in 1935, was promoted by both an architect, Sven Markelius, and a social reformer, Alva Myrdal. Myrdal, a young woman at that time, wrote about the inefficiency and isolation of women (each making her own meatballs in her own kitchen, the children bored and isolated. The building included a central restaurant, day care, and a laundry, along with the fifty-four apartments. Residents' meals were delivered up in one of four dumbwaiters, with dishes and laundry sent down the same way to the hired staff. At the time, a big fuss was made over these dwellings, seen as a threat to the nuclear family. In reality, the idea was not resident cooperation but maids in cooperation. The high differences in salaries between the servants and the upper-middle-class residents made this arrangement possible. The success of the enterprise was followed by eight other collective service buildings between 1935 and 1955, built by organizations or developers, many for specific groups of people—childless couples, single women, professionals, or working couples (Vestbro).[11]

The innovative developer, Olle Engkvist, built five collective buildings, including the Hässelby Hotel (1955), the most famous. Prospective Stockholm tenants for this "family hotel" found a restaurant, day care, shops and dry cleaners, elderly clinic, cafeteria, hobby room, a large dining-meeting hall, and housekeeping services among the amenities that came with the apartment. As impressive to the renter was the availability of all these services without ever walking outside—connected through an extensive corridor system to the 330 apartments (divided among seventeen buildings).

Meal tickets, whose costs were included in the rent, brought residents together to dine on a regular basis. The residents became well organized because of their familiarity with each other and their common need to negotiate with Olle Engkvist over dining problems, particularly the mandatory purchase of a minimum number of meals.

When Engkvist died in 1969, the new owners of the Hässelby were not interested in continuing to provide meals, in part because of rising staff salaries and in part because of the problems associated with providing good food service. For them, the best solution was to transform Hässelby into a normal apartment complex and rent out the common spaces for offices. The residents, however, argued that their contracts included the provision of meals, as well as use of common areas. When the new owners resisted attempts at compromising, the residents began to fight back by holding large meetings, writing articles, and contacting politicians. When they took over the dining room in a massive sit-in, they were forcibly removed by the police. Although the residents lost that battle, the Hässelby fight received a great deal of attention from the media and was one of the catalysts for the Swedish collaborative housing movement.

When chains and padlocks were placed on the dining hall doors, the residents decided to organize themselves to provide food, preparing it in their own rooms if necessary. Resident meal preparation began in 1976. In the first five years, 100-150 people ate communally every day. The meal preparation continues to this day, although the number of residents participating has reduced to about 50. (One of their main problems is that the owner, who controls the selection of new residents, prefers people who are not inclined toward shared dining.) "We've done it on our own now for fourteen years," says member Lennart Lindstrom. "It's more than successful; it's become a habit."

Another strong influence on Swedish collaborative housing, the BIG group, formed in Stockholm at the time of the Hässelby fight, developed a model of collective living based on an exchange of residents' labor. The group Bo i Gemenskap ("living in community"), or BIG as it came to be known, formed at the end of a women's architecture conference in response to the question, "How would we live if we could choose?" The ten women who set out to answer that question included architects, researchers, a journalist, older women, single women, and mothers with young children. They proposed a "little collective house" of twenty to fifty households. No employees would be necessary since the residents would share tasks. The BIG group made a model of their housing vision and followed it with a book in 1982 (BIG-gruppen).

The group felt strongly that this new type of housing should not be only for privileged groups, as was the service housing, and pro-

A photograph taken in 1935 of the restaurant in John Ericssonsgatan 6. *(Dick Urban Vestbro)*

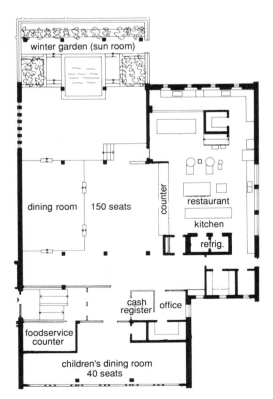

Right: Plan of the Hässelby Family Hotel restaurant. *Above:* Plan of an apartment at the hotel. *(Dick Urban Vestbro)*

Table 4.1   Swedish Collaborative Housing Data

Project	Management Type	Ownership	Move-in Date	Number of Units	Building Type
Arken	Tenant and company	Rental	1985	29	Rehabil tower
Blenda	Tenant and company	Rental	1983	24	2 midrise
Blomstret	Resident	Co-op*	1985	37	Tower
Fabriken	Mixed	Rental	1985	109	Lamel building†
Flygtrafiken	Tenant and company	Rental	1987	52	Lamel building
Fortuna	Tenant and company	Rental	1989	21	
Fristad	Service	Rental	1984	133	3 blocks (connected)
Fullt hus	Tenant and company	Rental	1988	26	Tower
Hässelby Hotel	Owner	Rental	1955	328	Tower and lamel building
Jakobsbergs	Tenant and company	Rental	1989	22	
Katthuvudet	Resident	Co-op	1986	18	Tower
Kupan	Resident	Co-op	1986	52	2 towers (connected)
Lergöken	Tenant and company	Rental	1985	26	Tower
Mattbandet	Tenant and company	Rental	1987	63	
Nålmakaren	Service	Rental	1983	102	
Orion	Tenant and company	Rental	1984	157	7 towers
Oxbacken	Service	Rental	1985	290	Block
Prästgårdshagen	Tenant and company	Rental	1984	31	Tower
Prästgårdsmarken	Mixed	Co-op	1984	56	9 midrise
Regnbågen (Rainbow)	Tenant and company	Rental	1989	19	Low rise
Rio	Service	Rental	1983	111	2 towers (connected)
Slånbäret	Tenant and company	Rental	1988	34	
Slottet	Resident	Co-op	1984	16	Rehabilitated
Södervärn	Tenant and company	Rental	1983	21	Rehabilitated
Södra Station	Tenant and company	Rental	1987	63	Tower
Solbringen	Service	Rental	1983	86	Block
Sörbyängen	Service	Co-op	1984	84	
Stacken	Tenant and company	Rental	1980	33	Rehabilitated
Stolplyckan	Service	Rental	1982	186	13 buildings
Svärdet	Tenant and company	Rental	1988	118	3 towers
Taljan	Tenant and company	Co-op/rent	1986	9	Tower
Trädet	Tenant and company	Rental	1985	38	Rehabilitated tower
Trapphuskollektivet	Tenant and company	Rental	1988	8	Lamel building
Trekanten	Tenant and company	Rental	1986	78	Tower
Tunnan	Tenant and company	Rental	1987	27	Rehabilitated tower
Vildkornet	Tenant and company	Rental	1988	82	2 blocks (connected)
Yxan 3	Tenant and company	Rental	1983	20	Rehabilitated lamel building

Source: Vestbro, Woodward, Lindén.
*In cooperative ownership, the residents decide whether or not to limit the resale value.
†The thin lamel building type was developed by Swedish functionalists to allow more light and air into apartments.

posed that public housing companies should build collaborative housing as publicly financed rentals. Unlike the Danes and the Dutch, whose original motivation was community, the BIG group envisioned togetherness as a by-product of cooperating on tasks.[12]

Architect Lars Ågren was influenced by both the Hässelby Hotel and the BIG group in his renovation of Stacken in 1979. In the following decade, other multi-unit buildings have been turned into collaborative housing (Table 4.1). The majority are rentals, where future tenants are selected in advance and are

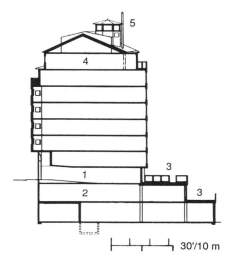

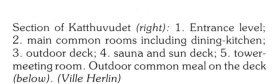

Section of Katthuvudet *(right):* 1. Entrance level; 2. main common rooms including dining-kitchen; 3. outdoor deck; 4. sauna and sun deck; 5. tower-meeting room. Outdoor common meal on the deck *(below). (Ville Herlin)*

involved in some design and planning. Their involvement is not as encompassing as in many Danish developments.

Tenants in the thirty-one-unit Prästgårds-hagen (1984) were selected two years in advance. Tenants now prepare five meals a week, organized in groups based on their dwelling floor level. The residents have contracts that spell out their influence on management and economic issues. The owner, a housing association, gives the tenant association about $9,000 for management, with the surplus used toward common area purchases (Arkitektur).[13]

Private collaborative housing is also being constructed through the initiative of architects and future residents. Katthuvudet ("Cat's Head") is an urban infill development in Stockholm (1986) initiated by Ville Herlin of Stacken architects. The design was the result of an intensive participatory process, with each of the eighteen apartments tailored to an individual household. The common space—2,690 square feet (250 square meters)—includes a kitchen and dining room, a workshop, a photo lab, a penthouse sauna, and a deck, with a 360-degree view tower. Members have dinner together three nights a week and work one evening a month.

To reduce costs, the project was fast tracked, with many design decisions made during construction. In addition, a day care center rents the common space during the day to help offset monthly costs. Nevertheless, the unanticipated high cost of these cooperative units, financed by the residents, has made the group reluctant to limit the equity on resale. The prime location of the property will soon escalate costs to the point where only those with high incomes will be able to afford to buy in, underscoring one of the problems faced by privately owned collaborative housing.

There are seven renovated collaborative housing developments in Sweden. A few, such as Stacken, are in renovated high rises. Others are in mid-rise buildings, such as Slottet ("the castle") in Lund (1985). This apartment building, built in 1924, was bought by a core group of residents. They located the common spaces in the basement and on the ground floor, as well as in the attic, of this five-story building, providing over 2,000 square feet of common area.

Although almost all Swedish collaborative housing is in multistory buildings, some of the more recent collaborative developments are closer to the Danish low-dense model. Rainbow (1989), is a small rental project of nineteen units, with the dwellings, circulation, and common areas under one roof. The residents had petitioned the municipality of Lund for a number of years to sponsor such a project. The result bears some similarity to the enclosed atmosphere of Jystrup Sawærket. Interesting differences are in the way the common spaces are visually connected to a public pedestrian street and the impressive kitchen design, truly the heart of this development and designed equally for efficiency and community.

THE SERVICE HOUSES

Unique to Sweden is the development of large-scale service houses that combine communal living with social services. The first of its kind, Stolplyckan, was developed in Linköping in 1979. The idea was to maximize use of common facilities and minimize expenses by combining both standard apartments and apartments for the elderly and handicapped with common services and amenities. The service houses add another alternative to the management of collaborative housing. In the other two management forms—tenant-managed housing (with a nonprofit housing company as owner) or management by owner–residents—those who live in the housing decide and provide services. In the service houses, the management provides many amenities such as cleaning or a hot meal. The strong role of the management in service houses alters both the development process and types of services. The residents must grapple together with these institutions on their role in development and management, and their use of the facilities. A closer look at Stolplyckan highlights the advantages

Building plan of Rainbow. *(Palm Lindén)*

1. Common area; 2. private dwelling; 3. hallway;
4. sitting area; 5. shared outdoor square; 6. public
pedestrian path.

Rainbow's front facade with the common rooms overlooking the pedestrian street.

In the large collaborative community at Stolplyckan, most of the thirteen stairwells are connected by only a ground-floor corridor. Their relative isolation creates a greater opportunity for residents in the same tower to know each other and have a "stairwell" dinner. *(Thor Balkhed)*

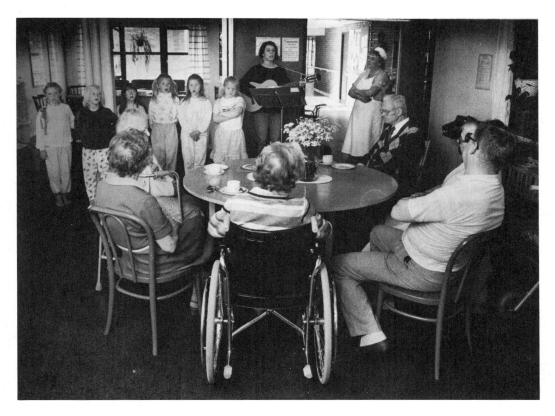

Children living in Stolplyckan and attending the "Stoly School" give a small performance in the café during the daytime for elderly and disabled residents. The house staff also listens. *(Thor Balkhed)*

and disadvantages of this larger-scale housing type.

STOLPLYCKAN: INCLUDING SOCIAL SERVICES WITHIN THE COMMUNITY

Units: 186
Ownership: Rental
Site: Suburban, 5 acres
Began/Moved in: 1977/1980
Architect: Höjer & Ljungqvist

In Stolplyckan, 141 collaborative apartments have been mixed with 36 apartments for the elderly and 9 units for the handicapped. The hope was that combining these three groups would reduce the overlap in services and

amenities. Another hope was that using common facilities and eating together would create a real sense of community and reduce the isolation of residents. The large size of the Stolplyckan community provided a real possibility for an intergenerational integration through the use of the common areas that totaled a half acre of floor space under one roof.*

A walk through Stolplyckan reveals the richness of its common facilities. The inclusion of the elderly brought government funding for a professional kitchen with a professional cook. At lunch, hot meals are prepared

---

*The common facilities (2,000 square meters) were provided by slightly reducing apartment sizes from the Swedish rental standard. The social service agencies provided funding for the kitchen and dining facilities.

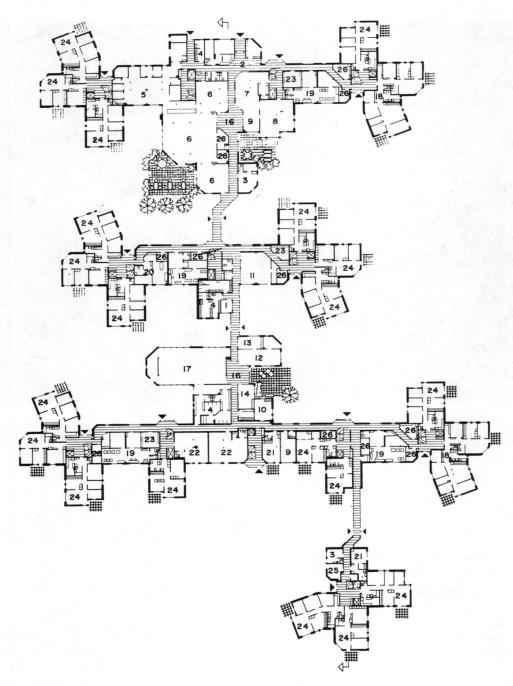

Plan of Stolplyckan. *(Höjer-Lungqvist)*

1. Reception; 2. entry; 3. staff lounge; 4. dressing room; 5. professional kitchen; 6. dining room-cafeteria and meeting room; 7. café; 8. library; 9. meeting room; 10. pottery room; 11. weaving room; 12. wood shop; 13. painting studio; 14. metal shop; 15. photo lab; 16. square; 17. playroom; 18. day care; 19. laundry; 20. beauty shop; 21. guest room; 22. rentable room; 23. wheelchair storage; 24. apartment; 25. garbage storage; 26. storage.

Almost every apartment in Stolplyckan has a unique element—an extra window or balcony facing in a different direction from the rest—and each top apartment has a roof deck. *(Thor Balkhed)*

for the elderly. (In addition, meals are delivered to qualifying elderly in the surrounding community.) The food is served cafeteria style in a large dining room, where the other residents can also eat by purchasing meal tickets. Nearby are the café and a library. Off the main passageway are the sewing and weaving room, the wood shop, and the ceramic studio. A gymnasium can be booked for badminton, exercise, or movement classes (sauna and showers are located directly behind the gym). Away from the main "street" are two guest rooms, available for about $5 each, although their popularity requires booking in advance. The residents have also created a music room by taking over part of the garage.

Perhaps the best amenity for families with children is the day care and the inclusion of the first three grades of elementary school—kindergarten and first and second grades. The children need only walk down the hallway to class. The class makes use of the gym and craft rooms and the children eat a hot lunch in a room adjoining the cafeteria.

The common amenities rarely sit unused. During the day, the older people and children use them, and in the evening, the other residents take over. Another benefit is the accessibility of the facilities through the extensive enclosed passageway, easy for children, the handicapped, and the elderly to negotiate. They can lead freer lives without extensive supervision. The ground-level passageways connect all the common amenities to the apartments, located among thirteen buildings (from three to seven stories high). Households are not segregated according to ages but can freely mix. Three buildings have a greater concentration of apartments for the handicapped to simplify service worker routines, but they also include nonhandicap units.

A New Model

The town of Linköping planned a new housing area of 200 to 300 houses. Their non-profit housing corporation hired the design firm of Höjer & Ljungqvist, with whom they had worked for many years. Ingvar Thornblom, an architect working at Höjer & Ljungqvist, had been a long-time resident of the Hässelby Hotel and had given much thought to creating collaborative housing; in fact, he had just written a pamphlet on the subject, with the Hässelby Hotel as the model. Thornblom and the director of the housing corporation combined political savvy and a housing vision, and they began to work out the initial concept for Stolplyckan.

The social service agency of Linköping—a powerful (and high-budget) organization in the town—came into the picture. It's director had more or less parallel ideas but a different vision on management and distribution. Soon conflicts arose between the architects and social service agencies, with the housing authority in the middle.

The idea of a common service core, financed in part by the municipal budget, was agreed upon, but many other features, such as residents' needing to commit themselves to a certain amount of work in the dining room per month or that tenants would take over the dining space from the social services in the evening, were refused.

An organization of the housing association, the social service agency, and the tenants' association was formed. They discussed ways of organizing the community, but the tenants' association had less power than the other two organizations.

A schedule was worked out so that future residents would meet each other months in advance of the move-in date. Thornblom said:

Being an architect, I think you create a scenario for people's lives, but I not only wanted to provide the scene, I also wrote some highlights of the play, based on what we did here [Hässelby]. I even made proposals of boat trips on a certain day in August and other events and meetings. I wanted to get them started, to initiate things. When the director of the housing authority retired, six months before residents were to move in, those in authority did not understand the importance of this, and it was not fully done.

When the tenants moved into the first building, they formed a tower committee with the idea of arranging a meeting with the next group moving into the second building, and each group would arrange a meeting with the next. These tower committees were formed in each of the thirteen towers, much to Thornblom's disappointment. He felt very strongly that an entire community committee should exist—not thirteen separate ones. After a few months, a common organization was formed for the entire building, with yearly dues to finance common activities.[14]

Common dining was also organized through the existing building committees, but the social service agency refused to allow the residents into the kitchen. Since the kitchen was a workplace for professionals, the city health authorities made rigorous demands about hygiene. Solving the conflict required active mediation by the social services. It took two years before the social services took that initiative.[15] A certain irony can be seen with the residents locked out of the kitchen and making common meals in their own kitchens, very much as the Hässelby Hotel residents had done five years earlier. The common meals at Stolplyckan moved from residents' apartments to the café, placing pressure on the social service agency to allow access to the kitchen, which it eventually granted.

Like the Hässelby residents, the Stolplyckan families began a long struggle to get into the common kitchen. Resident Mark Olson, an American from Virginia and a long-time resident, still recalls that struggle with anger: "We were paying half the rent for the place—including the kitchen. How can they possibly keep us out of the kitchen!" (Part of the monthly rent is for the common facilities.) Theirs was a successful fight. After about two years, they received permission, with several concessions, one being that each resident needs to be tested for tuberculosis.[16]

Stolplyckan Today

The many institutional aspects of Stolplyckan, not the least being a certain repetitive and massiveness of architecture, cannot entirely be altered by the residents, but they have tried. Teams of painters, including children, have transformed the institutional walls into lines of color. The long corridor walls are filled with the fruit of countless art and ceramic projects completed in the common facilities.

In the early evening, residents gather in the café—some leaning against the counter waiting for coffee and cake, families crowding around tables, along with several people in wheelchairs. An older man sits with a Down's syndrome boy, while another gets them coffee, the little boys run around underfoot. The walls of the room are decorated with drawings and other art by residents, and music is playing nearby. Amid the noise, someone sits in the corner reading.

In the Stolplyckan experiment, the designers—both social and architectural— hoped to create a family where old and young work together to support each other. While a community has been created, the closeness between different groups of people has not entirely materialized. The elderly, many over 75 or 80 years old and frail, have little interest in joining the other residents for common activities. They eat their big meal at lunch, and many are already in bed by 7:00 or 8:00 P.M. The other residents have shown little eagerness to join the elderly at lunchtime. Many are away at work, others feel the price of 33 crowns (around $5) is too high, and some do not like the meals.

Among the other residents, not everyone participates in the collaborative cooking and dining. Except the elderly, all tenants are required to do their share of cleaning but nothing more.[17] Among the thirteen buildings committees, some are more active than oth-

A large tree created out of boards and paint spread its branches near the junction of two corridors, creating a resting spot amid the fluorescent lights and long corridors. The residents created it with the help of an artist. *(Thor Balkhed)*

ers. The social service agency has created a cushion of responsibility with meals available each lunchtime, maintenance of many common areas, and its vested interest in keeping things running. When certain residents choose not to cooperate, as happens in all such large communities, it does not create much tension. Although the social service agency has created its share of problems, it has also brought a certain institutional stability and calm.

The elderly I interviewed had many positive things to say about their life in Stolplyckan, even without their joining into house activities. The few irritations—children skateboarding down the hallway or playing with the elevator—were minor compared to the many benefits they mentioned: being around the children, the wide range of spaces, the convenience of the meals, and the feeling of a community. A typical response was Brita Reidler's: "It's better to live here than by myself. Here I can look out and see children playing. I can always find company if I want to, and I can be alone too if I want that." Her son and family live a floor below her, and her two grandchildren are in the day care, her grandson being one of the first graduates of the Stolplyckan school.

The limitations and viewpoints of the elderly and disabled bring with them a different sense of time, responsibility, and notions of ability. Their acceptance asks for a separation from expectations. There is a peace here that has eluded other communities. It is the feeling of people simply accepting the society of each other.

Seven large service houses have been constructed in Sweden. Two in Stockholm, Rio and Fristad (1983–1984), combine equal numbers of elderly apartments (with alarm buzzers) and standard apartments. Although both have been functioning for over five years, a number of conflicts were found among the tenants in these two developments

The covered bridge at Fristad that divides the building for elderly housing from the other tenants. It may be closed because it contributes to tenant disharmony.

(Woodward, Vestbro, and Grossman). In Fristad, the elderly are separated into their own building, creating a greater division between them and the other tenants. (The buildings are connected by a bridge.) Some of the elderly residents complained about the noise and turmoil created by the children and wanted to separate the two parts (Vestbro). The other households are not enthusiastic about sharing common facilities with the elderly, most of them frail and in their eighties.

The social service agency does not want tenants cooking in the professional kitchen. Some of the tenants in Fristad have started preparing common evening meals together but not in the large kitchen. Other tenants prefer to have services provided by a paid staff but would like more control over them, such as the kind of food served (Woodward).

Similar conflicts can be found in Rio. The tenants have less influence over management decisions than in Fristad, especially concerning the amount and type of meals served. Cleaning and use of common facilities have also been a source of disagreement. As in Fristad, the tenant selection process did not stress community participation, with some tenants unaware of the intention behind the service houses until they had moved in. Researchers Alison Woodward, Dick Urban Vestbro and Maj-Britt Grossman concluded in their seven year study of both Rio and Fristad that these two service housing models "never really got a fair chance." They believe success in similar projects hinges on housing allocation that stresses motivated tenants and education of the administration, who often have little knowledge of this new way of living.

NOTES

1. The Million Program occurred between 1965 and 1975, when 1 million new units were built in Sweden, assembly-line fashion, to ease the housing shortage.
2. In Sweden, the nonprofit housing companies are municipality owned and managed, while in Denmark and Holland, they are independent, state-supported institutions. Swedish tenants have no direct participation in the companies; instead, their participation is based on negotiations (Cronberg 1985).
3. The thirty-five identical three-room apartments matched reasonably well with the number of households. Two were enlarged by combining apartments, two two-room and four-room apartments were created by moving the apartment party walls, and a few single adults agreed to share apartments.
4. Göteborgshem had previously converted the tower into its office space, with the conference room on the fifth floor, although it had moved out some time before the group's conversion.
5. The Social Democrats, who have governed Sweden almost continuously since 1932, have strong links to the trade unions and have started unions for other groups, such as the tenants' association. The Social Democrats have also started public housing companies, such as Göteborgshem. (The trade unions have their own large nonprofit housing company, Riksbyggen.)
6. Ågren (1984, p. 84) notes that fifty-five adults and twenty-five children moved in.
7. The "postmaterialist" tenants, as researcher Woodward (1987) calls certain public housing renters, "value quality of life over material quantity and . . . prioritize the satisfaction of nonmaterial needs."
8. A kitchen, a dining room with a seating area in the corner, the day care and children's play area, and a room for sewing with a large weaving room are located on the fifth floor. The wood shop, the music room, and the youth room—the café before the teenagers demanded their own space—are located off the entryway.
9. The costs have remained the same as for a "regular" apartment with the same number of rooms, with a slight decrease in size to create the common areas.
10. The groups often decide to limit the selling price of dwellings so that the housing remains affordable.
11. Gärdesgården (1942) for childless couples, Blackeberg (1952) for singles, Smaragden (1938) for single women, the YK House (1939) for professionals, and the Marieberg (1944) for working couples (Vestbro 1982).
12. Inga-lisa Sangregorio (1985), a member of the BIG group, writes: "The most impending problem for us hardly had to do with the lack of 'togetherness.' . . . When we were drawing our models for the little collective house we were looking at it as one way to solve the problems of the household work in a more reasonable, more fair and more fun way than what is possible or at least common in the nuclear family."

13. Residents saved $4,824 (34,000 Swedish crowns) between 1985 and 1988 on electrical and water bills (Kollektivhus i Stockholm 1989).

14. The yearly dues are 50 Swedish crowns ($7.50) for adults and 10 for children to pay for New Year's parties, block parties and new materials for the workshop, gymnasium, and other amenities. This organization, Stolplyckans kollektivhusforening, uses the informal tower groups to organize common projects. The common house organization has proved extremely valuable in negotiations with the housing authority and with the social service agency.

15. Although the social service agency was nominally interested in the residents' use of the kitchen, it did little the first two years to help them get in. This indifference was a threat to the pioneer efforts required by the residents to create common meals—meals necessary to the creation of collaborative housing.

16. Tenants waged their own fight with the authorities concerning health. A product called Flyt-Spackel was placed over the concrete floors to create a smooth, flat finish. Bacteria managed to grow underneath and produced ammonia after a few years. One of the residents, a doctor, became suspicious when his children developed watery eyes and eczema; another tenant working at the university began to run tests. Tenant Thor B recalls, "Because we live and work here together, we notice things and can organize much more efficiently than other tenants. We fought to have them fix the floors, and that was a very expensive repair." The other apartments built at the same time, but not part of Stolplyckan, benefited from the effort; their floors were also renovated.

17. Every ten weeks, each family is expected to act as the evening host at the café, serving coffee and cake, and cleaning the café and library afterward, giving an extra social aspect to common work.

REFERENCES

Ågren, L. 1984. *Kollektivhuset Stacken.* Gothenburg: CTH-Architecture Department/Korpen.

Arkitektur. 1985. Issue on collective housing. **85**:3-30.

BIG-gruppen. 1982. *Det lilla kollektivhuset: En modell för praktisk tillämpning.* Stockholm: Swedish Council for Building Research.

Caldenby, C., and Å. Walldén. 1984. *Kollektivhuset Stacken.* Gothenburg: Korpen.

Cronberg, Tarja. 1986. "Tenants' Involvement in the Management of Social Housing in the Nordic Countries." *Scandinavian Housing and Planning Research* **3**:65-87.

Kollektivhus i Stockholm. 1989. Stockholm Stads Uppföljningsgrupp för Kollektivhus.

Krantz, Birgit, and Britt Pedersen. 1989. "The Stolplyckan Concept—a Meeting Place of Communal Living and Social Service." In *Neue Wohnformen in Europa, Berichte des vierten Internationalen Wohnbund-Kongresses in Hamburg,* ed. Joachim Brech, pp. 332-340. Darmstadt: Wohnbund, Verlag Für Wissenschaftliche Publikationen (in English and German).

Palm Lindén, Karin, 1987. *Kollektivhuset Slottet-ett typiskt BIG-kollektiv.* Manus, Byggnadsfunktionslära. Lund: Lunds Universitet.

Lindén, Karen Palm. 1989. "The Physical Structure of the Swedish Collective House—Support or Limit the Inhabitants' Everyday Life." In *Neue Wohnformen in Europa. Berichte des vierten Internationalen Wohnbund-Kongresses in Hamburg,* ed. Joachim Brech, pp. 320-331. Darmstadt: Wohnbund, Verlag Für Wissenschaftliche Publikationen (in English and German).

Sangregorio, Inga-Lisa. 1985. "Nu kan det avslöjas! Bogemenskapen kamouflage för egoistiska kvinnors langtan efter privat liv!" (Now it can be revealed! Residential togetherness is a camoflage for egotistical women's longing for a private life.). *Arkitektur,* p. 29 (Jan./Feb.).

Vestbro, D. U. 1982. *Kollektivhus fran enkokshus till bogemenskap.* Stockholm: Swedish Council for Building Research.

Woodward, A. 1989. "Communal Housing in Sweden." In *New Households, New Housing,* ed. Karen Franck and Sherry Ahrentzen, pp. 71-94. New York: Van Nostrand Reinhold.

Woodward, A. 1987. "Public Housing Communes: Swedish Response to Post-material Demands." In *Housing and Neighborhoods,* ed. W. van Vliet—, H. Choldin, W. Michelson, and D. Popenoe, pp. 215-238. Westport, Conn.: Greenwood Press.

Woodward, Alison, Dick Urban Vestbro, and Maj-Britt Grossman. 1989. *Den Nya Generationen Kollektivhus.* Stockholm: Byggforskningsradet (English summary).

Two

American Collaborative Housing

. . . Sometimes I feel that we've found another way to live where it doesn't have to be hectic and crazy and competitive all the time, or lonely. It's a feeling . . . like together we can somehow do it, that we've become an extended family, part of each other. Then I don't dwell on the newspaper reports, or the bills, or the latest pressure at work. Its just a feeling of real joy and belonging—we're living the difference.

a collaborative housing resident

CHAPTER 5

But Would We Want
to Live There?

The European examples attest to the many benefits of living in collaborative communities—security, friendship, sharing of tasks, and a good environment for children. "That's all very well, but would I want to live there?" questioned a working mother at a talk on collaborative housing. Her concerns were the greater possibility of conflict within the group and a loss of personal freedom. She is not alone in her fears of interdependence. A magazine article on new housing, specifically redesigning the suburbs, received this comment: "With all its obvious drawbacks, the single house on a suburban lot allows more

A discussion among members of Muir Commons concerning an amendment to their bylaws. Decisions require the full consensus of the membership. *(Thor Balkhed)*

control over one's territory. . . . The American Dream is not just a box on a lawn. It's a chance for a small portion of creative independence."[1]

Collaborative communities require organization and interdependence among households that does not need to be dealt with in the typical detached home. Decisions that are generally made within the family or by the individual now move into the sphere of the group. Residents in these communities need different social and communication skills than individuals living in a typical neighborhood.

Clearly Americans have values, beliefs, and attitudes that are not the same as those of Europeans, but similar types of collaborative housing can be seen in the United States. Some developments, although they are only a handful, incorporate many of the same ideas. Collaboration has worked, and continues to work, in the United States.

These cousins of European communities give us the closest reading on the functioning and appearance of possible U.S. prototypes. There is not one particular housing prototype to point at; instead there is a spectrum of approaches and solutions.

In this chapter, we look at eight U.S. developments (Table 5.1). Like their European counterparts, they are maintained and managed by the residents, have complete private dwellings and common areas, and include a common house or rooms. Four were developed entirely by the group, under various tenures and legal agreements. In two (N Street and I Wonder If Herbie's Home Yet?) the group formed after initial purchase by an individual, and in two (the Amalgamated and the Reservoir), a nonprofit organization instigated the developments.

MOTIVATION AND ORGANIZATION

The motivation behind developing these U.S. examples was to create a socially supportive community for the residents. In most of the examples, obtaining affordable housing was also important. In Denmark, Holland, and Sweden, similar motivations were apparent. But in those countries, another motivation (particularly in the more recent communities) has been the many possibilities of working together with twenty or forty other households, creating new organizations and larger common areas.

In American collaborative communities, not as many activities occur in the common house or rooms, and they are not used quite as frequently as in those European countries. Meal preparation, for example, is organized on an individual basis, most often potlucks where one household prepares a main dish,

Table 5.1 U.S. Collaborative Communities

Community	Location	Completed	Developer	Tenure	Locale
The Amalgamated	Bronx, NY	1927	Nonprofit	Limited equity co-op	Urban
Bryn Gweled Homesteads	Southampton, PA	1939	Group	Land trust	Suburban
I Wonder If Herbie's Home Yet	Bainbridge Island, WA	1973	Architect	Planned unit development	Rural
Monan's Rill	St. Helena, CA	1974	Group	Partnership	Rural
N Street	Davis, CA	1984	Individuals	Home ownership	Suburban
Reservoir	Madison, WI	1988	Nonprofit	Leasing co-op	Urban
Santa Rosa Creek Commons	Santa Rosa, CA	1982	Group	Limited equity co-op	Urban
Sunlight	Portland, OR	1978–1979	Group	Condominium	Suburban

Residents of U.S. collaborative communities enjoy many social activities together. Here the folksong society performs for friends and neighbors at Bryn Gweled, Pennsylvania. The white building in the background is the common house. *(Robinson)*

and are held from once a week to once a month instead of several times a week.

Management, however, is organized in a similar way. In Sættedammen, Denmark, and Santa Rosa Creek Commons, California, residents manage and maintain their development. At monthly meetings, residents talk over problems and decide policies. (In Sættedammen, Denmark, members vote on many issues, whereas in Santa Rosa all decisions are made by consensus.) Committees are organized to deal with specific details and research issues, such as membership, the garden, or special events. In both communities, members are expected to contribute about 8 hours of time a month.

The American examples developed independently of European collaborative housing. The group that eventually developed Sunlight, in Oregon, began organizing in the 1970s along the lines of Danish cohousing but without any knowledge of others' developing similar communities. They decided among themselves to build a common house, share dining, and use a consensus decision-making process.

This dependence on others (and the realization that the rest of the group depends on the individual) may seem to outsiders a negative aspect of living collaboratively. But to residents, this is often the heart of living collaboratively. "For me, this is a real way of living. It is not a matter of portioning off a part of myself but living in a whole way, both giving and taking," explained a resident.

DESIGN

Most of the American collaborative examples have managed to blend into the surrounding neighborhood and do not call attention to

Although the Reservoir development (twenty-eight units) has a higher density than surrounding homes, it fits well into the neighborhood.

themselves. They stress a homelike quality and deemphasize an architecture of collective living. Two rural examples, Monan's Rill, California, and Herbie's in Washington, are a tribute to the individual family home. The image of the rural examples—individual homes surrounded by landscaping—remains strong in both suburban and urban examples. Developments in the city, such as Santa Rosa Creek Commons, also appear conventional from the street. The N Street suburban homes, in California, fade chameleonlike into the surrounding tract houses.

The building facades fit quietly into the surroundings. The Reservoir in Madison, Wisconsin, is a good example of higher-density housing carefully designed to fit comfortably into the 1920s style of the surrounding neighborhood through details such as bay windows, wide roof overhangs, and roomy porches. "Our biggest compliment," said architect Jim Glueck, who worked with Design Coalition Architects, "is that people think it's a renovation."

In the case of the Reservoir, pressure from neighbors had much to do with the appearance; in the Santa Rosa Creek Commons, money was a constraint against new forms. But beyond these obvious restraints, the members very much harbor an image of their community as a place that fits in with the surrounding neighborhood and does not stand out.[2]

Many of the early European developments were designed to blend quietly into the community. In Denmark, earlier collaborative housing had traditional rural designs, such as in Overdrevet. Some of the more recent developments take the opposite approach and go out of their way as provocative architecture, such as Adalen. The common house has also become more prominent and stands as a symbol of the community, such as in Kilen in the urban neighborhood developments,

Denmark, or Hilversumse Meent in Holland (see Part One).

ENVIRONMENT

Living harmoniously with the environment has been one of the goals of collaborative housing. These eight examples reflect the concerns, beliefs, and theories of their time.

In the 1920s, sunshine, open space, and clean air were considered the antidotes for crowded industrial cities. Gardens and open space were an important element in the design of the Amalgamated Houses, built as a cooperative in Brooklyn, in 1927. Almost 50% of the site is unbuilt, a large percentage for workers' housing of the time.

In 1939, when Bryn Gweled, Pennsylvania, was started, the concept of open space and spreading out on one's own land were still important. The depression gave impetus to the idea of small garden plots and self-sufficient home owners. In Bryn Gweled, each household was allotted a two-acre homestead, with the idea that food could be grown, as well as residents' organizing together.

With growing density, housing that spreads out has proved to be costly and environmentally unsound. In the 1970s, fueled in part by the oil crisis, energy conservation became an important focus. In Sunlight, Oregon, the houses are clustered together along two pedestrian streets, and the design incorporates many solar energy ideas.

In the 1980s, communities such as N Street and Monan's Rill placed an emphasis on organic gardening and permaculture (combining human culture and agriculture). Organic agriculture became a community task.

In the 1990s, environmentalists increasingly are taking a holistic approach to housing. The emphasis is on combining housing with gardening, shopping, and places to work. Examples are the Danish urban neighborhood and several pedestrian-oriented communities being developed in the United States.

The challenge has been financing innovative design that is energy efficient and environmentally compatible. The development of Santa Rosa Creek Commons illustrates the struggle to bring innovative ideas to reality and the eventual compromise that is often required.

FINANCING

The local government is conspicuously absent in the development of most of the U.S. examples, unlike most European models. The difficulty of obtaining government support is a common thread running through the lower-income developments.

European developments receive direct government support. The Danish government provides very good terms for cooperative developments, and the Dutch and Swedish governments subsidize rental cohousing. But lack of government support in the United States has required communities to rely on their members' resources. Dwellings have tended to be expensive, beyond the reach of those below median incomes. Many of the people best served by this housing type—the elderly, single parents, the handicapped, and young couples with children—are shut out of this option. The few affordable projects have relied on loans and grants.

Since housing is the biggest single investment most Americans ever make, there is little interest in limiting equity without some monetary incentive, for example, government loans. The Danes, Dutch, and Swedes know that the government will help provide housing and health care as they grow older. Housing is not their main investment for the retirement years, and they are more willing to accept rental and cooperative housing.[3] The United States is far behind these countries in housing options for low- and moderate-income residents. A large project like Stolplyckan in Sweden, with 194 households and numerous common facilities, can be developed relatively quickly with public support. In the United States, which lacks such support, the most basic type of affordable housing cannot seem to get off the ground.

Two examples are discussed in this part to show both the need and appreciation for a nonprofit collaborative housing option. The first and longest running is the Amalgamated, a cooperative in operation since 1923. The Amalgamated, in Brooklyn, provides apartments, child care, and common facilities at affordable prices. The Reservoir, in Wisconsin, is a leasing cooperative developed by a nonprofit housing association. The residents, a mix of incomes and ages, manage and maintain the development with the help of the housing association.

The European developments have also enjoyed technical and organizational support. The Dutch national collaborative organization, LVCW, provides a network of support for communities. In Denmark, the Danish Building Research Institute provides data and reports on a number of cohousing communities, plus books on development. Sweden has a large number of researchers who study various aspects of collective living, from history to floor layouts.

Most of the U.S. collaborative communities reinvent the wheel when they begin their development process. Of the eight communities mentioned, only two had heard of each other. Not only does this lack of knowledge create difficulties during development, but over time, as problems arise, the individual communities remain isolated, seeking solutions as best they can. This is particularly hard

on nonprofit collaborative developments, where there are many questions on organization, funding, and feasibility. To build affordable communities can be a long struggle, and harder still to include collaboration.

NOTES

1. The writer is N. I. Hilliard of Berkeley in the Letters section of the *San Francisco Examiner,* August 23, 1987.
2. The architecture of the most urban example, the Amalgamated, built in 1929, was originally in a Tudor style. In the 1920s, neo-Tudor architecture had become the symbol of suburban dwellings, in contrast to the sleek, modern style of avant-garde European buildings. The image was not a futuristic one but rather the opposite (Dolkart). There is no indication from the exterior of the cooperative interior life. Rather, the gardens stand out as the focal point.
3. In Denmark, the first communities were privately developed. Since 1981, limited equity cooperatives have been created and now account for about two-thirds of all cohousing, or over seventy communities.

REFERENCE

Dolkart, Andrew S. 1989. "Homes for People; Non-Profit Cooperatives in New York City 1916-1929." *Sites,* pp. 30-42.

CHAPTER 6

Santa Rosa Creek Commons: Learning to Compromise

A large vegetable garden is located at the center of the Commons.

Santa Rosa, California
Units: 27 (including 10 low-income
  units)
Tenure: Limited equity housing
  cooperative
Site: Urban, 2 acres
Began/Moved in: 1977/1982
Architects: Jacobsen, Silverstein and
  Winslow

Santa Rosa Creek Commons, located a block from city hall, is hidden from the street by a fabric of single-family homes. A row of covered parking spaces is revealed by following the driveway around an existing home, and beyond, the three wide-roofed buildings appear, surprisingly conventional. Beyond the buildings, the place unveils itself: a community garden, a play area, and a wide, grassy floodplain sloping down to the creek. The community is not unlike its setting—quiet and seemingly conventional.

Helen Perkins, an energetic woman in her seventies, lives in one of the downstairs units, right off the common garden. Almost from the beginning she has been the secretary for Santa Rosa Creek Commons. Her sister was one of the members who found the site and "got in touch with everyone she could think of." Most of them were in one way or another connected with the Society of Friends. A number of these people had begun thinking of creating a community where people of different ages, backgrounds, religions, and cultures could live together. They were not particularly well off, but felt that they could start such a community by combining their talents and resources: familiarity with working in groups, organizational skills, and participation in many causes of the past twenty years such as the development of food and housing cooperatives.

This group of ten interested people organized what eventually became Santa Rosa Creek Commons. Each put down $5,000 to purchase together an acre of land, with a house on it. A year later, each member put in an additional $2,500 to acquire the house and lot next door.

Helen Perkins is matter-of-fact about the hard road of development. She gathers up three thick notebooks and places them in front of me. Looking through the pages—from the beginning in January 1977, when Helen's sister first talked about the land, to moving in in June 1982—the count is 135 meetings.

THE DESIGN

One of the women in the group was taking a design course taught by architect Murray Silverstein, one of the coauthors of *A Pattern Language* (Alexander). The patterns extract design "best solutions" that can be used over and over again, without giving specific measurements or plans. They are described as a language of design that allows the articulation of infinite variations. Aside from teaching, Silverstein was in the process of opening an architectural office, JSW, with Max Jacobson and Barbara Winslow. The Santa Rosa Commons members interviewed other architects but were enthusiastic about the book and chose JSW because of the emphasis on participatory design.

The members hoped to build a real prototype, both social and egalitarian, and with energy-saving components. They hired a financial consultant with connections to the U.S. Department of Housing and Urban Development (HUD), hoping to get some government funding.

After some debate, the Commons members decided to develop an innovative prototype using solar components and design. This was a more elaborate scheme than first envisioned but embodied their philosophy of living responsibly on the land. A solar consultant, Peter Calthorpe, joined JSW, and together they began working out the various solar configurations that affected building design.

The architects dealt mainly with a small group of Commons members headed by Ruth Allen, who had an architectural background. They discussed drawings and sketches, manipulated various configurations, and constructed a model of the buildings. Presenta-

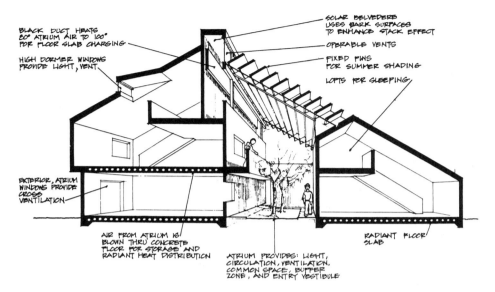

BLACK DUCT HEATS 80° ATRIUM AIR TO 100° FOR FLOOR SLAB CHARGING

HIGH DORMER WINDOWS PROVIDE LIGHT, VENT

SOLAR BELVEDERE USES DARK SURFACES TO ENHANCE STACK EFFECT

OPERABLE VENTS

FIXED FINS FOR SUMMER SHADING

LOFTS FOR SLEEPING

EXTERIOR, ATRIUM WINDOWS PROVIDE CROSS VENTILATION

AIR FROM ATRIUM IS BLOWN THRU CONCRETE FLOOR FOR STORAGE AND RADIANT HEAT DISTRIBUTION

ATRIUM PROVIDES: LIGHT, CIRCULATION, VENTILATION, COMMON SPACE, BUFFER ZONE, AND ENTRY VESTIBULE

RADIANT FLOOR SLAB

The initial design had three buildings with a central atrium-greenhouse that also served as the common solar collector for the surrounding seven to eight units. Each unit had concrete floors for radiant heat distribution, plus windows that opened directly into the atrium. *(JSW Architects)*

tions were made regularly to the large group and their concerns and suggestions relayed back to the architects.

The initial design had twenty-five units in three separate buildings, plus a community meeting hall, private yards or spacious balconies, and a central outdoor commons. Patterns from the book were not only included but often served double-duty by having an energy rationale. A design pattern for a cascade of roofs sloped at the correct angles for solar panels, the arcades could be used as a shading device, and the common areas at the heart (locating these areas centrally) were atrium greenhouses, which also served as the common solar collector for the surrounding units, complete with a system of operable fans and vents.

With the design complete, the architects were given the go-ahead to do a set of construction drawings, an expensive undertaking because of the novel design. Unfortunately, the funding sources were not as committed as the Commons members had believed, and their financial consultant, who had been so optimistic, suddenly disappeared.

The architects were in the process of applying for a building permit and had done some negotiations with the contractor when the Commons members decided they lacked sufficient financing. The programs that were available did not fund solar energy, and the project square foot cost was more than the HUD programs could support. "The whole thing came crashing down and fell apart," remembers Silverstein. "We let ourselves spend a lot of fairly visionary time," recalls Ruth Allen about working with the *Pattern Language,* "and when we got down to the actual building process—the permits and the loan from the city and things like that—we weren't able to realize the kind of visions that are outlined in the book."

Not only did the members feel themselves almost back at the starting point, but they faced architectural bills of about $60,000. It was a low point, and some people abandoned the whole idea, but a core stayed on, with an unshaken belief that they could find a solution. They paid JSW and kept looking around for a solution. The architect, however, believed that was the end of the project.

By 1979, two years after the land was purchased, interest rates were climbing, as were housing and construction prices. A new housing law, authored by Democratic assemblyman Tom Bates, created a new type of housing cooperative, called limited equity, based on a recent housing development in Berkeley, Savo Island townhouses. The idea was to create inflation-resistant housing by allowing only a limited profit for owners when selling their unit. Like former "stock" cooperatives, each household would not own its own unit but would own one share in the collective, and this collective of households owned all the units. Unlike a stock cooperative, the amount of profit the owner made on selling the unit was restricted, so that moderate-income buyers could afford this housing.

One of the consultants to the Savo Island townhouses and the new housing law was Al Bonnett, and it was to him that the Commons members turned. "When they came to me with Murry's original plans, I said they needed to throw it out," recalls Bonnett.

Combining innovative cooperative living, an innovative design, and innovative financing all in one project was too difficult; something had to give. Silverstein recalls,

After almost two years, they called me up, and it was as though they had risen from the ashes. They said we'd have to redesign and that we had to have the drawings done by a real specific date, which was very soon. I remember sitting here at this table with Bonnett and some other guys and saying we can do this [he takes a piece of paper and quickly sketches three rectangles and a curve for the parking]. Before, it had been this agonizing over the *Pattern Language,* and everyone had their input. And now it was this five-minute thing with Bonnett saying, "Yeah, just go with that; don't mess around."

In order to receive state money, the entire development had to fall within very strict guidelines that included tight budgets on how much the architect could be paid, the cost per square foot, and the kind of amenities that could be included in the design. There were no funds for a community room, and the laundry space was enlarged as much as possible so that it could also serve as a meeting space. Only the bare minimum was approved.

FINANCING

The term *patchwork* is how Bonnett describes the financing that helped get Santa Rosa Creek Commons off the ground. Today it would be described as creative financing. Bonnett came up with a financing package combining private, state, and federal money to create a limited-equity cooperative. The members pooled what money they had, borrowed more from friends, and came up with $80,000, not including the land and the existing buildings.

The linchpin in the scheme was the National Consumer's Cooperative Bank, located in Washington, D.C. This would be another first: the first new housing ever to be financed by the Coop Bank, and it was not eager. The bank, concerned with business and market-rate cooperatives, found the limited-equity concept hard to comprehend.

"Although several members of the Coop board were vociferous against such a loan, their local representative convinced them," recalls Bonnett. The bank committed to a loan of $759,500, with the understanding that the group would get low-income sponsorship. The Commons group was able to secure an additional loan of about $400,000 from the California Housing and Community Development Department by agreeing to include ten units for low income members. In order to get this state money, the city was required to pitch in also, and it gave $40,000. The members even managed to get a loan of over $20,000 from their contractor, Todd Construction. After four years of struggling, the financing fell into place.

When I talked to Bonnett, eight years later, about what it would take to get another Santa Rosa Creek Commons built, he said, "I don't know if you can reproduce it at all because of the many obstacles we had to overcome, including waivers to the law.[1] Savo Island, for example, was a good job of finding ways around the existing laws. The bottom line is that it's extremely difficult to do this type of housing cooperative. A series of warranties have been set up in the California constitution to protect consumers. The Department of Real Estate never considered the developer and consumer to be one and the same." For example, although the down payments of the members were in the bank, the state would not release the money until a project was completely built. Member Calvin Simons went with Bonnett to the Department of Real Estate and "argued ourselves red in the face, and it was no use." In the end the project was required to submit all the documentation required of the developer of a private subdivision. "It was one of the most successful projects I ever did because of the people," concluded Bonnett. "I don't know if you can ever reproduce the people and the motivation they had to persevere."

BUILDING

By the fall of 1981, the 2 acres had been leveled; the two front houses that faced the street had been kept. In early November, the first foundation was poured—a momentous occasion with invitations that went out to a number of people.

Many of the units had already been spoken for; only four of the unassisted remained available. There were over eighty names on the waiting list for the ten low-income units.[2]

The Commons members thought they could use their own people to finish the construction and lower some of the costs, but they could not find a contractor to work under those circumstances. "We're in a world that's not set up for doing things ourselves," said Ruth Allen. "It's one thing to hire a contractor and do your own homes, but to get loans from the National Consumers Coop Bank and the Housing Authority, we had to have complete plans bid by licensed contractors." Then she adds, "On the whole, it's remarkable how well they turned out."[3]

Members started to move into their apartments in June, and a large open house party was celebrated on September 25, 1982. Four

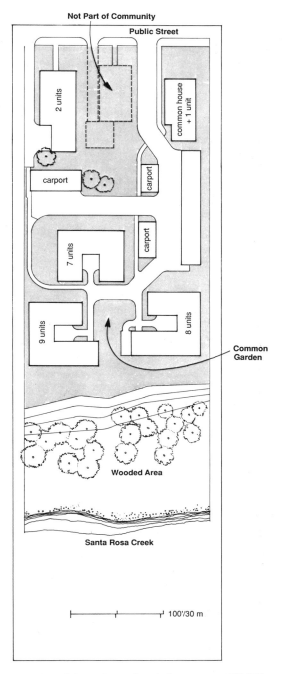

Site plan of Santa Rosa Creek Commons. *(SRCC)*

months later, HUD officials presented the Commons with a national merit award. It was the only thing HUD ever gave them.

COSTS

Members had hoped monthly payments would be below $300; in reality, they ranged from about $400 to $800. (In 1982, this range was about an average market rate for the area.) Member Lucy Forest mentions her worries that after all the years of working for the project, "It may well be that Jim and I can't afford to live there."[4]

Many of the residents, particularly the elderly, had assumed monthly payments would remain fixed or go down. Instead, both the fees and the carrying charges have risen about 30% since the project opened nine years ago. The reason is that the loans are not at a fixed rate. The Coop Bank loan required graduated payments in which the interest rate went up or down with the market. Refinancing, which the Commons is now seeking, is difficult because banks are unfamiliar with limited-equity cooperatives and are reluctant to make loans. The few banks that are willing to make loans have high interest rates.[5]

Nevertheless, members achieve home ownership with low down payments. In return, they make a modest gain on their investment. The increase that members are allowed for selling their membership never exceeds 10% annually of the original down payment. "No one's going to get rich on this," remarked Calvin Simons, one of the original investors.[6] Indeed, the members have voted consistently to raise membership costs only about 6% yearly. "Your initial investment is appreciating. Whether it will appreciate to the same degree as having the capital in the bank, which also is appreciating, is a big question," said a former member.

The Commons has a regulatory agreement with the state to house very low income people, the handicapped, and the elderly. The market-rate households do not carry the costs of the ten low-income apartments. Instead, the state gave the Commons a subsidy: a thirty-year no-interest loan to pay for the construction of the assisted apartments.

A hefty manual of instructions must be followed for the assisted apartments, and it is occasionally revised. To make it manageable for the Commons, the sections are divided among several people. There is a yearly inspection and recertification, which the committees help to organize. In other limited-equity housing cooperatives, an outside management firm usually handles all of these details, but the bottom line is higher rents. This community saves money by doing this work themselves. A former member feels that it would be easier "to even pay $50 a month more and let a manager deal with it." However, the consensus of the members is that to build a spirit of community, all the residents should be called on to maintain and beautify the community.

THE COMMONS TODAY

Thirty-two adults and a dozen children share ownership of the Commons, which has turned out to be an inviting place to live, even with the many budget cuts. The garden and outdoor areas are both serene and safe because the apartments have been separated from the parking area and street noise. To reduce the appearance of higher density, the apartments have been divided among the three buildings. Each U-shaped building has a cluster of seven to nine units sharing a small courtyard. But many of the extras, such as the wide balconies, and essentials, such as a large community room, have been reduced in size. The balconies are still there but adequate for only several flowerpots. The common room did not work well doubling as the laundry room, and eventually part of one of the front houses was converted into a meeting room. Although the budget cutbacks allow the community to function, the opportunity of creating a design that truly reflects this new way of living had to be modified.

The initial vision has changed in the process of being realized, and not only physically. Ruth Allen recalls that there was to have been one community meal a week: "Well, for one thing, we couldn't afford the community space, and for another, people began to realize that

The private entrances are grouped around common courts. Balconies above the entrances were reduced in size because of budget cuts.

it took a lot of energy to do some things cooperatively. We have now a good balance between doing some things privately and some things cooperatively."

Although community has not taken central stage, it is very much a part of the Commons. Aside from the community room, there are also shared laundry facilities, a guest sleeping area ($7 a night), a vegetable garden, a play area, shared tools, a recycling center, and a community vacuum cleaner.

The Commons is entirely self-managed.[7] Every member is expected to contribute at least 8 hours each month toward the community. Part of this time is taken up by a choice of two committee meetings, which each member is expected to join. The committees range over a wide and varied territory:

Building and grounds
Garden and landscaping
Membership and marketing
Social activities
Children's activities
Parents' support group
Education
Finance
Community room
Time and management[8]

"When you talk of 8 hours minimum, there's a lot more than that per person that's put in here," says Ed Duckles. He puts in between 20–30 hours a week, as does his wife, Jean. The bookkeeper puts in about 30 hours a week, and so does Helen Perkins. Most people faithfully put in a minimum of 8 hours, and a number put in more than that. A number of the members who work extra hours are retirees, and there is an agreement among them that full-time workers, especially single parents, are justifiably too busy to do much beyond the minimum required.

"You have to build it yourself. You have to

be interested to begin with if you're going to really make it work." said Ed Duckles with conviction. "By joining the Commons, every individual becomes a member of a community that has set a certain standard and quality of participation. It's a very subtle peer pressure that says if you join this co-op, you not only give a minimum of 8 hours a month, but you also meet the needs as they come along."

CHILDREN

About a dozen children live at the Commons.[9] The freedom to roam in a car-free area is a benefit not only to them but to their parents. The children can play outside in secure surrounding, and "it feels really safe because a lot of the neighbors are around."

Friends of various ages are a few steps away, as is the spacious play area near the floodplain. One father mentioned: "The neighbors had a daughter the same age as mine, and they were like sisters." Children can knock on a neighbor's doors and be welcomed. When they have a problem, they have a choice of people to turn to for assistance.

Neighbors help out with child care and baby sitting. One member took care of an 8 year old in the afternoon while her father, a single parent, worked. "I watch her when she comes home from school, and if I'm busy, the neighbors take turns keeping an eye." Older children are available to baby-sit for the youngest.

Two committees handle the policies on and activities of children. The Children's Activities Group plans parties, field trips, and children's holiday events.[10] The Parents' Support Group brings children and parents together to discuss ways to live together harmoniously. This group has helped defuse some of the problems that occur over community restrictions.

With the amount of attention and care bestowed by the community, it is hard to believe that children are also one of the main sources of conflict. The community has to decide on standards that are acceptable, as well as who

is to discipline the children. Some members think that children should be allowed to run around until nine at night; others do not. Some feel that a standard needs to be set for the kind of language children use; others do not.

In a diverse community with many different views, the amount of supervision considered acceptable requires constant revision. "Everyone has a different idea on how to bring up their children. You can imagine that some people are very allergic to forms of behavior that don't bother other people," said a former member.

DIVERSITY AND CONFLICT

The diversity of people—middle class, working class, elderly and young, athletic and handicapped, well educated and not—is a source of richness and difficulty. "We have single mothers, traditional families, and elder citizens," said Calvin Simons, describing the Commons. "We like diversity. It makes things interesting." To appreciate diversity requires not only tolerance but a certain acceptance of conflict. Learning to live together has brought many benefits—and created a few problems. Perhaps the most difficult has been deciding how much the community can tolerate and how much conflict is too much.

In their desire to be community minded and help people out, the residents accepted a family of seven into one of the low-income three-bedroom apartments in 1982. The five children, all of them aggressive, proved to be quite overwhelming to families of only one or two children. Cultural and other differences between this family and the other members compounded the situation. "They didn't cut the grass, they didn't weed, they hung their wet mops and boxes of things outdoors that they didn't have space for indoors," recalls a former Commons member. A few members wanted to evict these tenants. A great deal of effort, and a number of years, was spent on resolving conflicts with this family. Eventually a search for a larger residence was begun by the family and some members of the Com-

Working hard on "play day," members of all ages enjoy volleyball in the more secluded area behind the buildings.

mons, as well as by the Santa Rosa Housing Authority. In 1988, the family moved to a subsidized four-bedroom house in a nearby town.[11]

"People who need to be assisted are a special problem all by themselves," says a former member who believes they have sensitivities connected with their own individual survival. But other members of the Commons were quick to point out that some of the low-income members are among the more responsible contributors to the life of the community. Most members see no differences between the two types of household, a few do.[12]

The Commons has a six-step mediation process for resolving conflicts, with residents advised first to talk to each other and to try to understand and settle problems. Then a mediation panel, composed of member volunteers with special training, is set up. Three members are chosen by the parties in tension, and a meeting is scheduled. Each party relates its side of the story, and solutions are discussed. The process is sometimes successful, and sometimes it is not.

THE MONTHLY MEETING

At 3:00 P.M. on the second Saturday of each month is the all-member meeting. The chairs, in a circle so wide that their backs touch every wall of the meeting room, quickly fill up. Greetings are called out more loudly as more and more people come in. All members are expected to attend these monthly business meetings. Those who do not show up are excused; if they do not say why they will not attend, they are considered absent. About 90% of the members are in attendance, easily making the quorum—a majority of the twenty-seven households.

The people seem at their ease, relaxed, and cheerful, exchanging bits of news. The president of the board opens the meeting with a moment of silence. Stillness fills the room. When the meeting begins, the woman sitting next to me reaches into her handbag, pulls out a shirt, then a needle and thread, and begins sewing on a button.

Visitors are introduced and the previous month's minutes approved. A glance at the agenda tacked to the wall shows that at least eight of the ten committees will be reporting. Topics range from an annual education workshop to refinancing the buildings.

Until recently, nine members of the board of directors had the responsibility for most decisions. Now all twenty-seven households constitute the board. There is an executive committee of president, vice-president, secretary, and treasurer to see that the community runs smoothly, but their opinions count the same as those of everyone else.

Several people hoping to become members are attending this meeting. A single mother sits with her toddler, waiting for the membership committee to talk about her application. The little boy is impatient and squirms in her lap. Applicants are required to attend at least two monthly meetings. They write a letter to the community explaining why they want to join and include a personal history about themselves and their experience working with others. After that, several members of the membership committee visit the applicant's home. A decision is made only after further discussion among the members. The process takes at least several months, and when the applicant has finally been approved, there is often a wait for a vacant unit.

A good part of this meeting is not taken up with membership but with deciding on the removal of a tree whose roots are tearing up the asphalt and the planting of a new one. Everyone seems to have an opinion. The garden committee proposes an orange tree as a replacement. But B talks about frost and chill factors' killing the tree, while C points out that there is an orange tree flourishing three houses down; still, D does not want the old tree taken down, believing that it can be trimmed, and H says that would allow the car light to shine into her bedroom, so she advocates putting up a lattice while the orange tree grows. What if passer-bys help themselves to the fruit? wonders K, only to be told by L that this is a way to feed the hungry and by M that those are not the type to take the fruit in the first place. N reminds the rest that there is the pollution from the cars out front, and P brings up the question of how to cut down the old tree, and then chain saws are discussed. . . .

I am told by the woman sewing next to me that this topic was brought up at last month's meeting, to no conclusion. When the president asks, after 40 minutes of discussion, whether consensus can be reached to tear down the existing tree and let the garden committee decide on the replacement—and it does—they are satisfied, albeit some more than others. "Consensus is time-consuming but worth it," a member told me later. "Voting with two-thirds for and one-third against is faster but leaves ill feelings in the third against it."

After about an hour, there is a much-needed break. Everyone stretches, moves around, and socializes. Little bells ring from the toddler's shoes as he runs off, and several members talk to his mother.

When the meeting resumes, there is some fun and comic relief in the form of a weather report, a tradition carried out by one of the residents. Loud calls are heard for the weather report as soon as everyone sits down again. The weatherman rises. He has on a large, black plastic bag with a cut-out for his head, an old black hat, and an oversized red polka-dot tie. A clown's red nose completes his outfit. He clears his throat, but the laughter from the group only gets louder. He holds a report in his hands but cannot seem to see it because of his large nose. He takes off the nose and announces, "The weather has been cold." The members clap and hoot. He tells a joke that livens up the meeting and a few weather facts, and then the meeting gets back to business.

The finance report follows, with a stack of handouts. Members are attentive to the explanation of interest rates and refinancing terms. The original loan has an adjustable interest rate, and refinancing for a cooperative is difficult. Only one bank in California seems willing to give a loan, at a steep interest rate. A number of questions are raised, and a decision is made to write to the bank for more information. The meeting draws to an end with announcements of forthcoming events and who is going away on trips.

The end of the meeting is a good excuse for a covered-dish dinner. Patrick and Mary-anne Michaels (they met at the Commons) are in charge of preparing the meeting room. Chairs are moved, folding tables set up, and tablecloths spread as we have a conversation about the meeting. People appear at the door bearing plates of food and holding children by the hand. Guests pop in, loaves of bread appear, and the salad arrives. "Sometimes it's real hard, but when it's wonderful, it's wonderful," concludes Patrick.

NOTES

1. The low-income housing subsidies and laws change from year to year, although the difficulty of obtaining the subsidies remains. The exact development of Santa Rosa Creek Commons would be different if it was done today, but the group's struggle through financing, design, and realization would probably be similar.
2. The new buildings would add 17,000 square feet to the site at a construction cost of about $42.50 a square foot (the original hope was $35.00/square foot). The architect's fees and construction supervision came to $40,000.
3. A few unforeseen problems arose during construction. That spring had unusually heavy rainfall, swelling the clay soil. Member Ed Duckles believes, "One of the biggest problems is not design but the fact that these buildings were built in one of the wettest springs they've had in ten years. As the clay soil drys, the buildings are sinking a little and causing some minor cracks."
4. *Santa Rosa Press Democrat*, November 8, 1981.
5. Professor Alan Haskin of the University of California, Los Angeles, has undertaken a study of California limited-equity housing cooperatives (LEHC) with the objective of providing proposals for legislative reforms. Between 1979, when the legislation for LEHCs passed, and January 1989, the end of his study, only thirty LEHCs were developed. Haskin's study identified six basic problems with developing LEHCs, including the need to train prospective shareholders, property tax relief, and the difficulties of dealing with the Davis-Stirling Act (Haskin).
6. Nonassisted members pay a one-time membership fee that takes the place of a down payment when they move in. The fee varies between $7,000 and $9,000, depending on the apartment. The monthly payments are between $550 and $700 and include the unit's proportionate amount for maintenance, common facilities, and the garden. The assisted apartments require a fee between $1,500 and $1,900, with monthly payments based on 25% of the member's income. When a member moves, he or she will receive back the membership fee plus an added equity, limited by law not to exceed 10% of the base membership share each year. The equity to be added is set by the Commons board each year. This has been set at 6% the last three years.
7. The manager, one of the members, is paid a token fee of $50 a month. He does maintenance jobs himself or asks other members to help him; if the work requires higher skills, he hires professionals.
8. A committee that is looking into the reasons for nonparticipation at the fullest and suggesting alternatives.
9. The number of children is limited because most of the units are one and two bedrooms. There are only two family units (three bedrooms).
10. An example of activities to bring the adults and children together is Special Friends. Any interested adult fills out a small card that has written on it: "Activities I would enjoy sharing, Conditions, Restrictions, Best time to reach me, and Other Comments." These cards are posted. The children find the activity they like and find the adult. As one member explained it to me, "Any child can contact me about starting a stamp collection or baking cakes, and the two of us can negotiate." Although this seems to be a good idea, it does not seem to be currently appealing to the children.
11. Although the wear caused by the large family during their six years of occupancy was considerable, some of the costs were covered by the replacement reserve funds accumulated in the annual budget to put apartments into good condition for new occupants. The damage (not wear and tear) was deducted from the family's share value before it was returned to them.
12. Since the members make all decisions together and because the low-income subsidies are connected to specific apartments, residents know who the low-income families are.

REFERENCES

Alexander, Christopher, Sara Ishikawa, Murray Silverstein, Max Jacobsen, Ingrid Fiksdahl-King, and Schlomo Angel. 1977. *A Pattern Language*. New York: Oxford University Press.

Haskin, Allan. 1989. *Limited-Equity Housing Cooperatives in California: Proposals for a Legislative Reform*. Berkeley: California Policy Seminar, University of California.

CHAPTER 7

Other American Examples

SUNLIGHT: PASSIVE SOLAR DESIGN

Portland, Oregon
Units: 15
Tenure: Condominium

Site: Suburban, 7.5 acres
Began/Moved in: 1976/1978–1979
Architects: Church & Maslen

Lining Della Street and Lois Lane are fifteen single-family homes built in two rows. The

All of the houses in Sunlight have large windows facing the south and atriums for heat gain. *(Church)*

houses were built along a sloping south-facing hill to receive the maximum solar exposure. Located 7 minutes from downtown Portland, the community, covered with wild woods of maple, alder, and big firs, with a year-round creek, seems a world apart from the city.

The idea began with three singles and three couples who lived in the same neighborhood. "We wanted to save energy of various kinds. It seemed silly all of us running home and cooking. So we started a dinner group once or twice a week," recalls member Dot Dixon. "We all shared the same background of the sixties, and we had talked of buying land together. Halfway through the seventies was a time of many human potential movements, and we got inspired to link our talking with some action. So we said, 'Let's do it! Let's do it!'"

The group started by raising money to send one member, Bill Church, to the first U.S. solar conference, held in Albuquerque, New Mexico, in 1976. He became knowledgeable in the various solar energy alternatives. That same year, the group purchased 15.5 wooded acres, chosen for their south-facing slope. They agreed to divide the cost of the land and the community house equally among themselves under condominium ownership. Each household paid for the construction of its own house and owns it, including the land it sits on. The remaining land and the common house are owned and maintained together.

Architects Bill Church and John Maslen (who has been a resident for ten years) planned the community. Design guidelines were hammered out at group meetings, resulting in houses clustered on 3 acres, with the rest of the site left undeveloped. Parking is along one edge of the community, and residents walk to their homes. The homes have a passive solar design that includes a long, narrow floor plan with minimum openings on the north-facing facade. The weathered cedar exteriors help the individual houses blend into the surrounding woods.[1]

Each household followed the design guidelines, working out its house plan individually. They conferred with the architects to make sure their designs would work. Although the houses look similar from the exterior, the inside of each is very different. "We were aware how the standard house of the time—with a living room used only for formal occasions, a separate and rarely used dining room, and an isolated kitchen—didn't function well. We designed a large living-dining space, a good social space. Others in the community could drop by, sit in the living portion, and feel comfortable while someone else was working in the kitchen or eating," said Maslen.

The houses range from a studio (800 square feet) to a five-bedroom house (2,400 square feet). Members finance the housing through individual bank loans and sell at market rates to interested buyers. Current prices range from $75,000 to $140,000. "Money was the most disappointing thing. We had hoped because we would be building the homes at one time that we would save on the houses. We didn't! They are all different, all sizes; everyone wanted something special, something unique and expensive," said Dixon.[2]

An energy consultant, Ralph Bruinsslot, designed a system that included a solarium with a tile floor, and beneath the tile a 4-foot bin of rocks to store heat. In theory, a fan blows the air down a duct, pulls it through the rocks to get heated, and then sends it back up to the solarium. This system was not installed correctly and did not work, however. Solar panels were considered but did not make financial sense for the small amount of sun during the winter heating season.

The passive solar energy components were the most successful; they include thick insulation in walls and ceilings, a south-facing exposure, the solarium (minus the air rotation system), and clerestories in the bedrooms. The solariums have south ceilings sloped to the angle of the sun in December, with two walls sloped out to create a lens to capture the sun. (The backup system is electric heating and wood-burning stoves). For cooling, windows have been placed at the top of the house and at the bottom to create air suction, which works effectively to cool the interiors.

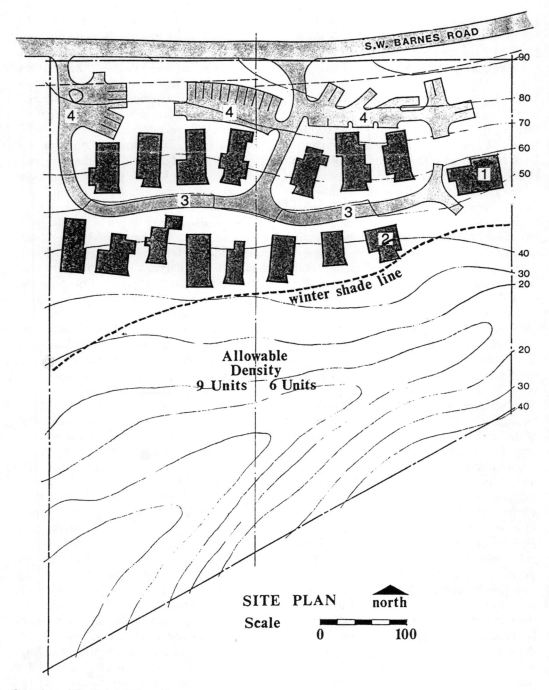

S.W. BARNES ROAD

4   4   4

3

1

3

2

winter shade line

Allowable
Density
9 Units   6 Units

SITE   PLAN   north
Scale
0   100

Site plan of Sunlight. (Church)

1. Common house.
2. Parking
3. Pedestrian street
4. Parking

"The whole idea wasn't solar energy; it was just one component. Our wanting to build this community has more to do with social relationships," says Maslen. During the design, long discussions took place about the location of the common house. No one wanted to live next to this potentially noisy building, and so it was placed at the end of the street. The common house contains a kitchen and dining area for fifty to seventy-five people, a library, a pottery room, a workshop with tools donated by members, and a storage area. The common house is used for meetings, a weekly common dinner, and parties and as a work space. With good insulation, the common house has not been a noise problem, and several members regret that it is not more centrally located.

Members share potluck meals on Wednesdays at the common house. Usually one person organizes the meal by making a main dish and setting up the dining room with tablecloths and silverware, while the others bring side dishes and desserts, although suppers of all bread and dessert have slipped in occasionally.

Once a month a community meeting is held following dinner at which maintenance and community issues are discussed. One of the five members of the board of directors facilitates the discussion. (Members rotate these positions every two years.) One recent topic has been about selling part of the site to reduce members' payments. For their size, they felt they needed only about half of their site. Recently the community sold 8 acres to a cohousing group forming in Portland. All decisions in the meetings are made by consensus. This particular decision has taken a number of years to decide.

There are few rules at Sunlight. "We are a pretty relaxed group," explains Barbara Church, one of the original members. There are conventional bylaws required by law, but members do not have a rule book.

No one looks over potential members. New members buy one of the houses when they are for sale. Under condominium ownership, the members have little to say about who will be moving in, and many do not

seem to mind. "It's not part of our system to throw people out. Actually I think it's fascinating how it all evolves—the comings and goings. I wouldn't want a stricter way to control people."

This tolerance does not mean the community is conflict free. Members have strong opinions, and they are not always in agreement. But after ten years, the issues are not as complicated as in the beginning, and a rhythm of past decisions guides the community.

The community celebrated its tenth anniversary in spring 1989, and everyone who had lived there was invited to celebrate. Dinner and a slide show were followed by dancing. "It's hard for me to imagine going back to live on a street where there isn't more of a connection as we have here. I really enjoy this. It's a different level of intimacy," says Barbara Church.

N STREET: AN EXPANDING COMMUNITY

Davis, California
Units: 7
Tenure: Mixed—individual home
   ownership and partnerships
Site: Suburban, 1 1/4 acres (density is
   six houses per acre)
Began: 1984

On April's Fool Day 1989, a large fence-tearing party was held for five suburban homes. Friends and neighbors gathered in several back yards with saws and hammers in hand. Inside one of these houses, several people were preparing food in the kitchen. Kevin Wolf, one of the main forces behind the party, was making a huge pot of chili beans—preparing the ingredients, reading the recipe, and explaining to several helpers the quickest way to chop onions. (On his back in a carrier sat his baby daughter.) Taking the handle of a long, sharp knife, he grabbed three onions in one hand, laid them on the cutting board, sliced off both ends, made a cut from top to

Tract housing back yards combined and transformed into an organic vegetable garden, with the addition of a small greenhouse and chicken coop. *(Balkhed)*

bottom and peeled off the skin, then bang—and he had chopped them in 5 seconds flat.

Outside the fence was undergoing a similar transformation. Eager hands helped to carry away the cut wood. When they finished, the familiar back yard view of fences had vanished, and there remained one long, wide, green yard, with a view of the house across the way. Afterward, people sat in the back eating and getting used to the new views. The removal of the fences was another step toward the transformation they hoped would follow.

The city of Davis is lined with typical suburban tracts, spreading out around the University of California. Ten miles to the east is Sacramento, California's state capital. The university attracts thousands of students who share these suburban houses to afford the rent. Many of the people living in the area are students or involved in the political organizations around Sacramento and Davis, particu-

larly alternative environmental lobbying. This combination of suburbs, environmental interests, and an eager pool of renters has helped the N Street community grow.

This community currently consists of seven contiguous tract houses and two leased houses (and two additional houses rented by community members). These nine houses share their back yards, which have been transformed into a large organic garden. There are compost bins and, instead of bermuda grass, a chicken run. The residents share a washing machine and are considering building a greenhouse. They share one meal weekly, which is cooked by two-person teams and the cost of which is shared equally.

The community is still in formation—motivated and somewhat unstructured—yet they are effectively taking over a middle-class tract suburb. This was not the intention when Kevin Wolf and four other renters moved into the first house in 1979. Every year, their land-

Site plan of the houses (long dashed lines indicate fencing). Surrounding neighbors have expressed an interest in the collaborative ideas.

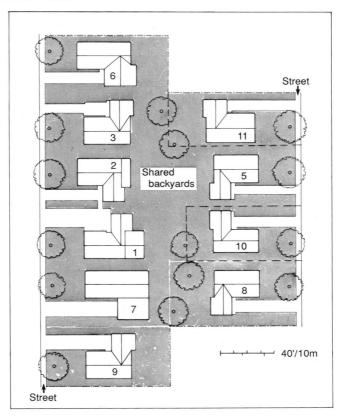

No.	Purchased	Bed/Bath	Price	Dwnpmt.	Ownership	Occupants
1	1984	5/3	$ 72,500	5%	Single family	5 Singles (renters)
2	1986	3/1	$ 80,000	12%	Single family	Couple with 1 child, and single parent with 1 child
3	1989	3/2	$103,000	20%	Partnership	3 Singles (renters)
4*	1988	4/2	$ 85,000	5%	Single family	3 Singles (renters)
5	1988	3/2	$105,000	25%	Partnership	Single parent with 1 child, and a renter
6	1989	3/2	$117,000	25%	Partnership	Couple with one teenager
7	1990	3/2	$130,000	25%	Partnership	Couple and 2 renters
8	Leased to community					Couple with 1 child, and single person (renters)
9	Rented to community					3 Single parents and 3 children
10	Negotiating on fence removal with owner					
11	Owner chose not to be part of community					

*Not shown (on a nearby street).

lord had talked of moving them out or selling the house. In frustration, Wolf bought the house in 1984. The rent was about equal to the mortgage payment, and he borrowed for the down payment. His roommates were not willing to make a commitment, so he bought the house on his own, rented it to his housemates, and continued to live there.

"Eventually we started dreaming of the house next door. We looked at the narrow side yards with no room to maneuver, and our yard, which had a garden and no room to stand, and thought, Wouldn't it be great if we could buy the yard next door?" Eventually he talked to the landlord, who was willing to sell for $5,000 over the market price. The owner required an option on the next contiguous house, which he also owned, believing that the group would turn the front lawn into a vegetable garden and lower the surrounding real estate values.[3]

The result of these negotiations was that Wolf, and later his wife, Linda Cloud, began educating themselves on financing, mortgages, and partnerships. By 1989, Wolf owned one house and had formed a partnership with Cloud on the second house and a partnership with another friend on the third adjacent house. Their vision expanded with each purchase, and this small group of owners and renters began talking to the landlords of surrounding houses, a high percentage of them rental properties. Some of the landlords were willing to sell and take advantage of the jump in real estate prices. The group began to line up friends for home ownership using the knowledge they had gained over the past two years to help them through the escrow process.

As does a real estate agent, the group receives some compensation for setting up buyer with seller, arranging financing, and working through the escrow process. The compensation, however, is not monetary. Kevin Wolf explains:

If we help someone buy a house, we want an easement on the back half of their yard, and that easement is on our title and their title. The easement ensures that neither party or future owner can do anything on their half of the back yard without a consensus from all the surrounding owners. We hope this will protect the community. If someone in five years sells and we're not able to buy, the new owner will need to find a buyer who is interested in sharing in the community. In addition, each new owner commits to purchasing 10% in the planned-for common house.

They select buyers on the basis of their willingness to agree to the basic easement rules and the concepts of a shared community. This agreement is being formalized.

The group has found friends to buy the houses, but there are not enough houses coming up for sale, so they are now trying to put a first option to buy on as many surrounding homes as possible. The group is approaching owners of adjacent houses about placing option money on other houses to give the group the first chance to put an offer on the property. They are also trying to secure long-term leases on some of the houses. The owner could use the option money as part of their down payment when selling or to put the fence back up if the house is not sold to the community. The group also will consider a long-term lease for those who want to move but keep the house. A house two blocks down has been purchased, to be traded eventually for a contiguous house.

Surrounding neighbors are encouraged by the group to buy into the houses they rent. One of these renters-turned-new-home-owner has been coming to the meetings and voicing her concern about privacy and the impact of children on her yard. She is hesitant about taking down all the fences and having a chicken coop bordering her yard. "There's a lot of things she has concerns about, and it will probably take her a year to get used to the concept—coming to dinners and getting involved in our community--before she decides whether this is something she wants to get involved in. We're not pushing her very hard, but we're making sure she is always included in the planning process and in knowing what is going on," explained Wolf.

Renters

The growing group can finance their houses because most of them convert their garages into an extra rental room. Through rent collection, they can afford $130,000 houses with $1,000 monthly house payments.

This house-buying system relies on renters. Two of the houses are rentals, and almost every home owner has at least one renter sharing the house. "The problem always is that renters have trouble keeping commitments to a place like an owner does," said Wolf.

Dave Fritz, a renter in the first house thinks "it's a lot better here than in a normal situation. We have more influence." Renter Risa Buck says, "I think that as far as upkeep and general maintenance, from your average tenant-renter situation, I think more work is done by us." In her four years living in the community, she has seen renter turnover and initial enthusiasm fade.

I like the idea of everyone sharing a back yard—in theory—but I think in real life, it's different. Part of the problem is that when people are renting, their investment is different unless they have some kind of ideological commitment to the concept of trying to build a community. I think it's very hard to find that kind of commitment from most people when they don't own it. When you just pay rent and don't intend to live there that long, people don't put out; they don't want to put out. I think the idea of ownership needs to somehow be extended to all parties involved because in order for this community to be nurtured, that can only happen by the inhabitants. And if the inhabitants don't have that as a priority, that's not going to happen.[4]

One of the group's many goals is to figure out how tenants can become owners. Although Davis has no rent control, several of the N Street home owners do not raise the rent as long as the renter stays. They are exploring ways in which renters with a long-term commitment can become part-owners.

The sixth and seventh houses, recently purchased, have been bought through a co-equity partnership. As other houses in the area escalate in price, partnerships will replace home ownership as the model of acquisition.

Of the ten partners who purchased the last house, seven are renters (five within the N Street community). Although only three of the renters live in the house, all the partners will gain from the house's appreciation. This model works well for those who only have $1,000 to $5,000 to invest and could not afford to buy a house. Pooling with others on the down payment allows the partners to purchase the house, and the rents equal the monthly mortgage.

Unlike a standard partnership, a partner cannot force the sale of the house. A partner who sells to a new member will receive 75% of the appreciated share. The other 25% will go into a nonprofit N Street organization.[5] The purpose of the organization will be to provide a revolving loan fund for further purchases. The organization will also help to establish the common house and other common amenities for the homes.

More Fence Tearing

Another fence-tearing party followed soon after the purchase of houses 6 and 7. A garden plan, completed by a university student as his thesis and already outdated by the purchase of two more homes, is soon to be updated and implemented. The long-term goal is to take the first rental house and turn it into a common house by enlarging the kitchen, tearing out some walls, and creating a large space for child care and dining, computer room, workshop, guest room, and even student rental rooms (or a childcare provider's apartment). The common house would be owned by the surrounding twelve houses, each with a 10% share. Since the house is owned by Wolf and Cloud, they can finance it at a low price and accept payments over time. When owners sell their house, they would then have to sell a share in the common house also.

Members bring their own plates, cups, and utensils to the once-a-week common meal, which now rotates among the homes. Eventually the group hopes to have a common house. (N Street)

While other collaborative communities work out their agreements before moving in, the home owners on N Street are doing just the opposite. They are now developing formal rules and policies concerning children, meals, common ownership of tools, decision making, and planning. Not much mutual cost has been involved, and the community is still building itself up.

Their next step is to establish themselves as a working group and adjust to their growing size. They planned that it would take five years to get six houses connected and are a little surprised that it has taken only two and a half years. Now their aim is for twelve homes, and they are negotiating with landlords farther down the block. "It's a hard process to do. The thing to realize is that the price of housing is skyrocketing, and every month it goes up another $1,000 to $5,000. I wish we could move even faster," says Wolf.

BRYN GWELED: TWO-ACRE HOMESTEADS

Southampton, Pennsylvania
Units: 74
Tenure: Leased land with privately owned homes
Site: 240 acres
Began: 1939

Bryn Gweled is a cooperative community of seventy-four homesteads on lush rolling fields and natural woodlands. Members lease a lot for a ninety-nine-year renewable term. Each lessee who builds or buys a home owns all such improvements but does not own the land. The land is owned by Bryn Gweled Homesteads Inc., of which each member is a shareholder.

In the summer of 1990, Bryn Gweled cele-

Sketch of the common house, a converted barn.
(Bryn Gweled Association)

brated its golden anniversary. As a fiftieth anniversary present, the community tripled its common house space to include a large meeting hall. Four hundred participants crowded inside for the big reunion party. Some of the pioneers who helped build up the community were participants.

Bryn Gweled was founded in 1939 by a dozen Philadelphia families who wanted to move to the country. (Bryn Gweled is Welsh for "Hill of Vision.") The founders were inspired by a successful businessman, Ralph Borsodi, who had bought a 100-acre site near New York City and turned it into a cooperative homestead. Visitors were invited to come on the weekend and see the self-sufficient community. Borsodi's talks on cooperative living, the ample gardens, farm buildings, and the women making homespun clothing out of their sheep's wool were inspiring in those lean times.

Herbert and Georgia Bergstrom's visit there in 1935 gave them "the idea and hope of someday being able to establish some kind of cooperative community." When they moved to Philadelphia, their idea grew. In the summer of 1938, they were further inspired by a trip to England and the Scandinavian countries where they visited housing developments to study private, public, and cooperative arrangements. Back in Philadelphia, the

Bergstroms began discussing the idea with their coworkers, neighbors, and friends:

Our first thought—who among our friends should we try to get together to discuss the idea? . . . Quickly we got in touch with others, who joined us in the early planning. We met every Sunday night, during all of 1939 and most of 1940. On a Sunday in December 1939, all the members of the group visited five of the most desirable sites [within an hour's commute from Philadelphia]. We selected the 240-acre site . . . which became Bryn Gweled Homesteads. The price was $18,000.[6]

Bryn Gweled was conceived during a depression, and some families had little hope of affording a house except through buying the land together. Several families who could not qualify for a loan were helped by personal loans from other families. The bankers were suspicious of housing on leased land, and a lot of negotiating and discussions were required to convince them.

Some of the discussions of that year, aside from financing, centered on how much should be done cooperatively—whether there should be shared dining facilities, bylaws, lot sizes, and committees.

Now that we owned the land, we set about determining what we should do with it. The decision to leave the wooded areas and streams and stream valleys totally unmolested was . . . spontaneous and unanimous. . . . It was simply taken for granted that these treasures would be set aside for the length of the community, whatever its future.

A small group of self-appointed experts met at one of the members' homes to lay out the roads. On the living room floor, they unfolded a large map of the site and laid out roads and walkways. The large amount of road building was estimated to require 900 hours of labor, all volunteered by the residents.

In 1941, a year and a half after the site was purchased, Bryn Gweled had grown to forty members. Business meetings were held in members' homes, but as World War II came to an end, the decision was made to have a commons house. The carriage shed was re-

The privately owned house sits on 2 acres of leased land. Homesteading has given way to the suburban commute into town. *(Robinson)*

modeled and became the community meeting room.

By mid-century, forty-four families lived at Bryn Gweled, and the homestead began to resemble the physical shape that is still evident thirty years later. Three thousand trees were planted as a community project. A gas co-op was opened in 1949 (a gallon cost twenty-five cents). Many meetings were held to discuss membership criteria, problems with children and dogs, and the need for capital. Jane Stewart, one of the homesteaders, recalls: "One of the major reasons for a need for capital was the decision—not lightly arrived at—to make our own swimming pool. We also found time to have fun together. Films were shown. . . . We had many parties: out-of-door suppers and picnics and square dances, winter holiday dinners for all."

By the 1960s, over sixty lots had been taken, and the surrounding area was being developed. The era of unlocked doors was disappearing, and reports of vandalism were on the rise. The residents established a voluntary patrol. Bryn Gweled was becoming suburban in appearance. The original idea of homesteading and working the land was no longer in evidence; most of Bryn Gweled residents now commuted to work (and the gasoline co-op was dispensing about 50,000 gallons of gasoline a year)

In the 1970s, Bryn Gweled entered portions of common land into the Bucks County Conservancy to keep the land undeveloped. All the lots had been taken; the community was complete.

Today Bryn Gweled's land covers 240 acres; 160 are divided into approximately 2-acre leaseholds to create about eighty homesteads.* Half of the remaining land has been

---

*Although the land is divided into eighty-one lots, three remain unbuilt (due primarily to difficult sites) and four homeowners have double lots resulting in seventy-four households.

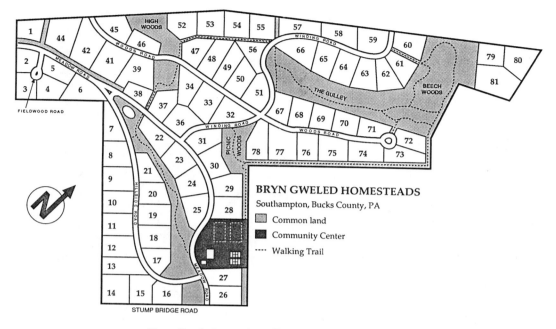

Bryn Gweled site plan. *(Bryn Gweled Association)*

placed in the land trust. The other half is used for common open space, the community buildings, roads, and other improvements.

Bryn Gweled members voluntarily perform the functions of officers, managers, book-keepers, and maintenance persons. Work parties are held once a month, with house-holds volunteering at least a half-day. Projects range from road maintenance to remodeling the community center. John Robinson, a recent resident whose interest in Bryn Gweled began when his daughter bought a home in the community, explains the volunteer work:

We have a work party once a month. In the mornings we cut grass or push back the woods, and then those who have participated snack at the community center. In the late afternoon, we have a covered dish dinner, and everyone brings some food to share. At 8:00 our meeting starts, and that usually lasts for two hours.[7]

The community house is now a large building, about 5,000 square feet. (A 2,000-square-foot addition is under construction.)

The upstairs has a large room with a kitchen for meetings, parties, and square dancing.[8] Outside is the swimming pool, heated by solar panels.

Each household pays a monthly assessment based on the year's budget, usually about $300. The budget covers such expenses as maintenance of community property and improvements, taxes on common land and unleased lots, and those of the many appointed and volunteer committees. Real estate taxes are paid separately—about $2,000 a year per house.

Getting on the waiting list for Bryn Gweled can be daunting. The nature of the membership procedure ensures a certain amount of compatibility by requiring the applicant family to meet with each of the seventy-five families at Bryn Gweled—and not more than three at once—a time-consuming process. Applicants who are accepted are placed on the waiting list until a house becomes available. Members are also restricted by this procedure, since they can sell only to those on the waiting list, and they cannot start negotiating until the ap-

Many hands help the work go quickly on this fall work day. Resident work parties undertake road maintenance, mowing, remodeling the community center, clearing paths, cutting wood, landscaping, and maintenance of all community structures. *(Robinson)*

plicants are approved. "If an applicant wants Bryn Gweled, fine; if they're after a particular house, forget it," was the explanation. If there are no applicants on the waiting list, the home seller can rent out the house until someone has been approved (who also wants to buy their house).

At this time, Bryn Gweled has no trouble attracting potential members; nine approved applicants are on the waiting list. The common thread is the desirability for community. The members range in age up to 86 years old and are a variety of races and religions. Of the 74 households, 35 are couples, 18 couples with children, 19 singles, and 2 single parents (127 adults and approximately 50 children).

With the large number of households, long-time member Marjorie Ewbank feels, "You don't get well acquainted with all, but we all still feel a part of a family." Her husband, John Ewbank, believes that there is a great emphasis on family autonomy, and differences between individual members are

considered their own business:[9] "We always try to work out our differences in the meetings. If the vote is close, we vote to reconsider the matter. We always try to respect the diversity of outlook." To him, that is the uniqueness of Bryn Gweled: "Here there's a desire to preserve diversity."

MONAN'S RILL: A RURAL RETREAT

St. Helena, California
Units: 9
Tenure: Partnership
Site: Rural, 440 acres
Began/Move in: 1972/1974

> The stag at eve had drunk his fill
> Where danced the moon
> on Monan's Rill.
> —Sir Walter Scott
> "Lady of the Lake"

Resident Russ Leisure built his own home by hand at Monan's Rill.

On the wine taster's trail in northern California sits the little town of St. Helena. Good wine and fanciful television shows featuring this area have brought attention to what was a quiet, rural place. Development has grown rapidly, and sites are being carved out in most directions. About twenty minutes outside St. Helena, reached by driving on winding roads that leave the developments behind, a row of mailboxes and a dirt road signal arrival at Monan's Rill (a rill is a creek). The landscape is dry with manzanita and oak trees, and hills follow hills into the background. The road leads past a common vegetable garden and orchard and then winds out to community-owned single-family homes.

Monan's Rill grew out of meetings in the early 1970s among a group of friends, many from Quaker backgrounds, who were trying to sort out what they meant by community. The families who came to the meetings "began to search for community among themselves and a place for it to grow." From the meetings, thirteen people—six couples and a single woman—committed themselves to form a community and began a search for land. This core group had in mind 50 acres with water, near electricity, and not far from roads. They ended up buying 440 acres for the water and paid $170,000. This turned out to be a wise move because the county's new general plan requires 40 acres per house for a building permit.

Moving to the site required time. People needed to find new employment nearby and began the difficult task of fencing the land, building roads, and putting in the water and sewage systems. Not everyone could move to the site immediately since there were no roads or houses. One of the couples, Russ and Mary Leisure, bought a trailer and moved onto the site. They cleared out a site and hand built their house. "Took me two and a half years to build," said Russ, "and when I started, I didn't know much about building a house." Most of the members knew little about construction when they bought the site but learned as they went: "Here we have our own income and responsibilities. No dogma or guru and didn't want one. We studied communities before we began. It's a high-risk venture."

The community began as a cooperative but gave up that idea when the county, without any experience with cooperatives, became afraid that a commune was about to be developed. The group decided instead to form a partnership with life use. The partnership owns the land and the improvements. This is not a common legal form because members cannot limit their individual liability, although the residents have made it work for them by spending many hours with a lawyer.

Each member is required to have a minimum liability coverage of $1 million.

The temptation of making a profit has been removed as an incentive. The partnership has a limited-equity clause. If the community is liquidated, each member's share will be paid off their and the profit given to a charity. Also, once a year, all the members discuss their wills. Many people have made a generous provision for the community.

Members' investments are returned when they move out, but the community has up to ten years to pay. When a young family recently moved out due to the long commute to work, Monan's Rill paid them off right away

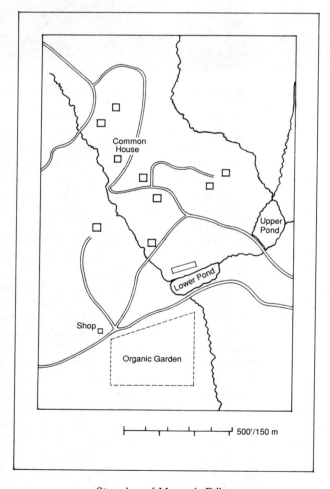

Site plan of Monan's Rill.

because they gave a discount on their home investment.

New members are required to make three investments: a nonrefundable membership fee of $2,500, a returnable investment calculated by age (from $5,000 to over $20,000), and a returnable investment for housing. In addition there is a monthly maintenance fee of $140 per member.

The community is gaining new members slowly, now numbering twenty one adults and six children, from 1 to 76 years old (four couples, five couples with children or teens, and three singles). It does not advertise and is not centrally located. Still, new members arrive. One hopeful candidate commutes from San Diego so that she can spend some time meeting the members.

Although Monan's Rill may not seem to be an appealing financial investment, the members feel there are many advantages to life outside the fast lane. Members share a large garden and orchard (certified organic). The children can go to any house and get attention. They have a swimming hole and acres of open space for playing.

The common house is used for potlucks, meetings, and celebrations. A new larger common house is being planned because the existing one is not located centrally or designed to everyone's satisfaction. Also shared are a small barn and a woodworking and equipment maintenance shop. Cooperation and mutual support are considered highly desirable, and responsibility for maintaining the gravel roads, fencing, equipment, wood cutting, and taking care of the animals is shared.

Mutual support is not limited to tasks. Russ Leisure recalls "a couple living here [who] decided to split up. They each had invited the community to help in their split. The community gave them assistance and helped them resolve their differences. We have professional counselors within the community who also worked with them, and they came together again. We had a big celebration, a sort of second marriage." But not all members find happy endings, and some have moved out. Conflicts also occur, and the immense amount

of work required to put in roads and build housing has at times caused friction.

Russ Leisure agrees the work is hard. He has worked long hours to help establish Monan's Rill. His house is now complete, with a unique interior. He has made a path that winds up from his house to the common house at an even 6 percent slope: "Mary and I are determined to spend the rest of our lives here, even if we have to get around in an electric wheelchair."

I WONDER IF HERBIE'S HOME YET?

Bainbridge Island, Washington
Units: 7
Ownership: Planned unit development
Site: Rural, 8 acres
Began/Move in: 1972/1973

Bill Isley, an architect with his own office in downtown Seattle, takes a half-hour ferry ride home to a rural island. He lives in a community with six other households, which he started seventeen years ago. Isley was trained as an architect and a city planner. During the 1960s, he worked all over the world and was inspired by the strong sense of community in less-developed countries. In Micronesia he saw villages with a common meeting house where the land was not owned individually, and in Malay the people took the best land for the community. "When I came back to Seattle, I had some money, and I decided to buy some land. I called up a number of friends and told them about it," recalls Isley, and adds, "because you can't be a community by yourself."

He found and bought 8 acres of land on an island located near the home where he grew up. The community name comes from a suggestion by Isley's then 5-year-old daughter. When asked for her opinion, she dug out a school book with the title *I Wonder If Herbie's Home Yet,* and that title seemed to include some of the words and feelings the group had been tossing around. The first structure they built, in 1973, was the common house, as a symbol of the neighborhood. Called the Barn, the large open-sided building (3,000 square feet) is constructed with salvaged material. The floor is half wood for playing basketball and dancing and half concrete for doing projects. On one side is the kitchen and in the center a huge stone fireplace. The Barn is surrounded by a series of gardens and lawns used for parties, weddings, and recreation. In the garden is a separate sauna building.

When the time came to locate the houses, the first question asked was how much land it takes to build a single-family home? They figured about 7,000 square feet would do, particularly if there is undeveloped land around the house. Two ideas for a site plan were considered: to build a cluster and leave the rest of the property in its natural form or to spread out the homes with abundant land in between. The latter became their plan. Isley explains, "Our reasons were privacy, resalability, and architecture. Some people didn't want to be near a road; some wanted to be up high; others wanted something else. We decided to spread out."

Each member, stake in hand, walked the site and stopped where he or she thought the center of the house should be. The stake was pounded in. A 50-foot rope was tied to the stake, and a circle was drawn, with the stake as its center. The result was seven round sites, each with a 100-foot circumference, about 8,000 square feet.[10] By using a circle, they did not need to lay out four stakes. Surprisingly, this method worked well; there was no overlap of circles because each person had chosen a different site.

There are seven homes on the 8-acre site. The 7 "leftover" acres are held in common. The parking area is to one side, and there is a short walk to the homes.

When the sites had been figured out, they went to a lawyer and asked, "How do we do that?" The lawyer used the state regulations for condominiums as a framework. Each lot was privately owned, with the rest of the land held in common (each household holds a

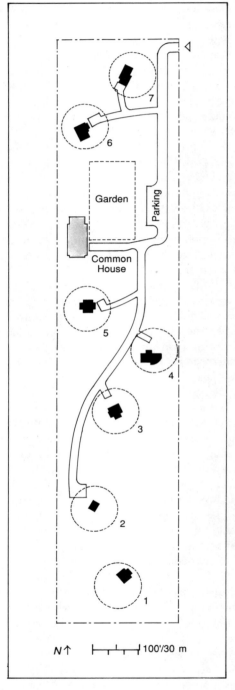

Site plan of Herbie's. The seven circles are the privately owned lots for the houses. The remaining land is owned in common.

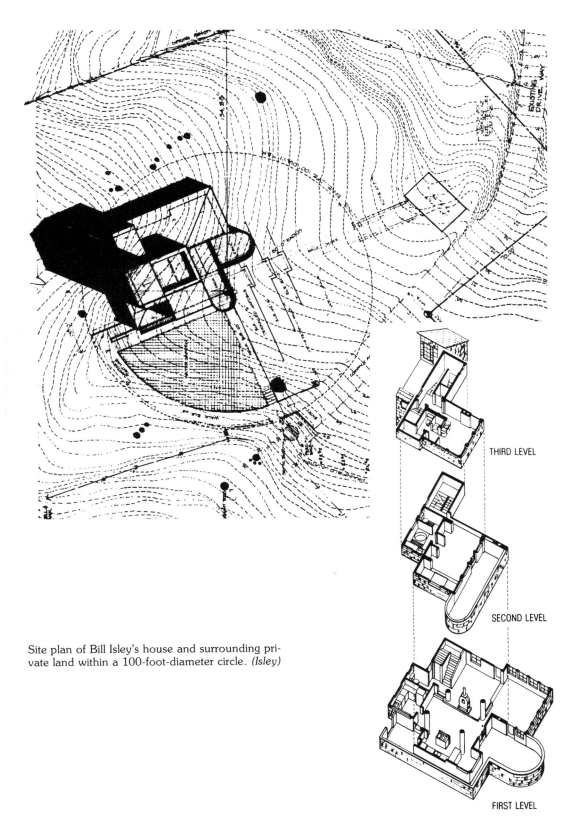

Site plan of Bill Isley's house and surrounding private land within a 100-foot-diameter circle. *(Isley)*

THIRD LEVEL

SECOND LEVEL

FIRST LEVEL

125

one-seventh share) and governed by a home owners' association. They filed to change the zoning into a planned unit development (PUD) in 1973. A hearing was required for developing condominiums, and there was quite an uproar from the neighborhood. The group, mostly architects and designers, had ideas about the land that the neighbors found hard to comprehend. Eventually the group prevailed.

Now the community is a model for the island. Most of the site is undeveloped, with many firs and huckleberries growing wild. Unlike surrounding developments, there are no fences, and only trails connect the houses. From the beginning, the group did not have any design controls. For a group with a large percentage of designers, this was probably as close as they would get on a design consensus. The houses are innovative and often remodeled. Their motto is that owners can "design what the hell they want, but we don't want anything offensive."

The first house, built in 1973, was 1,000 square feet. The community grew gradually, with the last house constructed in 1985. According to Isley:

When the community started, we had very little money. It makes sense, when you're starting out, to get a group of people and pool your money together to buy land. People could build a house who couldn't afford land because we did it collectively. We were in our early thirties with lots of energy. We dug trenches together and helped each other out.

The territorial aspects are different from condos. There's a built-in regard for the land. The regular condos try to fit people into the same socioeconomic place. The houses here—some are very expensive, some are quite small. The difference is nice. It's good that we have different prices.

The owners have organized themselves on everything, from lawn mowing to monthly board meetings. They decide what to fix, when to borrow money, and what amenities to build. In the beginning, each owner had to work five hours a month. Over time, this standard has become more relaxed, and now they say that the people who want to work are having fun—and the others aren't.

"Oh, we've had a few problems, minor problems," explains Isley. "A guy has a beat-up truck sitting in the driveway. We tow it away and charge him for it. A dog chews up other people's garden. But we have a forum for talking, both to plan fun things and talk about problems." He continues, "We had by-laws. Like a state legislation, we had so many. Every time there was a problem, we'd have another. But basically we realized that there were one or two people who caused this to happen, and when they moved out, we threw the laws away. You can't legislate everything."

The community of fourteen adults and ten children is like a little village town. They have their own water system and a monthly charge of $60 for capital improvements. Roads are fixed and trails added. New amenities are built, such as the large sauna that has just been finished. They also share insurance. The county did not know how to tax each home at first and finally decided to divide the property taxes seven ways. The households have annual elections and rotate positions on the condominium association's executive board.

Each person is free legally to sell. When an owner sells, the board has first right of refusal and can buy the house. The second right goes to individuals in the group. Screening of new members is not a formal procedure. The future owners are invited to a function, and so far none has been disliked. The people who want to buy a house have wanted it for the same reasons that motivated the start of the community: they like the idea of sharing, they like privacy, and they enjoy the rural setting.

NOTES

1. Many of the people were moving from large houses of their own to Sunlight. All wanted space around their houses; there was no interest in row houses.
2. The community won a design honor award from the American Institute of Architects. The award was in part because of the group's impetus in developing the community.
3. They were required to put $1,000 a year down for five years, and if at the end of the

five years they did not purchase the house at the agreed-upon middle of three appraisals, then they would forfeit the $5,000.

4. At the same time, she mentions her own disinclination to own any part of the house because she does not feel "it's a good investment." She also notes the reluctance of her housemates to make a strong commitment among the distractions of urban living. These renters are young, single, well educated, mobile, and relatively poor.

5. The next person who buys the share will buy at 75% of the actual cost. In this way it is easier for people to afford to buy a share in five or ten years, when the appreciation has risen. Assuming the house cost $100,000 and in ten years would be worth $200,000, it has appreciated $100,000. When refinancing, $25,000 (25%) could be available for the nonprofit organization.

6. The Bryn Gweled History Committee has put together *History of Bryn Gweled 1940–1980* with contributions from Herbert G. Bergstrom. The Bergstroms, members of the Society of Friends, were among the founders of Bryn Gweled and homesteaders for thirty-six years.

7. Community business is conducted at these meetings, usually held the first Saturday evening of each month. Everyone is expected to serve on at least one committee yearly, and members are encouraged to take part in various elected, appointed, and voluntary committees over the years. The committees span a wide range: Alternative Housing, Assessment and Budget, Bryn Gweled Supply, Children's Activities, Community Activities, Community Center Maintenance, Community News, Community Planning, Martin Luther King's birthday celebration, Soccer, Swimming Pool, and Tractor.

8. There are no formal daily services such as child care, although members informally eat at each other's homes and share child care.

9. One member is now suing another member over a business venture.

10. The computation: 3.17 (pi) × 50 × 50 = 7,925 square feet.

CHAPTER 8

Nonprofit Developments

AMALGAMATED HOUSES: GENERATIONS OF COOPERATION

Bronx, New York
Units: 1,228 (11 buildings)
Ownership: Limited dividend (limited
    equity) cooperative
Site: Urban, 10.64 acres
Began/Moved in: 1925/1927
Architect: Herman Jessor

An idea—cooperation—has elevated the lives of generations of families. This community is strong. It is healthy. It has persisted for one half century.[1]

Ira Manning's grandmother moved into the Amalgamated in 1927, the year it opened. His mother lived there during the depression. He remembers playing with children down the corridor in the common playroom. His children, the fourth generation to live in the Amalgamated, are now attending the resident-run preschool.

The Amalgamated is one of the oldest nonprofit housing cooperatives in the United States. Its inception began in the 1920s when groups of Jewish needle trade workers, many living in overcrowded slums, became involved in building decent homes from which they would be free of the worry of eviction. In 1925, the Amalgamated Clothing Workers Union helped finance the purchase of 13 acres in the Bronx, just south of Van Cortlandt Park. The Amalgamated Housing Corporation was created to develop the housing. The president, Abraham Kazan, conferred with architect Herman Jessor in the design of six buildings, all walk-ups of five stories. Their success led to the construction of two more buildings on the site. By 1932, 639 units had been constructed. (See Table 8.1.)

The costs were reasonable for the time; the down payment was $500 a room, and the monthly carrying charge was $11 per room. A one-bedroom unit (three rooms) cost $33 and a three bedroom $55 to $65. Carrying charges (similar to rent) remained low because the Amalgamated took advantage of a new state law that provided a twenty-year exemption from taxes for retaining low rents and a 6% limit on any profit margins.

The members shared a cooperative store, a library, an auditorium seating 300 people, a preschool, a music room, and classrooms.[2] The cooperators ran a laundry, a food store, and a day camp that cost $16 per child for the summer. They bought milk and electricity

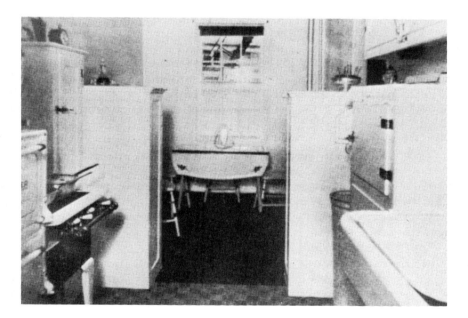

Top: Historic view of Amalgamated Houses. The Amalgamated was designed with 40% of the land in common open space, not typical of New York housing. The extensive gardens and open space allowed the maximum number of apartments to overlook greenery, in contrast to the overcrowded slums in which many of the residents had previously lived. *Bottom:* The original interior of an apartment, showing a typical kitchen. *(Dolkart & Sites)*

Table 8.1 Amalgamated Building Statistics

Building Number	Date Completed	Number of Stories	Building Size (Sq. Ft.)	Property Size (Acres)	Number of Apartments
6	1927	4	22,215	.51	55
7	1929	6	54,530	1.25	206
8	1950	12	70,925	1.62	282
9	1932	6	28,800	.66	115
10	1941	2	32,500	.74	48
11	1947	3	18,397	.42	30
12	1952	8	36,576	.84	139
13	1951	12	40,000	.91	151
14	1949	12	39,826	.91	145
TI	1969	20	60,724	1.39	156
TII	1971	20	60,724	1.39	156

Note: Building numbers 1 through 5 were demolished to make way for the Towers, TI and TII.

together at low prices and provided loans to new members. There was also a tearoom privately operated by a couple of residents.

Member Abe Bluestein moved into building 9 when it opened in 1932. "We'd go to the tearoom in the evenings to socialize; it was like a community center. I acted in plays there that we would produce every three months. There were all kinds of community activities."

During the depression years, over 60% of the members were unemployed, and many could not pay their carrying charges. Not one family was evicted. Instead 292 co-op members created loan funds by putting their money together, interest free. They lent money to members to pay for rent and food. Bluestein recalls, "When the depression was over and people back to work, every cent was paid back. There was a marvelously high moral code motivating the people."

After World War II, the Amalgamated Housing Corporation, under Kazan's leadership, continued to develop new housing cooperatives. They took advantage of various housing loan programs over the decades. In 1947, building 11 was constructed for veterans. In 1948, 800 apartments were built in Manhattan. In the late 1960s, the first walk-ups were demolished, and two twenty-story towers were built in their place, each with 155 units. By the 1970s, Amalgamated had developed 1,443 units, most on surrounding sites.

The many apartment buildings are all considered one cooperative under one board of directors, elected by the members. Since the stockholders share collectively in the whole cooperative, no separate building associations have formed. Members receive no profit on their share amount (their dividend is limited), leaving with exactly the same amount as when they moved in.[3]

Many changes have occurred over the years. The co-op is much more diverse than in 1927, with members from different cultures, races, and religions and with different beliefs. No one ethnic group reflects the incoming population of the members. Shared activities and services have changed with the needs of the members.[4] The summer camp went strong for forty-five years and then stopped. Fifteen years later, in 1987, it was resurrected and attracted 150 families. The preschool has expanded to include 75 families and is still run cooperatively by the parents. A café, serving snacks and dinner, has now become a popular meeting place.

As the economy changes over the years, so does the activity level in the cooperative. There are no longer full-time mothers to give some of their time during the day. Instead, members meet in the evenings or on weekends. Over the decades, interests have also changed. The computer club and senior club, both started in the 1980s, are popular. More recently, a teen program and recycling have started. Amenities, located in the various buildings, now include a ceramic studio, a photography lab, a general-purpose room, and a playroom, as well as the large auditorium.

Since the beginning, the Amalgamated has had an education department with weekly newsletters. Lynn Silver is the third education director in the co-op: "It's important to us that this community have a life other than bricks and stone. The pioneers who shared a common vision and built this up are aging. As they die, there are new people who come and don't understand or share this vision. We constantly work to replenish the cooperative vision and our leadership."

All of the activities are run by the same principles and policies as the cooperative at large.[5] The education director works with each committee to formulate policies, budgets, and services. The learning experience of a nursery school parent is then easily applied to the cooperative at large.

After more than fifty years, Abe Bluestein believes that "the original spirit persists. The leaders and volunteers today grew up in the co-op. They have a great love for the community, and they're very interested in it. To us, this assures continuity for the future."

THE RESERVOIR COOPERATIVE: MIXING INCOMES

Madison, Wisconsin
Units: 28
Ownership: Leasing cooperative
Site: Urban, 1.4 acres
Began/Moved in: 1986/1988
Architects: Design Coalition

The first day I was here, well, I looked out the back window and saw a mother there with her new baby, so I knew I was at the right place. I've looked at nursing homes, and when we get to the driveway and I see all the older people crumpled together, I told my son just to back out of there; I can't stand it—such a ghetto of old people. . . . That's the thing I love here—all the different generations, all the little children.

Agnes Myers

Agnes Myers leans out to the side of her motorized chair and pulls out another weed with her trowel. Agnes is on the gardening committee, and although she is 71 and has difficulty walking, she takes her turn keeping the weeds down. Three-year-old Alison, who lives above Agnes's apartment, runs outside to see what is going on. She puts her stuffed bear in the basket attached to Agnes's motorized chair and comes along to watch her work in the Reservoir's garden.

The Reservoir is a cooperative designed to meet the needs of an intergenerational mix of people. Parents can watch their children playing outside from the kitchen or dining room. The shared green with two play structures gives children a large area outside their door to run and play. For older adults and people with physical limitations, all first-floor units have been built without steps. Even the big front porches are at ground level. Four of the units are specifically designed barrier free. Light switches, the thermostat, door peepholes, and electrical outlets can be reached from a wheelchair; bathrooms are wide, with a roll-in shower; and kitchen counters are open for wheelchairs to roll under.

The twenty-eight dwellings are grouped into large "houses" of four-, five-, and eightplexes to fit into the neighborhood scale. Every four households share a central common room, used for meetings, socializing, and as a play area. Adjacent to each common room is a shared washer and dryer. All the households have access to a meeting room with a kitchen in the old livery, the only renovated building on the site.

The development process was handled by Madison Mutual Housing Association (MHA), under director Susan Hobart. A planning committee was set up consisting of local non-

The Reservoir has a mix of ages and incomes, with 15% of the units for handicapped people. The porch shown here has design details that are similar to surrounding homes but it has no steps, for barrier-free access.

Kitchen and dining areas have views to the back, allowing parents inside the house to watch their children play outside.

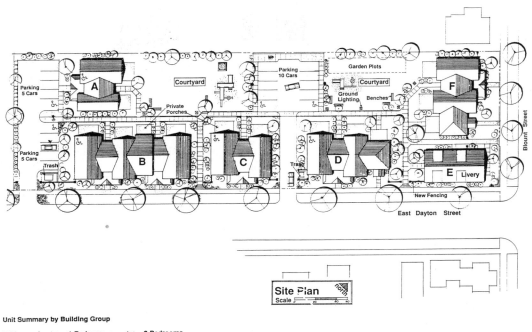

Unit Summary by Building Group

Building							
A	two	1-Bedroom +	two	2-Bedrooms		
B	two	1-Bedroom +	two	2-Bedrooms +	four	3-Bedrooms
C			two	2-Bedrooms +	two	3-Bedrooms
D			four	2-Bedrooms +	one	3-Bedrooms
E	one	1-Bedroom +	one	2-Bedrooms		
F			four	2-Bedrooms +	one	3-Bedrooms

Total: Five   **1-Bedrooms** +   fifteen   **2-Bedrooms** +   eight **3-Bedrooms**

Total Units: 28

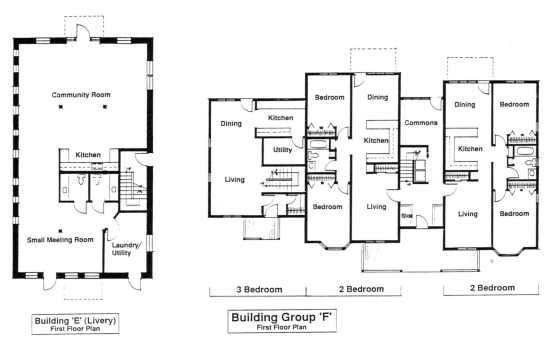

Plan of the Reservoir Cooperative. *(MMHA)*

133

profit organizations, a neighborhood resident, and two single parents.[6] The committee was influenced by the writings of architect Delores Hayden and the late Canadian architect Joan Simon, who both focused attention on the need to design housing for changing family structures. Project planning began in 1985 (Davis):

Summer 1985: Initial planning begins

Spring 1986: Proposal for Reservoir site submitted to city

Fall 1986: City awards site to MHA

June 1987: City issues revenue bonds as financing

June 1987: Groundbreaking, construction starts

October 1987: First units occupied

Spring 1988: Construction completed; full occupancy by June

Funding for the Reservoir came from tax-exempt bond proceeds ($975,000), a city second mortgage ($345,000), MHA equity ($191,610), and city financing on land purchase ($81,000 plus interest earnings of $7,500) for a total of $1,600,110.

Affordable housing was one of the main goals in developing the Reservoir. People with different incomes are mixed; a third of the apartments are for low-income people, a third for moderate incomes, and a third at market rate.[7] Members pay a membership fee equal to one month's rent (plus estimated utilities) when they move in and pay carrying charges (similar to rent) every month, under a leasing agreement with MHA. When they move out, this arrangement limits the equity members receive to their membership plus accrued interest, currently at 8.5%. New membership fees rise very little over the years.

At one corner of the Reservoir is the Livery, a renovated building with two apartments, office space, and common meeting room. Behind the Livery are the residences, all new construction. *(MMHA)*

In addition to affordability, the mix of unit sizes, from 680 to 1,300 square feet, helps attract singles, single parents, and families (Hobart). Residents like the downtown location, just south of the state capitol and within walking distance to downtown businesses, buses, and child care.

The Reservoir is owned by a mutual housing association. Mutuals are a popular concept in Europe but not as well known in the United States (see p. 198). The mutual establishes cooperatives by purchasing land, developing the housing, and training the first residents in cooperative management. Since it started in 1983, the MHA has developed cooperative clusters around Madison, including the Reservoir. All of the 206 units in these clusters share one board of directors and for legal purposes are considered one large scattered-site cooperative. The MHA and the cooperative are sister organizations but separate entities with separate boards of directors. The nonprofit MHA owns all the land and the common improvements and leases it to the cooperative. The cooperative, controlled by members, makes membership decisions and deals with day-to-day management and maintenance in all twelve cooperative clusters.[8]

Both organizations gain through combining their forces. The MHA has a broad vision for the neighborhood and leverages its ownership of 206 units into loans to develop more housing. Its nonprofit status gives it access to reasonable financing from government sources. For example, the Reservoir was mainly financed through a tax-exempt bond, issued by the city of Madison in combination with two other MHA developments. The cooperative gains because it can help accomplish tasks that smaller and isolated co-ops would find difficult, such as negotiating repairs at a cost discount because of volume. The cooperative can also subsidize repairs on older buildings from savings on newer buildings. On the minus side, the separate cooperatives give up some of their autonomy for their greater size.

There are various levels of decision making in the cooperative, of which the Reservoir is one member. The highest is the cooperative board (with one yearly meeting of all the members) where policy decisions are made that affect all the buildings. Second is the resident council, one for each of the twelve cooperative clusters (members meet once a month and elect a representative to the board).[9] In the Reservoir there is also another level of governance: meetings of four households once a month in their common room. The households discuss house rules, expenditures, and activities. All decisions are made by consensus.

So that new new residents will understand the structure of living in a co-op, there is a 12-hour training program during their first three months of residency. The program covers their responsibilities, as well as the history of the Reservoir, property management, finance, and decision making. One member commented, "The first time I came here I thought it was terrible; they had so many requirements and rules. But it's an experiment—we must work out how we will all get along."

New members are chosen for their commitment to cooperative management. After a year, if a resident does not participate in the training or does not attend meetings, a renewal agreement can be denied. "This is better than a typical rental situation, because it's demanded of people that they talk to each other," said Hobart. "People really have to take responsibility for living here. Responsibility empowers people."

NOTES

1. Robert Szold, a senior attorney and an Amalgamated director for forty-five years.
2. Classes included current events, literature, and Jewish history, and on Sunday mornings, topics of general interest were discussed (Dolkart).
3. There were years when excess operating budgets and carrying charges were divided among the members, but those days are long gone. Any monies left over after operating expenses are put back into the maintenance fund to cover the large number of repairs required on the older buildings. The newer buildings help offset the costs of the older ones.
4. The tearoom closed during World War II and

never reopened. The cooperative grocery store also closed, unable to provide the volume and variety that neighborhood competitors did. The library closed when the New York Public Library opened a branch nearby.

5. The cooperative is run on the Rochdale Principles. In 1844, the Rochdale Equitable Pioneers Society was established in England among twenty-eight unemployed weavers who opened a cooperative store. The eight principles formed the foundation of the American cooperative movement: open membership; one member, one vote; savings are returned to members in proportion to their patronage; neutral in religion and politics; cash trading; limited return on investment; constant education; and constant expansion. The Cooperative League of America, begun in 1916, spread information about the Rochdale Principles to the American public.

6. Madison Mutual Housing Association's planning committee included the local nonprofit Design Coalition, architects; Independent Living, an older-adults service provider; Access to Independence, an advocacy group for people with physical disabilities; Options in Community Living, a group assisting people with developmental disabilities to live independently; the Salvation Army Day Care; a member from the Old Market Place neighborhood association; and two co-op members.

7. Nine of the units have monthly carrying charges priced at 30% of a household's income whose income is 50% of the medium (HUD guidelines), nine of the units are priced at 30% of a household's income whose income is 80% of the median, and the remaining ten units are budgeted at market rents. The market-rate units help subsidize costs for the lower-income units. If a resident's income changes from low to median income, the household does not have to move, but the allotment of available median income units is reduced and the allotment for low-income units is increased.

8. Madison Mutual is not a cooperative but a private (not connected with the government) tax-exempt 501(c)3 nonprofit organization. Membership includes both co-op and community residents, and the mandate is to be a citywide affordable housing developer. The cooperative is not tax exempt, and membership is restricted to co-op residents, who control the co-op for their own benefit.

9. The resident councils work out problems and decide on rules, new members, and items that need to be repaired. Part of the monthly carrying charges include a housing fund for repairs and maintenance that members decide together how to spend.

REFERENCES

Davis, Martha. 1989. *Cooperative Housing. A Development Primer.* Washington, D.C.: National Cooperative Business Association.

Dolkart, Andrew S. 1989. "Homes for People; Non-Profit Cooperatives in New York City 1916—1929." *Sites,* pp. 30—42.

Hobart, Susan. 1988. "The Reservoir Cooperative: Developing One American Co-op. In *Women and Environments* **10** (Spring):16—17.

"Madison Mutual Housing Association." 1986. *Economic Development and Law Center Report* (issue on women, Spring 1986):31.

Martell, Chris. "Miracle at the Reservoir." *Wisconsin State Journal,* February 5, 1989, p. 12G.

CHAPTER 9

Four Imagined Scenarios

The eight communities described are modest examples of the potential for this new way of living, barely explored in the United States. After two decades, collaborative living in Denmark, Holland, and Sweden has become an accepted housing form. Each of these countries has adapted this concept to its specific housing types. Collaboration can also be adapted to a variety of American forms and need not be tied to a specific ownership or housing construction.

Following are four communities of the imagination designed to explore what the many European ideas would look like if they were translated into an American context. Four different sites were chosen and four developments drawn.

The first scenario, an urban apartment building, uses the stairway to link common rooms and apartments. The second, a renovated industrial building, includes some businesses with housing around a courtyard. The third combines three housing clusters with three common houses along a pedestrian street. The fourth, a suburban development, includes a common back garden.

In comparing developments in Denmark, Holland, Sweden, and the United States, there are some basic patterns, common to successful communities. These are the under-

lying themes that appear throughout the housing and commons in all four scenarios:

Site

Houses grouped together to provide common open space.

One primary pathway is used, usually a pedestrian street, a central green, or a plaza, to encourage residents to meet and see each other.

The center of the development is car free. Parking is restricted to the periphery of the site to create a pedestrian area safe for children.

The housing tries not to clash with the existing homes in the neighborhood by using similar styles, heights, and materials.

The outdoor areas allow for a variety of uses and meeting areas of different sizes so that several households or the whole group can find a place to meet comfortably.

Private Dwellings

Each household has its own private dwelling.

Each dwelling is slightly reduced in area in order that common rooms can be afforded.

The interiors of the dwellings are divided into zones, with the more private functions in the back (such as bedrooms) and the more public rooms (such as the dining and kitchen area) facing out to the common areas.

Areas in front of each dwelling, such as small front gardens or front porches, encourage casual socializing.

A variety of unit sizes, from studios to five bedrooms, allows a variety of household sizes.

Common Areas

The main common areas are grouped together to create a center of activity.

Common areas are located along a primary route, where residents are likely to see and use them.

The common house is located next to the open space so that activities in one area can expand.

These basic patterns have been used in a variety of combinations in these schemes. Each scheme emphasizes different areas used by all the members of the community—a staircase in the apartment building, a courtyard in the industrial building, a pedestrian street in the interconnected clusters, and common backyards in the suburban scheme. Each also has different common spaces and amenities. Although none of the illustrations shows housing that exists today, they provide a preview of types that could be developed. (The designs are by Peter Bosselmann and Paul Lukezy.)

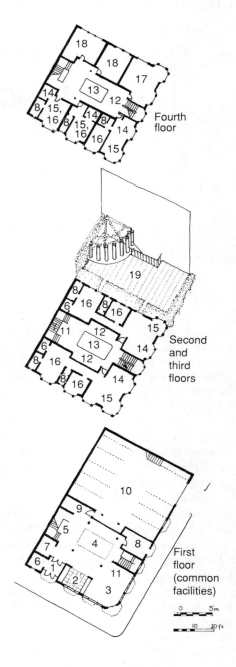

Fourth floor

Second and third floors

First floor (common facilities)

1. Entrance
2. Common kitchen
3. Common dining area
4. Sitting room
5. Fireplace
6. Closet
7. Mail
8. Bathroom
9. Mechanical
10. Parking garage
11. Stairs
12. Hall
13. Open to below
14. Kitchen
15. Living-dining
16. Bedroom
17. One bedroom apartment
18. Studio apartment
19. Common garden

APARTMENT BUILDING: THE VERTICAL STREET

In this first example, an inner-city building is renovated into collaborative housing. A small core group purchased the four-story walk-up, confident that they could take on a small number of apartments. They occupy the building during the renovation and gain members as more apartments are renovated.

The ground floor of the building was originally a corner grocery that went out of business. The grocery has been converted into the common kitchen and dining area, with parking in the back. The second floor retains the original floor plan of two-bedroom apartments, each with a kitchen and bath. A roof garden has been added over the parking area, accessible from the ground floor. (At some future time, another common room can be located upstairs and provide access to the second-floor garden for all the residents by converting a two-bedroom apartment into a one-bedroom unit.) The top floor in this example is divided into studios, each with a bathroom. The studios can be rented out to students or used as workspace, or the entire floor could be considered as one shared unit. The areas that are normally used individually—the staircase and landings—become jointly used as common areas.

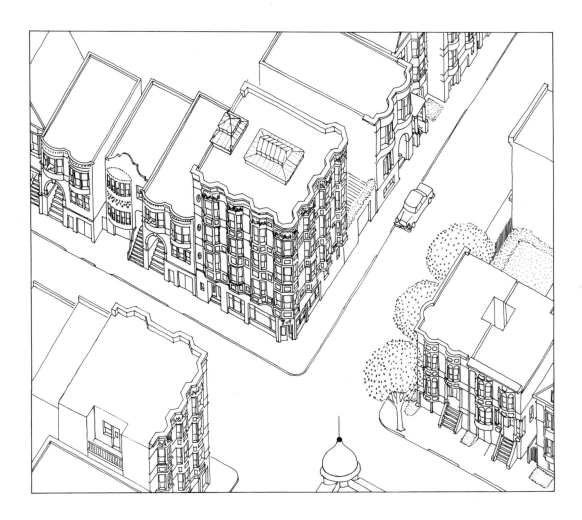

The Stairway

The stairway is the link between apartments and the common spaces, similar to a pedestrian street along a cluster of houses. The most-used common spaces (the dining-kitchen area area and sitting areas) are grouped together and centrally located between the entrance-way and the stairs. Daily, residents can see who is there as they come and go through the lobby.

Areas generally underused, such as the corridors, passageways, and landings, are now jointly furnished and used in common. Along these areas are places to perch, sit, and talk.

Hallways can become an extension of the resident's apartment. Individual entrance doors and the area in front of the private apartments open out to the landing. A window overlooking the stairway or a dutch door allows views and conversation both into and out of the apartment.

The lobby.

A hallway landing.

Ownership

The group could decide to turn the apartments into condominiums or a cooperative. Many cities restrict the conversion of rentals to condominiums, so a cooperative might be chosen, allowing the residents more control over membership selection. Although the former tenants can be invited to join the cooperative, most will move out because of the added costs and new responsibilities they will have to assume.[1]

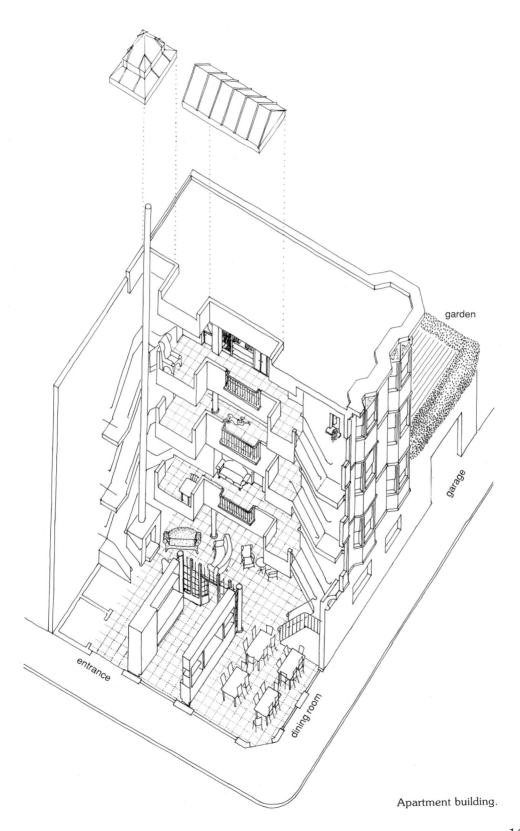

garden

garage

entrance

dining room

Apartment building.

RENOVATED INDUSTRIAL BUILDING: HOUSING AND WORKSPACE

Collaborative designs can be adapted to a variety of existing buildings, from old schools to industrial warehouses. In this scenario, a 1910 brewery is renovated into thirteen dwellings, with an additional eight multipurpose rooms. An existing office building on the site is leased to several businesses. The rent received can reduce each person's individual rent or be used for maintenance or capital improvement.

The brewery went out of business in the 1930s. Since that time, a warehouse has been added, and the buildings have been divided into a conglomerate of spaces and rented out.[2] After the renovation, the original boiler house became the common house. The brew house and the warehouse have been renovated into residences around the central courtyard.

The private dwellings are small, with loft space upstairs. All units have kitchenettes with windows to the large shared area and small front yards. The row houses in the back also have private back yards. The open floor

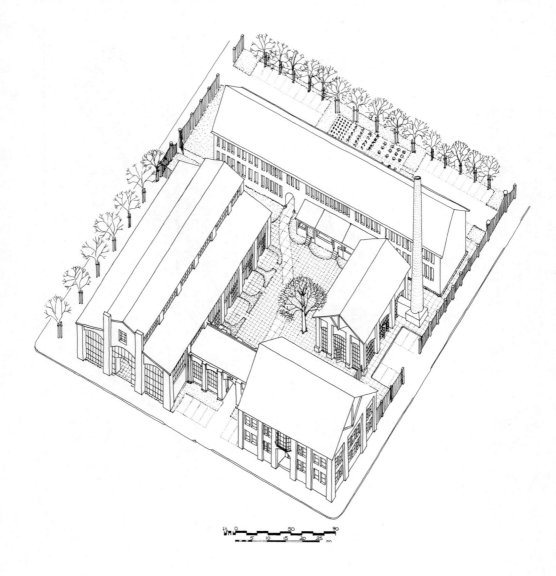

plan, with a loft, allows light to reach inside the long, narrow space.

To reduce costs, the interiors are not finished. Residents can complete the job themselves or decide to work together as a group, with each person learning one task and repeating it in each of the units. By using their own sweat equity, the residents reduce costs and learn quickly how to work with each other.[3]

Ownership

This development could be owned by the people who live there or leased by a group of residents from a company. Let us assume that the buildings are leased, and the residents draw up a contract with the company. They must deal with the issues of vacancy, collecting rent, and enforcing rules. Since the residents do not own the housing, the turnover rate will be somewhat higher than if home owners were living in the development.

1. Common house
2. Office building
3. Three bedroom row houses
4. Studio apartments
5. Live-work spaces
6. Parking
7. Common garden
8. Courtyard
9. Private yards

The corner office building could be part of the community, managed by a committee that oversees rentals or leased separately. The advantages of income-generated property need to be weighed against the possibility of rent increases should the building be hard to rent.

The Courtyard

The courtyard is located next to the common rooms. Activities such as dining outdoors or meetings can spill out into this space.

All the dwellings have direct access to the courtyard, and their front entrances are designed to enhance the use of the court by providing a place for sitting and talking with views into the court.

The small private yards between the court and the dwellings also provide screening from the views and noise of the courtyard.

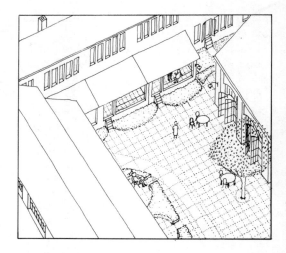

Common courtyard.

Live / Work as a Business Alternative

Part of this former brewery has been designed for small live-in businesses. The six multipurpose rooms have the possibility of opening their back facade to the street as small shops (photography, art studio, craft shop) or offices. The back doors open onto a loading dock that serves as a raised street.

One of the multipurpose rooms has been turned into an arts and crafts space with a kiln, shared by all the residents. Another room is being rented by four residents as an office. They share the cost of a computer, copier, fax machine, and part-time bookkeeper. Those working can meet together at the common house for a coffee break, lessening the isolation of working at home.[4]

An organization can work with interested residents to develop a home-based enterprise by providing starting capital and marketing and technical assistance. Affordable housing, with the provision of child care and some evening meals, can provide a supportive environment for this kind of cottage industry.

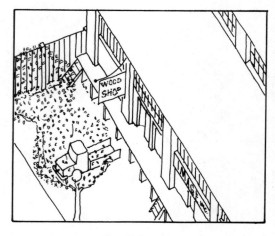

Small shops.

THREE INTERCONNECTED CLUSTERS

This scenario illustrates a medium-density development, most likely if a site is available in an established neighborhood, such as a school site. The neighbors fear that such a development could lower property values and bring increased traffic into the area. Lengthy discussions might be resolved by having part of the site remain available for neighborhood use, perhaps as a park.

The Site Plan

In this solution, we assume a large, expensive site requiring the construction of seventy units to justify the development cost. The large number of units are divided into three independently functioning communities that co-exist.

The design creates a U-shaped pedestrian street that connects these three separate housing groups. Each housing group has its own common house. Car parking is located

1. Common house
2. Common green
3. Public park
4. Public street
5. Pedestrian path
6. Parking/automobile traffic
7. Outdoor space (use to be decided by housing cluster)
8. Plaza
9. Private dwelling
10. Front yard
11. Private back yard

around the perimeter of the site. Common spaces are left undeveloped, to be completed by the residents later.[5] Each of the three clusters has the possibility of developing the common space on its own or in conjunction with another cluster and creating a larger common area together. Deciding on the common house or children's play equipment can help bring residents together.

Ownership

In this example, a nonprofit organization could finance affordable housing by building a large number of units in stages. If necessary, the nonprofit organization can sell one of the housing groups at market rates, with the profit used to finance the construction of the other two housing groups. The housing can be managed with the residents as rentals.[6] In this way, those less privileged in their ability to develop or finance the housing can also benefit from living collaboratively.

The Housing

The households are divided into groups of thirty to forty dwellings to increase a sense of identity and security. Each housing group has a clear separation from the other and is a distinct place. The houses are lined along a pedestrian street, with the common house centrally located.

Activities such as walking home, playing, and completing daily tasks create additional community life when they are interconnected with places to stop, watch, and stay. Porches, low walls, benches, and well-located stairs provide a place to sit and relax or view the action without being in the middle of it.[7]

The Neighborhood

The design does not ignore the larger surrounding community. The housing blends into the surrounding neighborhood through use of similar materials and massing. The design includes a park at the end of the common outdoor area. Located adjacent to the public street, it is open during the day for neighborhood use. The central common house at the other end of the site, through height and design, can be seen as a symbol of the development from the public street. From the public street, the pedestrian entrance is narrowed to indicate a more private path. A change of level occurs between the common outdoor space and the park.

Three interconnected clusters.

Services for the Residents

The nonprofit organization has targeted twenty units for low-income elderly and ten for single-parent residents.

Health services for the elderly: Depending on the number of elderly, space could be set aside for a small health clinic with a nurse. This kind of health care exists in Sweden and Denmark and could work in the United States if funded by the elderly. For low-income elderly, a subsidy would be required.

Special dwellings are designed for the elderly and handicapped, including such features as wider doors and lower cabinets. These dwellings are mixed among the other housing units so that separate groups are not formed.

Club: A pub or cafe for residents and their guests is located in the central common house, with space to move out to the plaza on warm evenings. This refreshment club could meet several evenings a week, and be organized and run by volunteers. Committees and the governing association could provide a flow of members.

Day care: A day care center is located in the central common house, with access to a yard and the large recreational space. Residents and neighbors drop off their children in the morning and can pick them up coming home from work.

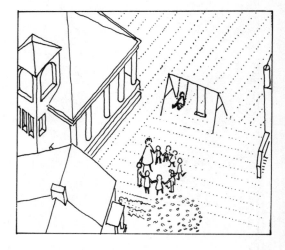

An association of residents from each of the three clusters would help coordinate the services.

SUBURBAN SCHEME: HOME OWNERSHIP AND GARDENS

While the idea of collaborative housing may appeal to families, there is reluctance in letting go of the dream of a single-family home. This model combines sizable detached houses (from 1,200 square feet) with shared common areas in a suburban housing arrangement. A greater collaboration with neighbors helps create a close sense of community and offsets some of the disadvantages of living in the suburbs. Collaborative housing is especially appropriate for new subdivisions being built far from the center of town, where land is relatively cheap. For working couples, commut-

ing leaves less time for cooking and socializing, and those who work or take care of children at home can feel isolated, far from services and friends.

In this model, typical suburban housing is developed on lots a third of an acre in size (100 × 160 feet). One block of the development is set aside for collaborative housing, with lots 10% smaller (90 × 120 feet) to create a central garden and sites for two small common houses.

The surrounding home owners have a strong desire to keep the character of the neighborhood as is. Therefore, this suburban model tries to incorporate the collaborative idea into the single-family neighborhood.

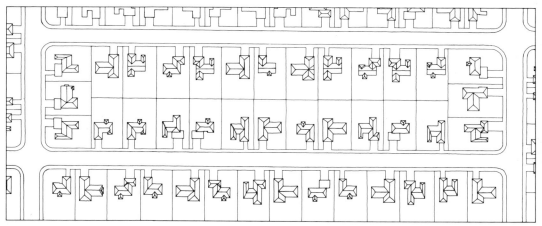

A typical layout for 100′ × 160′ lots.

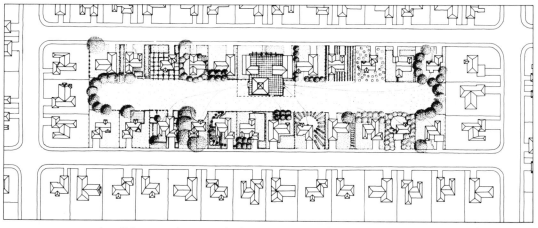

A collaborative layout with shared gardens for 90′ × 120′ lots.

Ownership

Traditional single-family ownership is the simplest for owning part of the back yard in common. An easement can be placed on a certain portion of each home owner's back yard and recorded in the deed. The easement requires that the other households are allowed access onto that portion of the property and that no fences be built on that portion. Since a certain percentage of the common house would need to be owned by each household, a condominium or cooperative ownership for the community as a whole has advantages, allowing a forum for common governance.

Fitting into the Neighborhood

The appearance of these houses would not differ from the surrounding subdivision. The same types of houses have been incorporated, but their floor area and lots have been reduced by 10%. Each household contributes this 10% to create two additional lots for the common house and for open space.[8] The 10% reduction in space has occurred by decreasing the size of the living room, dining room, and kitchen. The residents can decide whether the kitchen and dining room face to the back common area or turn toward the street.

Common Areas

Two common houses are built in the same style as the other houses, with an altered floor plan. The exterior of these common buildings can be designed to blend into the block or appear more prominent.

Outdoor space for each house includes a private deck and yard. The back third of each lot (40 × 90 feet) becomes available for shared use. A vegetable garden, play space, or a large, open area are all possibilities for such an arrangement. Changes in levels, planting heights, and views denote a change in the degree of privacy between the back yards and the common garden.

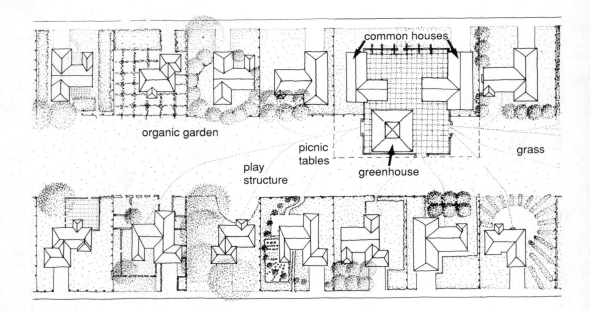

organic garden

common houses

play structure

picnic tables

greenhouse

grass

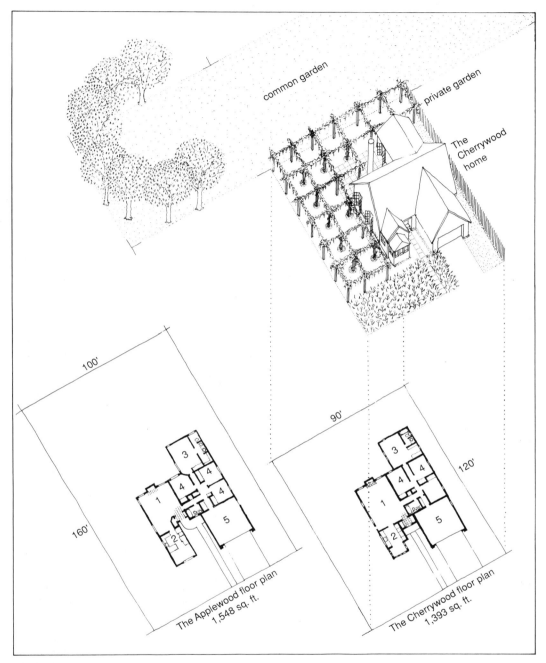

The Cherrywood plan is 10% smaller than the Applewood to allow for two common houses and a common garden.

1. Living-dining room; 2. kitchen; 3. master bedroom; 4. bedroom; 5. garage.

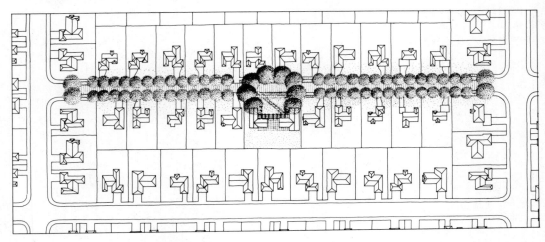

Sharing the street, 90' × 160' lots.

In a more prominent type of configuration, the common area moves out to the front, based around the street. (The houses have private back yards.) The street itself is turned into a *woonerf,* a Dutch concept where cars share the street with other uses (Moudon). Bollards and signs designate a woonerf street; paving and planting slow cars down, and a narrower street allows wider sidewalk areas. Places to sit and play are created. Suburban streets, usually a third to a half wider than necessary and with little traffic, are ideal for such a conversion.[8]

NOTES

1. A nonprofit organization could purchase the property and convert it into affordable housing for low-income tenants. Madison Mutual Housing in Wisconsin has specialized in turning rental buildings into leasing cooperatives. Director Susan Hobart finds that in a conversion (where the building is already occupied by people), three years are necessary for residents to become "self-sufficient financially and mentally." She finds that there is about a 50% attrition after a year and a half of those residents used to a tenant-landlord situation: "People move out because they don't want to deal with it, or get evicted because in the past they never had a lease, so they didn't have to take care of their dog."

   In city centers, an additional problem is faced by low-income collaborative housing in that people will be attracted to the price and location but not necessarily to the idea.

2. Several potential problems face industrial renovators. The first is the previous use of the facility and possible poisoning of the grounds from heavy metals or chemicals. The second is zoning ordinances that prohibit residential uses in manufacturing and commercial districts. In the past few years, a number of cities have passed a new use category, the live/ work unit, which combines residential and nonresidential activities, although this zoning can be limited to arts-related activities.

3. This possibility is feasible if bank loans are not raised to a higher interest rate for uncompleted units. Another important requirement is time and effort to organize such an undertaking and the ability to motivate people to finish the job.

4. Working at home or in the common house requires agreements among all the residents before moving in that such options are permissible and rules concerning noise levels, hours of operation, and so on.

5. All the units are built slightly smaller to afford common facilities. Part of the money is placed in a trust until the residents move in. The residents are allowed a year to decide how to spend these additional funds on common fa-

cilities. New housing groups in Denmark, built with minimal participation by future residents, are trying this method to spark community formation.

6. In the collaborative model, the nonprofit organization and the residents become equal partners in management, or the nonprofit group is involved in the administrative tasks such as bookkeeping or prescreening new members. The difference between such a model and congregate-type housing is that in congregates, the management and service tasks are not directed by the residents.

7. Urban planner Jan Gehl describes soft edges that provide a transition from private to public spaces—for example, a small front yard. He explains that "something happens because something happens because something happens," meaning that if one person lingers in the front yard and waters the plants, someone will come by and chat, a third person will then be tempted to stop and say hello to these two people, and so on.

8. Shared driveways, common in houses built earlier in this century, and back-to-back garages could be an option that gives a larger open-space lot.

9. A suburban street can average 66 feet across (42-foot roadway plus 12 feet for sidewalks on each side).

REFERENCES

Moudon, Anne Vernez. 1989. *Public Streets for Public Uses.* New York: Van Nostrand Reinhold.

Gehl, Jan. 1987. *Life between Buildings.* New York: Van Nostrand Reinhold.

Three

Development of Collaborative Communities

I thought of it as practical things, as organization—so I thought of schemes and how it could be done. I had been trying to make community life out of schemes, and I was dealing with human beings. I found that the only possible way to get the schemes working is to get the people working.

Lars Ågren, architect of Stacken, Sweden.

CHAPTER 10

How Is a Sense of Community Created?

What transforms housing and people into a collaborative community? When intentionally developing this type of housing, we wonder what the ingredients are that will help a sense of community grow. A relationship of close neighboring and caring can often take years to appear. Yet in the previous examples, residents both work and talk over their conflicts as they move into the housing and sustain that level of commitment for many years.

Developers, architects, and future residents juggle the many different aspects of collaborative housing with their limited time and budget. Is shared ownership and governance (with monetary and legal aspects tying members together) an essential ingredient? Is it primarily design with common areas to encourage socializing, as many architects believe? In looking at the various ingredients, the way these communities are developed stands out as one of the best indicators of a strong sense of community.

Skråplanet, now in its eighteenth year, has a celebration party. (*Gudmand-Høyer*)

SHARED OWNERSHIP AND GOVERNANCE

Condominiums and cooperatives provide a good source of information on shared ownership and governance. (By the year 2000, 50% of Americans are predicted to live in housing with shared facilities or open space.)[1] Under condominium ownership there is private ownership of the dwellings and common ownership of the land. A recent California study of 600 condominium home owners' associations and governing board of directors revealed a great deal of apathy: "Although the association's powers are broad and its activities directly affect residents' quality of life and owner's property values, participation in the association is usually sparse" (Silverman and Barton). The number of residents serving on committees or volunteering was 5%. Almost 40% of boards reported that members "did not care one way or another."

Shared ownership, and the responsibility of residential government, did not create a community glue. On the contrary, many conflicts developed:

Residents often did not understand, questioned, or even rejected the legitimacy of the collective dimension of association life. . . . The community in these associations is a fragile one because it is dependent upon utilitarian notions of collective action. It cannot support real differences because there is no group ethic which transcends individualistic notions. When differences arose, they then most often take a hostile form. (Silverman and Barton).

Perhaps limited-equity cooperatives, where a stronger board of directors has a greater jurisdiction over residents and where the seller's profit is limited, might fare better. A study of thirty-seven limited equity cooperatives reveals that a number of the co-ops had problems equal to or greater than those of condominiums (Heskin).

There are, of course, communities where common ownership has helped create stronger ties between neighbors. But in and of itself, common ownership does not create a will toward community. In fact, studies indicate that indifference, and even disharmony, can result.

DESIGN

Many condominiums and cooperative developments are built with privacy, not community, in mind. Some argue, as architect Lars Lerup has, that condominiums are "just vastly reduced single-family dwellings, small, stacked together, two or three stories, kerplunked down on the land with a little moustache of greenery around the walkway. It's really poorly done."

If housing is designed with community in mind, with common meeting spaces to allow residents the opportunity to socialize and plan activities together, will the result be a strong sense of community? No one really knows. Chance plays a large role. Architect Lerup admits his solution—the Double House, a duplex for single mothers and their children with bedrooms and kitchens off a large common room—could be "possibly a disaster."

Recent architectural designs, some already built, try to address the limitations of standard housing (Frank and Ahrentzen). While the ideas capture the imagination and many are successful, there is an increasing number with shared spaces that are not working.

In Cambridge, Massachusetts, architect and developer Gwen Rono redesigned a rectory into ten complete apartments, with additional common spaces: shared living room, kitchen, and guest room.[2] The architect not only had residents sign a Common Area and Shared Living Agreement but included the services of an experienced social worker, Jean Mason, for an initial period in the purchase price. People bought the units professing an interest in sharing but either were not very committed to the idea or did not stay. For example, an older couple from New York bought a unit for retirement and then rented it out. "They tried very consciously to rent to those who'd be interested. When people came by, they said, 'Great idea,'" and once they moved in, that was the last we'd see of them," explained one resident. Although there is less of a central focus on creating a community, residents do know each other and appreciate the common spaces (Frank and Ahrentzen), but the supportive community that Rono initially intended has not formed—a source of disappointment to some of the original buyers. Explains a resident:

The place started primarily as an alternative living style, but it hasn't worked out as proposed or conceived. I'm almost given up on this concept, but if we had a few more of us interested, we'd be off like the Celtics into a good second half. Just got overwhelming with people's attitude is "I don't care." Once in a while there is a party in this wonderful living room we share, but not for the house, just for someone's own social circle. That's great but not what we envisioned.

The residents now face a number of problems, including management and maintenance of their building. Most of them are not interested in taking on these responsibilities. The sensitive design, with its provision for common use, has some effect on a sense of community, but good design, in and of itself, does not create a strong community.

THE COLLABORATIVE ATTITUDE

In collaborative development, a sense of community appears long before walls have been built and the legal papers signed. A sense of community encompasses *membership*, a feeling of belonging to the group; *contact*, that members are in proximity and available to each other; *influence*, where each person can have some effect on the group; *fulfillment of needs*, knowing that the group can help meet each member's needs; and a *common history* and sharing of common experiences (McMillan).

The development process begins by forming the individuals into members of a core group. They commit themselves to meet regularly. Each member of the group takes on some of the development tasks and can influ-

ence many of the decisions made. Together, the members talk about their needs and find a way to fulfill them. Through this struggle to develop the housing, members begin to share a common history.

This process of creating collaborative groups is distinctly different from the process of participation. In a participatory design process, the architect manages the participation and chooses the degree of involvement. The future residents' involvement stems from "the goodwill of the professionals," as architect Ralph Erskine has observed. Conflict is kept to a minimum and solved by the architect. A solution is found within the parameters of site layout, number of stories, circulation, entrance location, and so on.

In a collaborative process, the group members deal with fundamental decisions and resolve differences among themselves. The future residents decide the amount of public and private area and their interdependencies. They have a vision of their community before the architect is hired. When the residents eventually move in, their managing skills, learned collaboratively, are put to use.

This attitude is a process in which people switch from an individual mode of thinking to one of an awareness and care of the group. Wanting to become a cohesive group does not create such a group (as witnessed by a number of groups that break apart) nor do people divide into those who naturally have this attitude and those who do not. Rather, it appears to be a process that involves the active participation of all members—their finding an order of working together through conflict. We could call this the managing community because each member learns to delegate authority, plan for the future, make decisions (and compromise), organize, and coordinate. (If only a few members had these skills, no agreements could be reached to delegate authority or make decisions.)

The development process is the training ground for resident management. Group competence in the various phases of development paves the way for a well-organized community after moving in. To the extent that decisions are made for the future residents, then the skills of setting goals, reaching decisions, and learning to trust one another are not experienced.

OUTLINE OF THE DEVELOPMENT PROCESS

An outline of the development process—combining information from European cohousing, existing American collaborative housing, and U.S. cohousing groups that are forming—appears on the facing page. The order will vary for each community, but the basic tasks will remain the same.

There are three basic ways to develop the housing:

1. The group members can decide to take on the entire housing development process themselves. They search for a site, find the financing, and design and build the buildings. Most groups do not have financial, design, or construction expertise, and they hire consultants for assistance. Nevertheless, the group directs the development and oversees the work of consultants.
2. Future residents can hire a developer to buy the land, select the architect, and construct the housing. The predevelopment costs, which are often subsidized in Denmark, Sweden, and Holland by the government, are now borne by the developer. The members lose some of their decision-making power but gain help in the development process.
3. The group can also negotiate with a nonprofit housing developer to help them develop the community. The nonprofit organization owns the property and rents or leases the units to the residents. In this way, more affordable housing can be realized.

Groups in Denmark have predominantly developed housing themselves. This could be seen as the ideal method because the group is always in control.[3] In Holland and Sweden, the housing is most often developed with a nonprofit sponsor, and the group negotiates its role in the process. In the United States, the hard road of development and rising housing costs have attracted groups to work with developers to speed up the process.

EXAMPLE COMMUNITIES

To illustrate these three development paths, projects are drawn from the European and American examples described in Parts I and II. In addition, three other American communities now in the development process are discussed; one in California, Muir Commons, and two in Washington state, Winslow Cohousing and Coho Cohousing Community.

Muir Commons

Muir Commons, in the town of Davis, California, a 15-minute drive from the state capital in Sacramento, has a 3-acre site, part of a planned community developed by West Davis Associates (WDA). Virginia Thigpen of WDA was familiar with the collaborative concept through Danish friends and had recently attended a slide show on cohousing given by designers McCamant and Durrett. Thigpen wanted to include cohousing as part of the city's affordable housing requirement for their planned community. Independently, a group of people interested in locating a site began to form. The group agreed to work with the developers because they hoped to speed up the development process and because the housing was more affordable. The developers, in turn, by including innovative housing were able to obtain building allocations for their entire project, a difficult feat in this town that would rather not grow.

Along with the positive aspects, Muir Commons illustrates some of the difficulties when a group works with a developer. "When I first went into it I only looked at the benefits," recalls Thigpen. "Now I see why I would have a hard time persuading other developers. The

Formation (and Information)

Growing a group
Discussing goals
Running meetings
Making decisions
Orienting new members

Structuring the Development

Committee tasks
Membership agreements
Schedule and budget
Consultants and/or developers

Site Search

Selecting a site
Cost considerations
Development requirements
General plan and zoning issues

Legal and Financial Options

Membership fees
Money for development
Financing options
Types of ownership

Design

Design strategies
Achieving consensus
Elements of the design program

Building

Bids
Construction
Sweat equity

Issues of Community Life

Before moving in
Conflicts
Conflict resolution and empowerment

Outline of the development process.

disadvantage is the amount of time required; the quality of the time, which can be intense; and the lapsed time necessary for the group to know itself and learn to make group decisions." Nevertheless, the $2.6 million community of twenty-six attached houses, plus common house, has taken about 2 years from the group's initial meeting to the beginning of construction.

Winslow Cohousing

In contrast, the members of the Winslow group on Bainbridge Island, Washington, a 30-minute ferry ride from downtown Seattle, wanted to handle the development themselves. The group, initiated by member Chris Hanson in January, 1989, decided to meet a minimum of 4 hours each week to plan the community. In addition to Hanson's development experience, the group included an architect, engineer, landscape architect, journeyman carpenter, and lawyer. Initially the group turned to its members to help start the project. Several weeks after its first meeting, Hanson found a site. In April he independently formed the nonprofit Northwest Community Housing Foundation to provide a development consultant service for Winslow as well as for a number of other cohousing groups forming in the area. Member architect Lynn Perkins teamed up with an outside architect, Bob Small, and began the design process. Members eventually replaced their architects with the design firm of Edward Weinstein Associates. Winslow illustrates how a group works with a development consultant and how group members take on developmental tasks themselves.

The $3.9 million community is located on 5 acres and includes thirty units, a common house, guest house, an orchard, and a half-acre vegetable garden. Aside from common dinners, members hope to establish a day care, elderly care, and a recycling center. This group's vision of providing a real community with dinners available five nights a week is similar to Muir Commons, but the path of development has been different.

Coho Cohousing Community

The Coho Cohousing Community purchased 28 acres of woodland on Vashon Island, Washington, the next large island south of Bainbridge. The group began meeting in January 1989; its members had no development expertise. Three months later they hired the nonprofit Northwest Community Foundation as consultant-developers. Coho members' goals were similar to those of the other two groups. "We are excited to create a living community that reflects our values: regard for the land, a safe environment for kids, and sharing with our neighbors," said member Deb Sweet.

The development, estimated at $2.5 million for twenty units and a common house, was designed by Bassetti Norton Metler Rekevics, Architects. Unlike the site plans of Muir Commons and Winslow with attached houses on both sides of a pedestrian street, Coho will have a mix of duplexes and single-family detached homes with extensive gardens.

DIRECTIONS

Dozens of other groups have formed in the United States, some more extensive in their goals than the examples just given. These three pioneering developments, one urban and two rural, have a modest budget with common areas ranging from a quarter to half the construction cost. All three model themselves after the Danish cohousing concept, with attached homes and a separate common house clustered to provide open space. (They vary from an overall density of eight units to the acre in Muir Commons to almost one unit to the acre in Coho.) Since these are some of the first collaborative housing communities in the United States, we can learn from their experiences.

Part three does not attempt a complete explanation of the entire housing development process, but an overview that presents some of the major steps other communities have gone through in the hope of aiding fledgling groups and design professionals. It begins with the group formation process, continues through the development process, and ends with some of the conflicts collaborative communities have faced after moving in. Readers can skip to chapters that most directly apply to their own situations.

NOTES

1. U.S. Department of Housing and Urban Development, *Questions about Condominiums* (Washington, D.C.: Government Printing Office, 1980).
2. The housing has ten units, and there is an intergenerational mix of residents. About 30% of the residents are elderly, and there is a mix of renters and owners (Frank and Ahrentzen; Hayden).
3. Future residents' working with developers is a form not encouraged in European cohousing. In Denmark, under the popular form of cooperative ownership, groups are forbidden to work with developers. How this form will evolve in the United States cannot be predicted.

REFERENCES

Erskine, Ralph. 1984. "Designing between Client and Users." *The Scope of Social Architecture.* C. Richard Hatch, (ed.). New York: Van Nostrand Reinhold, pp. 188–193.

Frank, Karen S., and Sherry Ahrentzen. 1989. *New Households, New Housing.* New York: Van Nostrand Reinhold.

Heskin, Allan. 1989. *Limited-Equity Housing Cooperatives in California: Proposals for Legislative Reform.* Berkeley: California Policy Seminar, University of California.

Hayden, Delores. 1984. *Redesigning the American Dream: The Future of Housing, Work, and Family Life.* New York: W. W. Norton & Co.

McMillan, David W. 1986. "Sense of Community: A Definition and a Theory." *Journal of Community Psychology* **14**(January):6–23.

Silverman, Carol J., and Stephen E. Barton. 1986. "Private Property and Private Government: Tensions between Individualism and Community in Condominiums." Working Paper 451. December. Berkeley: Institute of Urban and Regional Development, University of California.

CHAPTER 11

Formation
(and Information)

People want more than efficiency from their groups, they want to experience it as an occasion of being together with others.
Michael Avery et al.

Collaborative communities begin with individuals who are dissatisfied with their housing options and are interested in hearing about new possibilities. People come together with a general interest in the subject. Often an umbrella organization forms to act as a clearinghouse of information. Eventually the members of the organization split up into core groups, with specific goals, area of development, and price range in mind. Members of the core group begin by sharing goals and ideas. As first steps, they learn how to run a meeting, make decisions together, and deal with new members. Through the formation process, members begin to grow a group, discuss goals, run meetings, make decisions, and orient new members.

GROWING A GROUP

In Denmark and Holland, a small group of friends take the initiative through informal discussions among their friends or church and political contacts, often placing an ad in the local newspaper to enlarge the group. In the United States, where the collaborative housing idea is often referred to as cohousing and not as well known, slide show presentations of the European models are a popular method to attract new people. Flyers and advertising announce a meeting time and place, with a brief explanation of the concept. Following a presentation, a discussion takes place, and interested people are contacted to form a group. This initial group often becomes a catchall, where members can explore the idea without committing themselves to a specific development.

As the group becomes more familiar with the concept and begins finding sites and discussing goals, several smaller groups usually form around different housing possibilities—more urban or more rural, new construction or an existing building, a large amount of open space or perhaps a former factory. Often there is reluctance and some fear in dividing the members into smaller core groups because members have become comfortable with each other. But the large group generally cannot please everyone and still move forward quickly to obtain a site. Therefore, the

An Organizational Model:
Umbrella and Core Groups

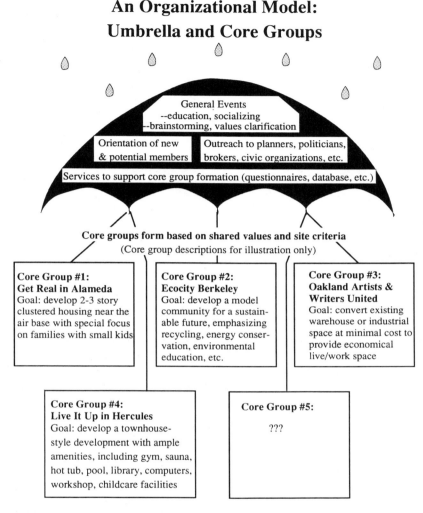

Core groups form based on shared values and site criteria
(Core group descriptions for illustration only)

Core Group #1:
Get Real in Alameda
Goal: develop 2-3 story clustered housing near the air base with special focus on families with small kids

Core Group #2:
Ecocity Berkeley
Goal: develop a model community for a sustainable future, emphasizing recycling, energy conservation, environmental education, etc.

Core Group #3:
Oakland Artists & Writers United
Goal: convert existing warehouse or industrial space at minimal cost to provide economical live/work space

Core Group #4:
Live It Up in Hercules
Goal: develop a townhouse-style development with ample amenities, including gym, sauna, hot tub, pool, library, computers, workshop, childcare facilities

Core Group #5:

???

Illustration of the Oakland, California, umbrella organization from the group's newsletter. *(Don Lindemann)*

first of many divisions occurs, with members moving in and out of groups.

In Seattle, Washington, an umbrella organization formed for disseminating information and educating new members recruited new members and organized workshops. Within a year, the members divided into a number of core groups with different site locations and interests in mind. The umbrella organization has changed its role, continuing to meet once a month with a representative of each of the core groups to trade information and keep up with the others' progress.

A small, dedicated group is required to create a core for collective activity. Core groups are most efficient if they take on a workable size of five to twenty people at the beginning of the development process. Formation of the core group begins by people choosing each other and making time and monetary commitments to a specific site area and type of housing.

DISCUSSING GOALS

The core group considers the type of development they envision—the size, the location, the community emphasis, the financial expectations, and the amount of participation. These discussions, which can take several months, allow people the opportunity to know each other.

Some groups close themselves to new members in order to consider shared goals. Others are open and need to find a process for integrating new members without sidetracking to explain the concept or reconsider previous agreements during the meeting. Once the core group reaches agreement on the basics of the development, they can advertise for new members to help with the mounting tasks of researching development questions and finding and financing a site.

RUNNING GENERAL MEETINGS

Decisions take longer to make in a group because groups listen to what all members have to say and bring up many more questions and alternatives than an individual. But groups of people can and do make decisions fast and efficiently with good organization. A number of books have been written about group dynamics (Knowles, Luft), running meetings (Auvine et al., Doyle), and making decisions (Avery et al.).

There are two types of meetings members will regularly attend: the general or business meeting where decisions are made, and committee meetings to work on specific tasks. General meetings are attended by all members and last from 3 to 6 hours, from two to four times a month. The general meeting can be uplifting and inspiring, but most beginning groups experience a certain level of frustration when they meet. Often members will not have the skills to work efficiently within a large group of people where everyone's opinion is counted equally, where the focus is development of housing, and the rules are made up along the way. A determined group usually picks up the skills within about five to eight months. At that time they can run meetings fairly efficiently, make decisions, and delegate the work. Until then, a few setbacks and frustrations are to be expected.

There are three parts to running enjoyable and efficient meetings: preparation for the meeting, the meeting itself, and closing the meeting.

The Preparation

At least half the work of a meeting goes into the preparation:

Setting an agenda: Generally a committee of members meets a few weeks before a general meeting to set the agenda. Issues are gathered from the previous meeting, from other membership committees, and from members who request to discuss an item. The items are prioritized, and time limits are set for each one. Members can change the agenda or add items at the beginning of the general meeting, with others' approval.

Choosing a chairperson: The chair rotates every few months among the group so that all members share the challenge of getting through an agenda and bringing people together on a decision. Some groups choose to have cochairs, acknowledging that one person may have difficulty moving the meetings along. By doubling up, one chair can be more experienced and help out a less experienced one. One chair can pay attention to the agenda and the other to the group. Consultants and nonprofit developers often take on the role of chair. Clearly this should be temporary and is not a recommended solution since the group does not learn how to lead itself.

Prior notification: A mailing prior to the meeting that includes the previous meeting's minutes and the next meeting's agenda gives members time to think, react, and come up with ideas. Particularly helpful is a three-month calendar that points out goals and directions. A larger community of interest can be created through a newsletter.

A newsletter is effective in its ability to link people at many different levels of participation—from active members to people who like the concept but are not quite ready, from design professionals to local authorities and nonprofit agencies. The advantages need to be considered with the difficulties of putting a newsletter together properly for any length of time.[1]

Committee work: Committees work on the tasks set by the general meeting. Members meet from 2 to 4 hours, from once to four times a month. Members generally join at least one committee and often several. Depending on the agenda of the general meeting, the appropriate committee makes a short presentation on the subject, bringing to the group clarity and factual information. Without active committees, two or three people become overburdened with tasks and hold too much responsibility. Meetings are often spent dealing with side issues best relegated to a committee or piecing together information that should have been researched and presented.

Time and location: The incentive to attend meetings increases when members are familiar with their time and location. If necessary, pick two days or locations and rotate them consistently. Meeting in other members' homes works well for a small group, but a meeting room is more appropriate for a growing group so that members can see each other and feel they have an equal opportunity to participate. Since gatherings are not only a time for listening but also a time for socializing, a meeting room should allow eating as well as rearranging of furniture.

When setting the place and time of the meetings, consider difficulties members may encounter when trying to reach a meeting—transportation, handicapped accessibility, parking, and child care. Generally parents rotate the child care in a separate room or, to reduce interruptions, in a separate house near the meeting place. In some groups, part of the dues are paid to hire a baby-sitter or teen members to watch the children.

The Meeting

Meetings are a time for both socializing and getting work accomplished. They work best when the two are separated, and socializing takes place before or after the meeting. There are some simple techniques for moving meetings along:

Post goals: Post the goals or agenda of the meeting. Be specific. If members know where the group is going, they can help to move it there.

Record minutes: The many advantages of having a written record of the meeting outweigh the difficulties in convincing someone to do the job. Minutes summarize meetings for those who did not attend, they are a written record of decisions, and they

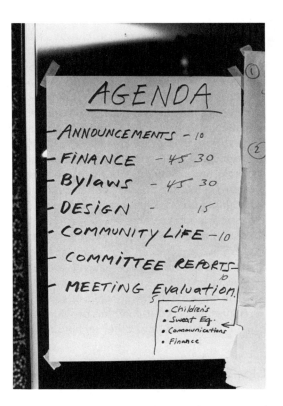

A clearly posted agenda indicating the amount of time to be taken for each item moves meetings along. *(Thor Balkhed)*

help the group refrain from backtracking. All meetings should be recorded, even if only with a few sentences. The meeting name, date, location, members attending, and the minute taker need to be recorded in a consistent format. The minutes include the agenda, the techniques or steps taken to reach a solution, major objections, decisions made, persons taking on responsibilities, and the next meeting date. Generally two notebooks of the compiled minutes are kept—one lent to new members and the other brought out when the original notebook disappears.

Pick a timekeeper: A timekeeper calls out when the agreed-upon time limit has run out—especially useful when each member is given a few minutes to present opinions.

Write issues visibly: The standard technique is to take a large roll of paper or butcher block and post it on the wall. As ideas are discussed, they can be written down. The advantage is that everyone can follow the discussion, a general direction can be picked out, and specific points can be organized under topic headings. This is an easy method to manage complicated subjects with many issues and many opinions.

Use group techniques: A number of techniques can be used to get information and ideas from the group. Brainstorming is useful when ideas on a topic are called out randomly by any member, with no regard to finding a realistic answer. In this way, ideas are generated quickly. In a round robin discussion, each member speaks in turn, ensuring that everyone gets a chance to voice an opinion. Dividing into small groups of four to six members is especially useful for hearing opinions. Each group reports back to the large meeting with ideas or solutions. (A number of group manuals provide information on these and other techniques.)

Closing the Meeting

Before members leave, take a last look at how the meeting went and follow these steps:

Mark points of consensus: A quick summary of areas that were covered and decisions reached gives a sense of moving forward and clarifies that a decision was made.

Discuss next steps: What needs to be done before the next meeting? What is the next big hurdle? Briefly discuss the next steps, what each committee should accomplish, and the topic for the next meeting. If a new subject will be tackled at the next meeting, a small presentation at the end of the meeting prepares members. Issues and ideas will begin to formulate, and members are better prepared when the topic is presented.

Evaluate the process: Occasionally evaluate the meeting by allowing each member a few minutes at the end to comment on the way the meeting worked. The evaluation process is meant to be brief. If problems to avoid in the future outweigh accomplishments, more time will need to be spent on the issues, perhaps by a special committee.

Organize social events: When members know each other, meetings move along at a different tempo. People are willing to let others make decisions and take over tasks because a basic trust in the group has grown. Social events give members an opportunity to meet and talk, often resulting in more open communications at meetings.

MAKING DECISIONS

Cohousing groups strive to reach a common agreement among themselves through some form of consensus. Consensus decision making requires skills and patience not needed when voting (parliamentary procedure, where the majority rules). Voting is quick and simple, but the minority may not accept the decision, creating divisions among the members.

Consensus takes about a third longer than reaching a decision through voting, but the quality of the solution and the commitment to its implementation are often higher. Although conflict is important to both methods as a means of understanding the issues, consensus aims at resolving the conflict to a greater extent than voting.

Consensus Process

A vocabulary of consensus needs to be understood because the process is more complicated and lengthy than voting. There are six steps in the consensus process:

1. *Issue:* A problem is stated.
2. *Discussion:* What needs to be decided is discussed, as well as concerns.
3. *Amendments:* As members bring up ideas and solutions, others add to them or alter suggestions. As one member explained, "It's not consensus if you don't have the benefit of the other person's wisdom."
4. *Test for consensus:* The facilitator draws the discussion to an end by stating a proposal that summarizes the group's direction or preference. The group agrees or disagrees, and more discussion follows.
5. *Proposal:* If agreed, a formal proposal is stated, and there is a call for any concerns about it.
6. *Formal consensus:* The concerns are discussed until consensus is reached.

Blocking is a refusal by a member to go along with a proposal and can give the individual the power to block the group.[2] There are several levels to blocking; for example, a member can agree to step aside from the decision making or to have his or her objections recorded. Most collaborative housing groups have adapted a form of modified consensus, which includes a provision to decide by majority rule if they get stuck and consensus cannot be reached.[3]

Reaching consensus in a group requires practice. Members who share similar motives and a certain affinity will have less difficulty; a shared goal is critical to reaching consensus. In the beginning, there is a certain level of frustration when the group cannot make a decision and becomes sidetracked or stuck. With about three to five months of practice,

groups make decisions rapidly and efficiently. Nevertheless, decisions involving money and basic design issues will take longer to find consensus than issues on membership or bylaws.

Signals

In a large group of people, hand signals or cards speed up the process of consensus. The Winslow group uses a system of five colored cards to show how much agreement there is in the group: approval, neutral, unsure, not preferred, or definitely opposed. Another method uses four cards: green for agreement, yellow for question, red for not in agreement, and orange for point of information. Agreement, disagreement, or the need for more discussion can be seen quickly by asking the group's response and scanning the room. During a discussion, a raised card clues the chairperson that someone wants to ask a question, add information, or show agreement. Another method is to use hand signals (Nearing):

Hand up: Call on me. The chairperson jots down the names in order so that members hold up their hand only briefly.
Single finger raised: A point of information; used only for facts, not opinions.
Thumb up: Agreement.
Thumb down: Not in agreement.
Thumb to the side: Member stands aside. The person has concerns but will allow the decision-making process to go on without participating.
Two hands raised facing each other: Need for focus; usually indicates when a disruption occurs, such as two people arguing or noise.
Two hands up and fingers wiggling: Silent cheer, indicating agreement with an idea.

ORIENTING NEW MEMBERS

The group is likely to deal with new members throughout the development process and beyond. Beginning groups grow and shrink as

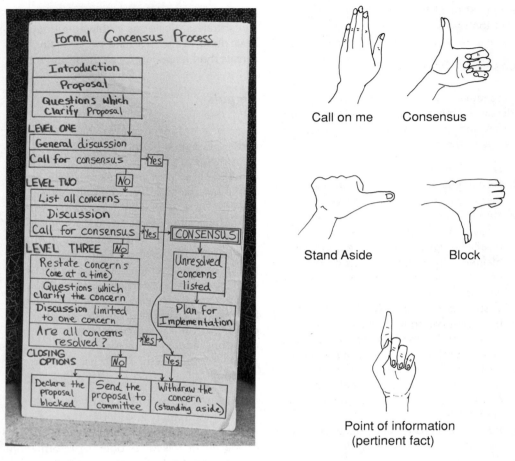

Chart of the consensus process on display at Muir Commons meeting (photo) and a diagram showing hand movement for consensus.

members decide whether to commit themselves. Once the location is chosen and money is committed, the group stabilizes, but members continue to drop out occasionally for various reasons—monetary constraints, not enough time, new jobs.

New members add different perspectives and bring new skills to the group, but they can also be disruptive. They question decisions already made, make new requests, and can slow down meetings by asking questions on basic issues.

A method of bringing in new people and making them feel comfortable eases the transition from interest in an idea to becoming working members. Such a method can be simply to have a monthly new membership orientation before the general meeting and teaming new members with a few old-timers. A group in Seattle provides new members with a handout describing the decision-making process, the bylaws and goals, and copies of contracts and agreements and urges them to read through the past minutes. Originally members were accepted on a first-come, first-serve basis without screening. Then the group realized the advantages of spelling out tasks and goals as a means of restricting who entered the group: "In the beginning we hadn't worked anything out—no consensus, no bylaws, no basic value statement. A few members who joined don't participate, and some inactive members would reactivate themselves." A number of groups further restrict new members by requiring that they attend a certain number of meetings or receive approval from the membership.

Aside from deciding how a person becomes a member and how membership is ended, many groups have different membership levels. Tiered membership provides a way of taking on financial costs and responsibilities over time. Generally fully paid members can vote and veto proposals, and associate members pay a small fee and cannot vote or veto.

Finally, contacting members who have decided to leave is also important. In some instances, they may have concerns or problems with the group that other members have not yet voiced and need to be discussed.

Maintaining a Members' List

An up-to-date list of member households can include the following information: name(s), age(s), address, telephone number(s), status (tenant or owner), annual income, maximum down payment, and maximum monthly payments. An up-to-date list with such information allows the group to assess quickly what they can afford if a site or building becomes available and how many can share the costs. Such a list is useful for revealing the composition of the group and helping to target new members.

In their aim to create a diverse community, a group may look at its membership and decide that there are not enough families with children, or elderly, or singles. Advertising for specific types of people and choosing members solely based on such criteria is a form of discrimination. Advertising can be placed in special interest magazines and newsletters, such as those for parents or retirees, emphasizing the advantages of cohousing for those specific groups. Sometimes if a specific group is not attracted by advertising, outreach into the community can be organized through presentations or meetings arranged through nonprofit organizations or churches.

Involving Children and Teenagers

Children do not have a vote and are not usually involved in meetings, but they can participate in social activities. Perhaps a few of the older children or teenagers would be interested in baby-sitting the younger ones at a meeting. At some point when the project is moving along, encourage children and parents to meet together and talk about the kind of places and activities they envision in the new community.

The collaborative housing concept can be explained to children in a manner they can understand. If there is a social time or a sharing time at the beginning of the meeting, they can participate. Involving older children and teenagers is important. If teenagers are willing to share in the work, they should be allowed to vote. By involving them, later divisions between them and adults can be minimized. Once the project gains momentum, teenagers can help design areas that will affect them— perhaps a basketball court, a teen room, padded music room, or separate rooms for them to rent. For some teenagers, these are the years that they are seeking independence, and community making may not be one of their priorities.

NOTES

1. Many groups begin a newsletter with information about meetings, relevant articles, book reviews, and housing issues, all put together by one member. That member soon feels overwhelmed with other development issues, and the newsletter dies. Even with the help of desktop publishing, the tasks of coordinating information, writing articles, and mailing are time-consuming. Break up the tasks into manageable chunks, with a committee where one member is in charge of subscriptions, another layout, a third announcements, and so on.
2. Quakers, who have made decisions using consensus for over 200 years, believe blocking is an essential ingredient in consensus but does not give the individual power to stop the majority. Laura Magnani, a Quaker, says, "We don't believe in it as a personal veto power. If the group has heard the concern, they can either move forward without the dis-

172 Formation (and Information)

senter, or someone in the group can say that we should pay closer attention to the concern of the dissenter. It is given to the whole group to allow one person to dissent."

3. For example, in Kilen, Denmark, all decisions require consensus, but when consensus cannot be reached on an issue, the residents vote. Sættedammen in Denmark makes decisions by voting, but certain rules that involve fundamental issues of voting rights or financial matters require a consensus to alter.

REFERENCES

Auvine, Brian; Betsy Densmore; Mary Extrom; Scott Poole; and Michel Shanklin. 1978. *A Manual for Group Facilitators.* Madison: Center for Conflict Resolution.

Avery, Michael; Brian Auvine; Barbara Streibel; and Lonnie Weiss. 1981. *Building United Judgement: A Handbook for Consensus Decision Making.* Madison: Center for Conflict Resolution.

Doyle, Michael, and David Straus. 1982. *How to Make Meetings Work: The New Interaction Method.* New York: Jove Publications.

Knowles, Malcolm and Hulda. 1972. *Introduction to Group Dynamics.* New York: Association Press.

Luft, Joseph. 1970. *Group Process: An Introduction to Group Dynamics.* Palo Alto, Calif.: Mayfield Publishing Co.

Nearing, Mary Beth. 1990. "Steps to a Consensus Decision." *Earth First!* February 2, p. 24.

Structuring
the Development

The tasks facing a group may seem overwhelming and require attention in all different directions at once. At first, many members of the group will have little idea of the steps needed to achieve housing or of how time-consuming the process can be. The group needs an overview of the housing development process.

The basic tasks are discussed and divided among committees. An agreement is reached on a preliminary budget and schedule. Bylaws and collecting dues are also part of the group formation process. Once the group is structured, the topic of hiring consultants or working with a developer will be discussed.

As the group begins to plan and organize, the members will begin to find out how much structure members are willing to accept. "There is a real conflict between order and freedom," explains architect Lynn Perkins who worked with the Winslow group in Seattle. Some members are interested in seeing a product; they want to move in tomorrow and would like a fast-paced development process. Others are interested in process; they want members to know each other well and make decisions in an unhurried pace. The trick is to balance the two, since both are important to creating collaborative housing. Committees, a schedule and budget, and selection of consul-

tants or developer help to structure the development.

COMMITTEE TASKS

We thought it was a practical arrangement, but it was a psychological solution, because people felt at ease in the smaller groups and could see their influence.

Lars Ågren

Dividing into committees of five to fifteen people allows the work to be organized into categories and be delegated for further discussion. These small groups report their findings and recommendations to a meeting of all the members. Although the groups work separately, solutions to their tasks are interconnected. The committee searching for a site depends on the committee that handles financing for the purchase; the financing committee depends on the membership committee; and so on. Each individual committee is dependent on the entire membership to make decisions and decide on specific tasks.

The beginning group can have three or four committees, such as those working on site location, legal and financial research, and membership. As the group expands and more organization and research is required, additional committees form.

In most groups, each member is required to join at least one committee, as well as attend the monthly group meeting. The monthly meeting of all members lasts about 2-3 hours, while committee meetings vary from 1 to 3 hours and require outside research or work. A member of each committee rotates as coordinator and generally attends a monthly coordination meeting.

Following is a sample list of committees; clearly they vary from group to group:

Coordinating Committee

Steers the general meeting by deciding on the agenda and prioritizing tasks.
Coordinates the committees.
Composed of one member from all the other committees.
Officially represents the group in signing contracts and dealing with consultants, the media, and other organizations.

Membership and Records Committee

Maintains current list of members (and attendance).
Advertises and prepares presentations and information for new members.
Maintains a waiting list.
Coordinates child care and special needs of members.

Communications Committee

Produces a newsletter that it mails to members.
Files minutes, reports, and contracts.
Maintains two copies of all minutes and newsletters.

Finance/Legal Committee

Researches and recommends specific financial and legal forms for the development.
Maintains subgroups on bylaws, insurance, funding applications, nonprofit status, and similar matters.

Community Committee

Oversees the well-being of the group process by promoting communications, as well as social events.
Monitors the efficiency and democracy of meetings.
Develops a method to address grievances and conflicts within the group.

Site Committee

Researches potential sites, land values, and buildings for renovation.
Checks on zoning, neighborhood opposition, and development requirements.
Eventually blends into design committee.

Design Committee

Works with the architect and other design consultants.
Sets up subgroups on design topics such as energy research, playground equipment, landscaping and gardening, sweat equity, and other related issues.

Treasurer

Collects membership dues, fees, and other required payments.
Pays the bills. (Groups of over twenty households may have a bookkeeper to maintain the group account balance.)
Sends warnings for overdue payments.
Maintains a copy of all contracts.

The general or business meeting provides the setting for making communal decisions and allows for the highest authority in decision making. Some decisions cannot be made by all the members because there is not enough information or the issue is too detailed or too technical. A committee is then asked to do further research or is delegated the authority to decide the issue.

Brian Dempsey of the Muir Woods group in Davis, California, feels that meetings were difficult in the beginning, but now they are efficient: "The group has become experts at meetings. We know when we're stuck, and we've got a 30-second technique to get un-stuck at meetings. We say, 'Put this in a committee.' Everyone knows it now, not just one or two people. We have no interest in staying till midnight."

MEMBERSHIP AGREEMENTS

Members agree among themselves how their group should be governed. Membership by-laws detail the procedures for membership, making decisions, dividing tasks, selecting houses, and other items important to group functioning. Generally the bylaws are not legally binding.

Eventually members will be required to invest substantial amounts of money together, and membership agreements form the basis for these legal documents. Groups working with developers usually do not invest capital until construction begins and therefore their agreements are not as extensive as members purchasing a site.

The Muir Commons group has a membership agreement hammered out through many meetings, and amended as the group moves through the design process (see Appendix D). No legally binding agreement covering membership investment was required since the developer owns the land.

The Winslow group has a number of agreements among the members. Since they have purchased a site, they chose to limit their liability by becoming a nonprofit association until the housing is developed. Their Articles of Association, about twenty pages long, include the purpose, powers, dues and fees, and criteria for membership in their association. Their agreements include a description of the kind of community they plan to build— with common facilities, cars segregated from the housing, and private units. They also have an explanation of procedures for reaching decisions through consensus, estimated development costs, and capital contribution agreements. Their disclosure statement can be found at the end of Appendix D.

SCHEDULE AND BUDGET

A preliminary schedule and budget need to be made at the early stages of development. Some indications of costs are required to assure members that their participation should result in housing they can afford. Schedules indicate movement forward, and planning six months or a year in advance helps set goals. When consultants are hired, having a schedule and budget saves time and misunderstanding.

Schedule

The sequence of events for the development can be projected and discussed, but the timing varies enormously depending on the capability of the group and the community they are developing within. It takes an average of 1 1/2 to 3 years to go through the various stages, assuming the group is organized and capable of making decisions efficiently and the surrounding community is not resistant to the development. Many groups require 6 to 12 months for the individuals to get to know each other, to figure out a process of deciding on goals and to feel confident enough in members to truly commit themselves. It is not uncommon for groups to meet regularly for a year or two and still be contemplating a statement of goals. These groups do not have the impetus of land investment driving them forward and often have no overall plan or structure.

The functions required from the start of development to moving in would include many of the following items, some of which are ongoing and overlap:

Introductory meeting
Discussion of goals
Committee meetings
Preliminary membership agreements,
   budget, and schedule
An event (social, a lecture, or something
   else)
Site tours and financing research

Finalize membership agreement
Monthly monetary commitment
Hiring consultants
Serious financial discussions
A social event
Concentration on sites
Site analyses
Option site
Tenure discussions
Outreach to new members
Research financing sources
More social events
Begin the design
Site design
Start planning approval process
Line up financing for construction loan
Research legal agreements
Common house design
Weekend retreat
Individual dwelling design
Discuss feasibility and consequences of
   sweat equity
Obtain all planning approvals
Finalize design
Architect begins working drawings
Discussions on community life
Working drawings completed
Appraisal on working drawings
Finalize legal and management agree-
   ments and check with lawyer
Bids
Construction and mortgage loan
   commitment
Close the construction loan
Begin construction
Celebration
Common House furnishings determined
Finalize member rules and agreements
Members do finish work on site (sweat
   equity)
Move in
Close mortgage loan (retire construction loan)
House warming party!

Before a site or building has been located, the group's schedule will be only tentative. After a site has been purchased or the decision to renovate a specific building made, the schedule becomes more detailed and exact.

Design Timeline

A timeline becomes important to keep the participatory process from bogging down. Design professionals' complaint on designing with groups is often "time and money." The architect understands the tasks to be done and wishes to proceed quickly, while the future residents want to understand the issues and make their decisions slowly. Architect Dick Metler of Bassetti Norton and Rekevics, Architects, working with the Coho group, said, "We could see immediately that if given the opportunity, the group would take as long as needed and then would expect the architects to work miracles and get the working drawings done on time. We said we need design decisions made on these days with time limits. If we miss these for any reasons, then all the schedule is off."

The Winslow group's design team prepared monthly schedules for 5 months detailing the phases of the design process. The schedule was too tight, and, in retrospect, the architects would have preferred to have a 12-month period to allow for several cost iterations as well as flexibility during the permit process.

Multistory collaborative housing requires strict scheduling and coordination. Architect Wille Herlin of Stacken Architects designed the structure of the multistory Cat's Head in Sweden and applied for a building permit before the group design process began. The group could decide on their apartment layout and the type and location of the common facilities—the infill, but not the structural decisions. For the design process, the architect created a chart noting each week of the design process, the issues to be discussed, and the date at which a decision must be reached. An agreement was made about decisions that were not decided by that date: they were made by the architect or a three-person committee. The group with the architect could decide to move decisions around to some extent if necessary.

The tighter the schedule is, the more pressure is placed on the group to make decisions

June 1990						
Monday	Tuesday	Wednesday	Thursday	Friday	Saturday	Sunday
				• Assemble Base Information: Site Drawings Soils Information Utility Information Permit Research **1**	**2**	**3**
• Study Site Plan • Study Previous Unit Designs **4**	• Study Site Plan • Study Previous Unit Designs **5**	• Schematic Design Charette @ EWA with D & B / NCF FULL DAY **6**	**7**	• Schematic Design Alternatives Generation **8**	**9**	**10**
• Schematic Design Alternatives Generation **11**	• Schematic Design Alternatives Generation **12**	• Schematic Design Alternatives Generation **13**	• Review Schematic Design Alternatives with ACT / NCF HALF DAY 3:00-6:00 **14**	• Integrate Comments • Package Alternatives Presentation **15**	• Schematic Design Alternatives Presentation to Group HALF DAY ● 8:00-12:00 NCF Office **16**	**17**
• Refine Selected Schematic Design • Informational Package to PCI Comments to NCF **18**	• Refine Selected Schematic Design Comments to EWA 12:00-1:30 ACT/NCF **19**	• Refine Selected Schematic Design **20**	• Refine Selected Schematic Design **21**	• Refine Selected Schematic Design **22**	**23**	**24**
• Refine Selected Schematic Design **25**	• Review Schematic Design Alternatives Refinement with ACT/ NCF HALF DAY ◐ 3:00-6:00 **26**	• Integrate Comments • Finalize Schematic Design **27**	• Finalize Schematic Design **28**	• Finalize Schematic Design **29**	• Final Schematic Design Presentation to Group HALF DAY ● 8:00-12:00 NCF Office **30**	

A monthly schedule was produced by the design team for the Winslow group. Abbreviations used: EWA, the architect; NCF, the developer manager; PCI, the contractor; D & B, the group's design and building committee; ACT, the group's architectural coordination team. *(Edward Weinstein Associates, Architects)*

quickly and the less happy the group as a whole will be with the process. An open-ended schedule results in a great deal of group process, with decisions taking a long time.

Budget

How is the budget set? At the start of the development, members do not know how much things will cost, they do not know what the interest rate will be when construction begins, they do not know what season construction will start, or whether a large contingency will be required. The budget is only a best guess.

If the budget is set conservatively, and therefore high, the architect may be encouraged to design to the budget limit. The contractors bids often end up 5 to 10% higher than the set budget. So the high budget grows higher. Financing becomes more difficult to obtain. However, if the budget is set low, it will encourage members to join who will not be able to afford a unit. After working hard for several years to develop the community, such members will be forced to drop out. Also, if the budget is underestimated, there may not be enough money to complete the project.

Chris Hanson, of the nonprofit Northwest Community Housing Foundation, says, "There is a strong motivation to set the budget lower for architects and higher for members. But you can't work with two budgets." He recommends that members estimate their unit price plus 20%. "A lot of people have had to drop out (of the Winslow group) because they chose a unit on the estimate and when the final budget came in at 5% more, they were priced out."

Preparing budgets is one thing, keeping to them is another. Not only is there a budget for the housing, but the organization itself needs to be run within certain monetary limits. The group begins to take in a substantial amount of money and disseminate it over long periods of time. If no one in the group is familiar with budgeting, a professional should be hired to give a perspective from a neutral position on cost control and cash flow: "If you don't have someone who runs their own business, then how can they do a budget and plan when money will be needed? It's a big stumbling block for groups," notes Hanson.

Keeping the design within budget has traditionally been the role of the architect. From the experience of American and European collaborative groups, the ability of architects to keep within a tight budget has not been particularly good. A multiunit development directed by a number of individuals has a high tendency to be customized. A stern and strict individual needs to keep an eye over this tendency.

Revising Budgets and Schedules

New information requires revising budgets and schedules. Sometimes the group cannot come to a decision as quickly as hoped or factors beyond the group affect decisions. For example, a decision on ownership will have an impact on obtaining financing. One member noted, "You say, 'O.K. This is it, and we stick to it.' But then we say, 'Next time we're *really* going to stick to it.' It's not how a business does development—they stay on schedule and on budget. But we're not in the business of making money. We're making community, and our priorities affect those goals."

CONSULTANTS AND/OR DEVELOPERS

Groups can take on the development process themselves or work with a developer. If the members decide to act as their own developers, they will hire various consultants to help them through the development process. Taking on the project tasks will be hard, time-consuming work, but the group will retain control of most decisions. The Winslow group decided to take on many of the development tasks themselves. Members spend about 7 hours at the general meeting and 2 hours in committee meetings each week, an average of 40 to 45 hours a month.

The nonprofit or for-profit developer working with the group will help them to reach their housing goal, but in exchange, a certain amount of group autonomy will be lost. Control over many decisions may leave the hands of the group, and at the same time, the developer will need to be educated in giving up some of his or her decision-making power. The Muir Commons group, working with a developer, has less control over many decisions. Its members spend 3 hours twice a month in general meetings and about the same amount of time in committees, an average of 12 hours a month. The group can decide to select consultants, a developer (for profit or nonprofit), or a developer-consultant.

Consultants

Among the consultants that provide technical expertise are financial consultants, architects, lawyers, engineers, and realtors. Choosing a consultant is often the first big decision a group makes. "In the very beginning everything is nebulous. We would make decisions by saying we can commit to this and change our minds. But hiring the architect seemed our first irreversible decision," said Doug Murray, a cohousing member.

In choosing a consultant, the appropriate committee decides on a list of names gathered through professional organizations and word of mouth. A letter is sent to each person explaining the task and requesting a resume, an indication of fees, and an interview.

Prior to the interview, a list of questions and issues is written out, and the same ones are asked of each person interviewed. A recommendation is given to the group by the committee, and a final decision is made by the group. Any contractual agreement should be looked over by a lawyer.

Choosing an Architect

The main problem facing the group is not to design housing, but to design housing that can be affordably built. Hiring a housing or financial consultant first—someone who knows financing requirements and all the separate pieces that go into development—can save time and money. With a clear budget and time frame in hand, an architect can then be chosen.

If the list of potential architects is long, several members can meet informally with the architects to discuss the development in a general way. A letter is then sent to a shorter list of architects explaining the project and requesting a page or two describing the architect's preliminary ideas, similar projects, and their work with participatory design. Interviews are set up with qualifying architects and the design committee (open to all members). An architect's presentation, followed by question and answers, will take from 1 to 2 hours (not including group evaluation). A second interview may take longer. Important factors to consider are the architect's style of working, previous experience in building multifamily housing, ability to work with a group, ability to stay within budget, and particular design bias. Will they attend meetings and involve the participants? Architects often come with a team providing various services, and major team members, such as the landscape architect, also should be interviewed.

Architectural services include site analysis, building code and zoning review, cost estimates, and obtaining approvals, aside from the design documents. There are five stages in which the architect is usually involved:

1. schematic drawings (includes programming)
2. design development
3. contract documents
4. bidding and negotiating
5. contract administration

In the programming phase, all the requirements for the development are written out, as well as relationships of the site plan, the houses, and the common spaces. The architect then presents an interpretation of the programming in loose drawings and sketches, called schematic drawings. In design development, architectural plans, sections, and elevations delineate the buildings and grounds. The contract (working) drawings include the nuts and bolts of the buildings, used to obtain a building permit and contractors' bids.

In a community for twenty-five average homes, the programming (and perhaps schematics) can take three to five months, with meetings of the architect and the group two to five times a month.[1] As a rough estimate, the architect will spend about 180–240 hours for twenty five households in group work. The costs can be paid in installments during the design process. If a member drops out, the new member is required to reimburse his or her design costs.

The design development and working drawings are paid as a percentage of the entire development costs—generally 3–6%. Architects also provide construction supervision during the building phase. The whole design process can take from one to three years for new construction; remodeling can sometimes be a faster process.

Design/Build

The design/build team offers the services of designing and contracting under one roof. The team can include an architect and contractor, or the leader may combine both skills. The advantage of contracting only once for many of the development services needs to be balanced with the loss of some control.

By hiring an architect and contractor separately, each role is clear. The architect oversees the contractor and reports problems to the client. When the roles are combined, the job is often completed faster but not necessarily better. The contract would spell out the role of the group and needs to be written with good legal advice to guarantee that the group's suggestions are followed.

Member–Consultants

The more or less objective process of design is skewed when members within the group are hired as consultants. The member-consultant needs to wear two hats—at some moments being the consultant, at other moments a member. One of the first Danish cohousing communities, Skråplanet, was organized and designed by a member who was also the architect. More recent communities, such as Cat's Head in Sweden, also have an architect-member. The position is not without strife, balanced out by the fact that the architect is often the initiator of the development and without her or him the community would not have been started.

Some group members believe that consultant-members have their own bias and cannot be truly objective. A group forming on Bainbridge Island near Seattle has used members for architectural design, development consultations, and legal advice. In each case, the member-consultant has teamed up with outside consultants, and when there is a question of conflict, the other team member then gives advice. For some, member-consultants are a convenient and inexpensive solution. For others, member-consultants are not neutral enough in their opinions and are felt to have too definite a point of view.[2] (The Bainbridge Island group eventually fired their architect, and she dropped out of the group.)

Developers

Members of a collaborative housing group may decide not to develop the housing themselves. Perhaps they have difficulty locating a site or obtaining predevelopment financing; perhaps they are impatient to have the housing completed and believe that the development tasks take too long for their group to complete on their own.

In considering working with a developer, the group can find out how much influence they will have over the development process. Can they negotiate

The choice of the architect?
The choice of contractor?
The choice of the site and site plan?
Participation in development and construction meetings?
Possibility of bringing in outside consultants?
Financing?
Size and style of common rooms and private units?
Selection of members?
How disagreements and conflicts are resolved?
Agreement that group members have first selection of housing?
Agreements concerning future management (nonprofit housing)?

Types of Developers

A *for-profit developer* works with groups that can afford to purchase their homes once constructed. This kind of developer provides the advantage of a fast development process for a percentage of the profit. When group members cannot qualify for a bank loan, a *nonprofit developer* can help develop affordable housing by obtaining government financing. Usually the housing is not owned by the group or the equity is limited on resale to keep the housing permanently affordable.* There is also a rare but growing service called

---

*The differences between for-profit and nonprofit developers are becoming smaller and smaller. Regulatory and political procedures slow down the development time, not the actual construction. For-profit developers may not be faster in these areas, and may not know how to work with groups. The main difference between these two types of developers is in their agendas.

the *development manager,* who aids the group to be their own developers.

For-Profit Developers. A developer will take on the risk of financing the site purchase and construction. Their familiarity with the development process results in housing being built fast and efficiently. Groups in urban areas are drawn to developers because housing prices are on the rise. Groups have difficulty competing with other interested buyers to option the sites that may appear on the market for one or two days before being sold; in addition, inflation makes delays very costly.

Member Juli Ingels, of the Muir Commons group, feels there are many advantages and disadvantages to working with a developer:

We didn't get to go out and pick our land. We didn't get to go out and pick our architect, pick our developer, pick this that and the other. The developer approached us and said, 'I will save this piece of land for your group and supply you with everything you need.' We as a group were willing to make the sacrifice and accept a smaller site than we wanted, less of a choice on our housing, on the common house, on a lot of things.

But the process goes faster because we have all these things—the site and the architect and the developer. We are going at a much faster pace, and we can move in quicker.

Without a developer, members will invest thousands of dollars in a site, as well as work many hours to push the housing development process along. With a developer, sometimes a commitment of money is not made until after the design is completed, and if members do not push quite as hard, the process still continues.

For-profit developers have their own agenda in developing housing—perhaps to make a profit on land sales, perhaps to gain certain development rights such as a waiver of a water moratorium, or to also be the contractor and make a profit on the construction.

Most developers will take the risk calculating a certain amount of profit—from 10% to 15% of the development price. They will usually insist on their choice of consultants and contractors to ensure a timely completion.

Many features may be predetermined, such as the housing type and the size of the common house.

Since the group will have many of its fundamental building (and economic) questions resolved, it may need a strong structure to stay cohesive. The Muir Commons group has hired its own team of design consultants to work on the programming phase, paid for by members. They also require members to attend a minimum of three meetings a month.

Most developers are not interested in working with a group. A member of another cohousing group in Seattle said, "We wanted a developer to put up risk capital. But it's hard to find a developer who is sympathetic and who would do what we want done at a reasonable price. They are really used to coming up with a concept, and then they do 'em. They think that's risky enough."

Working with a developer raises fundamental issues of decision making and power, particularly if the developer initiates the group formation. Since no regulations exist on developing collaborative communities, there is no outside assurance that the process of group participation will be followed. The difference between collaborative housing and a normal condominium development might be only superficial if the developer is leading the process.

Nonprofit Development and Management. A group of low-income or mixed-income members negotiates with a nonprofit housing developer on the extent of the housing and their influence. The financing is obtained through the developer from conventional and government grant and loan programs. The nonprofit sponsor requires a guarantee that the units will remain affordable over time. Therefore the sponsor may rent or lease the units and help manage them. The units can also be turned into a leasing cooperative, where tenant influence is stronger. (Nonprofit organizations also develop housing without managing it but usually as a limited-equity cooperative, a land trust, or other types of ownership restrictions on the equity buildup.)

Nonprofit organizations have their own agenda in addition to developing the housing—perhaps to provide housing for low-income people, to house specific groups of people (handicapped, elderly, single parents), to upgrade a deteriorating neighborhood, or some other program.[3] A group will need to accept this agenda when working with the organization.

In addition, public monies come with many constraints on who can be housed, as well as regulations governing costs, square footage, and amenities (which reduce the overall costs and the design options). As a far from average rule, nonprofit developers will charge about 8% of the total development

costs. This cost is not paid by the members directly but out of public funding and management fees.

Nonprofit organizations have several methods to involve future residents in the design. One, common in Holland, is to wait for a group to form and contact the organization and then negotiate with the group on the development. Another method, such as that of Tinggården in Denmark, is for the nonprofit organization to advertise for a small working group that participates in the design with the architect (but will not necessarily move in). Both methods require extra funding for the architect during the participatory design process.

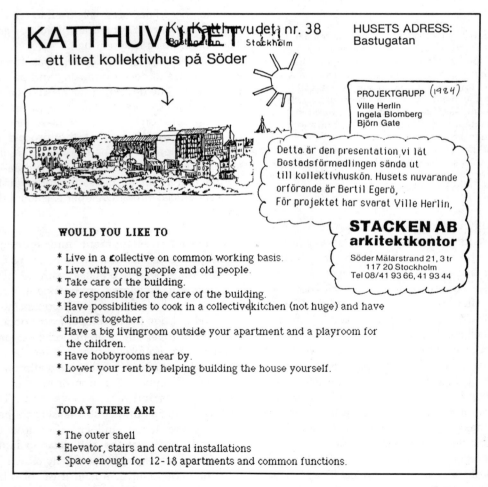

Advertising for members for the future Cat's Head in Stockholm, Sweden. The architect-developer sent these flyers to interested members on the city's housing list. *(Herlin)*

Development Manager. The develop-ment manager is an experienced developer who advises the group on how to take on the development role. The group takes the finan-cial risk and therefore pays the manager less profit than it would in a normal developer-cli-ent relationship. In developments that entail many different aspects, such as putting in roads, sewers, water, electricity, earthwork, and so on, the group could find the tasks overwhelming to coordinate and needs the service of a manager who oversees all the work.

The Northwest Community Housing Foun-dation, a nonprofit development manager in Seattle, facilitates several groups through the development process. It manages the budget, coordinates financing, acts as the agent for land acquisition, and aids in the selection of consultants and contractors, as well as in many other aspects of development. If a con-sultant is needed, the manager will aid the group in coming up with a list of candidates. The group and the manager then reduce the list to a manageable size and evaluate the pro-posals. The manager will recommend who should not be considered, and the group makes the final decision.

The Northwest Community Housing Foun-dation charges a fee of 5–7% of the total proj-ect costs. On the team is a realtor, who re-ceives the commission on the land purchase (and subtracts that amount from the group's bill). The contract stipulates 60% of the fee due at the close of the construction loan, which is the beginning of the building phase. During construction, it is paid on the same draws as the contractor.

An architect prefers to be paid for the work done; a manager may be willing to defer pay-ment and works hard to see that the project is realized.

It is a rare developer who is experienced enough to advise well and who could take the financial risk of the development but, instead, decides to work with the group in developing collaborative housing. Unlike the name *archi-tect*, which is regulated, almost anyone can describe himself or herself as a development consultant.

Developer Postscript

From the developer's viewpoint, the easiest method is to work with the group when the site plan, financing, and housing types have been worked out. But the future success of the community is strongly connected to the involvement of the group at the early stages of the housing development process (Cronberg).

When the group is involved in the initiative phase, the result is a higher level of interest in collaborating. The group has a voice in the selection of the site or building and the con-sultants. From the start, members of the Dutch Hilversumse Meent worked with a nonprofit housing agency to realize their rental community. They negotiated for a voice in the entire developmental process, in-cluding their choice of architect.

Nevertheless, somewhere along the line some compromises will need to be made if collaborative living is to become an accessible and affordable option. While group members look forward to having a say in all aspects of the development, this may not be a realistic possibility.

Collaborative housing has also been suc-cessfully developed with group involvement after the land has been optioned and the con-sultants hired—at the start of the design phase. In making these basic decisions, the developer retains more control in the process. Residents in Muir Commons, California, worked with a for-profit developer after she had obtained a site and construction financ-ing. They did not choose their architect, the site, or the basic style of the housing. They did decide on the site plan, the house plans, and common house design.

Attempts to form the group at the end of the design phase, or during the building phase have not been promising, particularly under condominium ownership. Least suc-cessful concerning the level of cooperation is bringing in residents at the end of the building stage with the hope that a group will form. Nonprofit organizations such as the Reservoir in Wisconsin have been able to form a some-what cohesive group after the housing has been completed because of the strict rules that can be imposed on residents through a cooperative ownership structure.[4]

NOTES

1. Three to five design weekends are another approach, with supplemental hours by individuals during the week.
2. Some collaborative communities in Europe have architect-members. Not an easy role to maintain, the long-term relationship between the architect and the group has been strained in several instances. In Skråplanet, members sued the architect for leaky roofs; in Cat's Head, the architect and the group had a major disagreement about the ownership form.
3. Nonprofit and government sponsors may be inclined to include people who have social problems (for example, substance abusers) in the belief that the supportive atmosphere in cohousing will be beneficial for them. In Holland and Sweden, such individuals have disrupted the community. One very different approach has proved successful: the group itself decides to provide certain services (for example, to help handicapped people or young adults) and chooses the individuals through interviews.
4. While the residents manage and maintain their community, their level of collaboration is not as high as in a community such as Santa Rosa Creek Commons, where the members took the initiative.

REFERENCES

Ågren, L. 1984. *Kollektivhuset Stacken.* Gothenburg: CTH-Architecture Department/Korpen.
Cronberg, Tarja, and Erik B. Jantzen. 1982. "Building for People: The Theory in Practice." *Building Research and Practice,* pp. 20-28 (Jan./Feb.).

Site Search

When available sites are few and far between, compromises will be necessary. Although each group member has an image of a dream site, eventually the market brings in a note of reality. Only when members have a sense of the market and potential sites and are aware of their options can they act quickly.

Groups need clear site criteria, money set aside, and a representative with the authority to act on a site. The time needed by the group to obtain approval from the members and collect option money can be a disadvantage compared to quick-moving developers. Reasonably priced sites are not on the market for long.

Members need to be aware of the different possibilities of controlling the site, such as leases and options. In many cases, the group might lose its money if it cannot obtain a building permit or financing within a certain length of time.

The day finally comes when the group does option a site. This is a great milestone in the development process, but the members may not feel like celebrating because optioning a site is often divisive for the group as a whole. Some members immediately drop out because they do not like the site. They may decide to band together and find another location. Other members may have financing difficulties.

New members are also attracted to the group. Nothing spurs enthusiasm like the possibility of moving forward toward construction. People (or other groups) may approach members with an interest in the site, although they may have different ideas in mind. Some members may be particularly eager to accept new people because they may be worried about their investment and the need to attract more members. For these reasons, membership criteria and specific agreements should be worked out before the site is optioned or purchased.

SELECTING A SITE

The group begins by getting an overview of the site selection process. They discuss various issues of site selection and determine which are most important for them. Finding and selecting the right site is a time-consuming process. Many groups become discouraged at this point in the development, never locating an ideal site. In a tight market, remaining flexible is one of the essential criteria for selecting a site. Undeveloped sites or usable buildings do exist but are not necessarily on the market. Legwork and diligence are required to find these sites, locate the owners, and negotiate with them. A developer-con-

Renovation is a good alternative to new construction. An older apartment building in Slottet, Sweden, has been renovated into sixteen apartments with common rooms on the ground floor and basement.

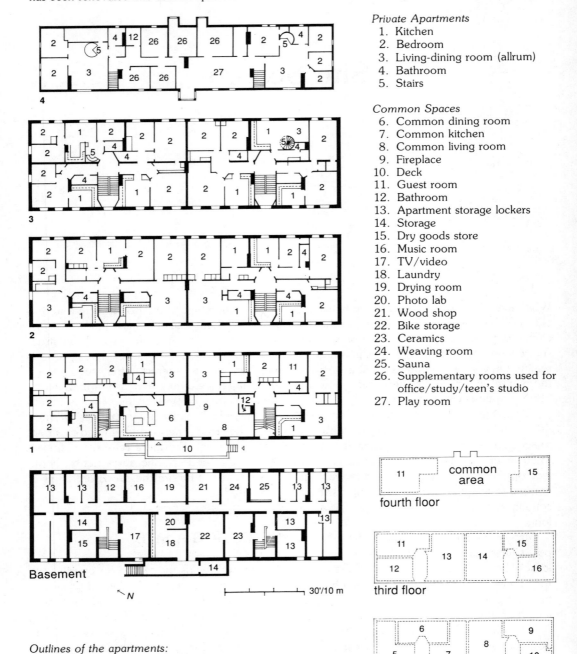

Private Apartments
1. Kitchen
2. Bedroom
3. Living-dining room (allrum)
4. Bathroom
5. Stairs

Common Spaces
6. Common dining room
7. Common kitchen
8. Common living room
9. Fireplace
10. Deck
11. Guest room
12. Bathroom
13. Apartment storage lockers
14. Storage
15. Dry goods store
16. Music room
17. TV/video
18. Laundry
19. Drying room
20. Photo lab
21. Wood shop
22. Bike storage
23. Ceramics
24. Weaving room
25. Sauna
26. Supplementary rooms used for office/study/teen's studio
27. Play room

Outlines of the apartments:

First floor: 1. Couple with two children; 2. elderly woman; 3. single woman; 4. single woman.

Second floor: 5. Couple with two children; 6. single man; 7. couple with teen; 8. single parent with one child; 9. couple; 10. single woman.

Third floor: 11. Couple with three teens; 12. single man; 13. couple; 14. single parent with two children; 15. couple with four children; 16. single man.

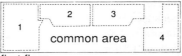

sultant or real-estate agents familiar with the area can be hired to work with the group on this task.

Groups should consider the advantages of renovating an existing building. In an urban area, a suitable building may be easier to locate than an undeveloped site, with the benefit of being in an established neighborhood within walking distance of shops and services. Renovation generally takes a shorter amount of time than new construction. The resulting units could cost less if they are completed within a year or two, instead of three or four. Collaborative communities have been established in renovated apartment buildings, factories, school buildings, and clusters of single family homes.

For groups determined to build a new community, teaming up with a developer is one way through a limited site market. Another possibility is to locate problem sites— for example, those with zoning difficulties, poor soil, or a high price—and try to negotiate some solution to the problem. Working with a nonprofit organization provides access to sites that might otherwise not be available for development.

Educating officials, nonprofit agencies, and influential special interest groups about collaborative living can also uncover site and building leads. Government or church land may be made available because of the interest that these groups might have in this kind of concept.

Some groups work out a formal process for finding and evaluating a site while others simply drive around hoping to find a piece of land. Rarely does everyone in the group find one site to be ideal. More often, some will be adamant about settling on a site, and others will feel that something better will come along soon.

"To help in a selection of a site, we set up criteria and specific steps," explained Dave Miller, of Miller/Hull architects. They are working with a group called Taproot that has had a difficult time searching for a suburban site near Seattle, Washington. They began by considering preliminary site selection criteria for their area that included the following:

Accessibility

Proximity and ease of access to public transportation and major traffic routes.
Proximity and ease of access for handicapped, pedestrians, bicycle traffic, and public schools.

Permits

Absence of zoning problems and adverse environmental impacts.
Absence of permit requirements.

Cost Considerations

Land acquisition.
Cost of site development and site preparation.

Quality Potential

Opportunity to provide on-site amenities.
Proximity to urban spaces, user services, and open space.

Environmental Impact

Air quality.
Proximity and impact of traffic noise and air traffic.

In a site selection workshop, each of these topics was discussed. Under the topic of *accessibility*, the group decided that there should be handicapped accessibility to the common house and some units. Under *quality potential*, there was interest in having a pond, swamp, or creek on the site.

The group took their multitude of desires and divided them into negotiable items, such as potential to expand, and nonnegotiable items such as specific transportation distances (in minutes both during rush hour and non-rush hour). Each of these items was to be ranked from 1 to 6 for each site.

Agreement was reached on the site criteria and then listed in a site selection manual. Also included was an evaluation checklist: preliminary costs for land acquisition, site development, site preparation, site access, permits, and resale value. A fourth part of the manual included general observations of the neighborhood—was there community diversity, accessibility to schools, and so on. Members take the manual to a potential site, and each member fills it out. The architects also fill out the criteria and help decide which site is best for the group.

The Winslow Group found their site on Bainbridge Island two weeks after their first meeting. The group had no formal criteria or selection process. A member recalls that "those who wanted to live in Winslow would drive around after the meetings." But member Chris Hanson, who found the site, had his own selection process, "I started by only looking at land zoned multifamily or commercial, knowing it would delay the process a substantial amount of time to rezone. So the first priority was to have it legal; the second, affordable; the third, available, and the fourth, centrally located between schools and transportation." The site was not on the market, but the sellers made it available because they liked the concept, asking for a $5000 nonrefundable deposit by May 1989.

Two factions formed within the group—those interested in the site in the town of Winslow on Bainbridge Island and those who wanted a more rural location. The original group of thirty to forty members dropped to eighteen when a nonrefundable $100 was requested, then to thirteen as more money was required to hold the site, then down to nine members when the site money became nonrefundable. Lynn Perkins recalls the ups and downs of their site acquisition:

People had reservations about the site. Some thought it was too small, some too dark, some too long a commute to work; some felt we were going too fast; some didn't like the group. Nine felt comfortable with each other and said, "Let's go for it!" We didn't know much about each other, but the land felt like home to me. You look people in the eye and think that they're not playing games and that they'll work to make it happen. Then came the time when the money would become nonrefundable. Each remaining member had to add more money to cover the amount taken out by those leaving.

Then we decided to obtain the adjacent site by purchasing someone else's option. People hesitated to join the group. It became an unknown situation about that land. Some who had left came back—there were sunnier areas on the land now, and the site was bigger. In those early days, the number of members was very flexible.

The other site did become available and the nine families committed a total of $35,000 (nonrefundable) toward the $578,000 purchase price for the two sites. By September, four more families had joined, and all thirteen brought their capital contribution up to 10 percent of estimated costs, an average of $100,000 per family. Six months later, the group, with twenty-six members, had raised $270,000 in capital contributions and paid off $200,000 for consultants, land, and "hundreds of dollars worth of copies." All thirty units had downpayments by summer 1990 although members continued to drop out and others join in.[1]

In contrast, the Muir Commons group in Davis agreed early on in the process to work with a developer who already had a site in hand. Although the site did not meet some of the members ideals, the advantages of having a site and working with a developer outweighed their other criteria. Members made no financial commitment to hold the site, although membership dues and fees for the design consultants were required. Shortly after construction began, members paid a fully refundable $1000 reservation deposit to the developer. A 3% deposit followed after the Department of Real Estate approval, with nothing more to the developer until moving in.

COST CONSIDERATIONS

The costs for obtaining a buildable site can be considerable. They include:

Preliminary Costs (Before Land Is Found)

Planning and design consultants
Financial consultant
Organizational costs (dues, photocopying, mailing)

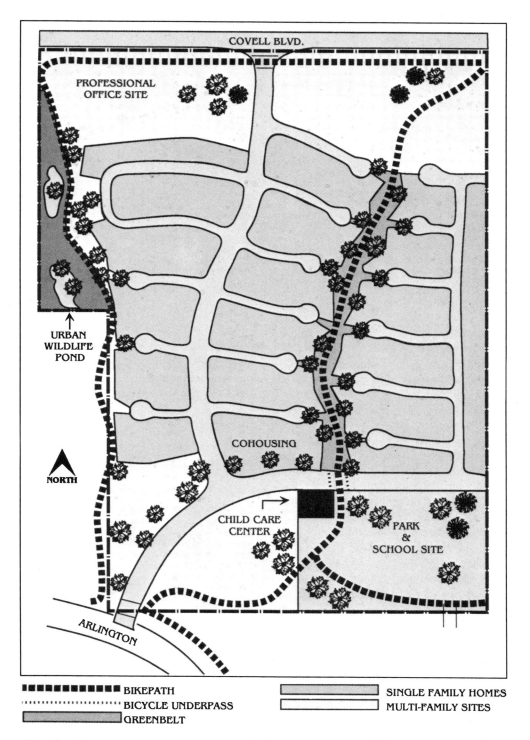

COVELL BLVD.

PROFESSIONAL
OFFICE SITE

URBAN
WILDLIFE
POND

NORTH

COHOUSING

CHILD CARE
CENTER

PARK
&
SCHOOL SITE

ARLINGTON

▰▰▰▰▰▰▰▰▰▰ BIKEPATH
∙∙∙∙∙∙∙∙∙∙∙∙∙∙∙∙∙∙∙∙∙ BICYCLE UNDERPASS
▭▭▭▭ GREENBELT

▭▭▭▭ SINGLE FAMILY HOMES
▭▭▭▭ MULTI-FAMILY SITES

The Muir Commons group teamed up with the developers of a new 110-acre community. The developers set aside a 3-acre lot for affordable cohousing that helped convince the city council to issue a building permit for the entire development. The group, in turn, was able to secure a buildable lot with no money down. *(West Davis Associates)*

Costs to Option a Site

Capital to hold option
Surveying
Various site tests (soil and toxic reports, environmental inspections)
Technical assistance (developer manager, architect, lawyer)

Site Acquisition

Capital to purchase site
Fees to realtor and title company
Maintenance of the site
Planning approval fees
Unexpected costs (special permits, preparation for public hearings)

Group members need to be prepared to put up $2,000-$10,000 per household to hold a site for any length of time. The money can be nonrefundable if the group does not follow through on its commitment to buy the site. Groups working with a developer (or nonprofit developer) may not be required to make a large financial deposit to acquire a site.

Before members commit large sums of money, a number of items need to have been worked out: membership agreements and a statement of goals, a legal agreement, an estimate of total final costs, and prequalification by the bank (determining the amount of mortgage loan a member can receive).

Members require time and trust among each other to commit large amounts of money. Legal agreements and guarantees cannot replace a certain feeling of comfort that evolves among group members.

DEVELOPMENT REQUIREMENTS

Before investing, an investigation of the site is necessary. The site may have obvious restrictions, such as steep slopes, or hidden problems that need testing or analysis. The following items must be considered in selecting a site:

The General Plan
Zoning

Environmental restrictions
Building moratoriums
Difficult neighbors
Difficult access
Site restrictions of funding source
Sliding area
Fault zone
Flooding area
Toxic chemicals
Poor soil

When a potential site is located, it needs a preliminary evaluation. If the site becomes the group's first choice, feasibility studies are often necessary to determine its suitability. Development costs are analyzed, soil and engineering reports are obtained, and the number of possible units is determined.

Site problems can be very costly to fix. A steep slope, for example, can add 20% to the construction costs. The Vashon group in Washington State purchased land with surface water and later had to work with the local wetlands law concerning development. Investigating the site thoroughly will decrease the risk of spending more money later.

General Plan and Zoning Issues

The General Plan sets into law how a town should conserve its resources and develop its potentials. This law determines where growth can occur and sets policies regarding transportation, housing, commerce, open space and all aspects of how land will be used.

Zoning is the tool for implementing a General Plan by defining the uses for designated parcels of land. The zoning has implications on the development plans and designs of buildings, including restrictions on building heights and density. Zoning often places limits on "mixed occupancy," such as combining living areas with work spaces or a childcare center.

Mid-size cities generally have approximately forty use district designations that are variations of residential, commercial, and industrial districts. Only in multifamily and in most mixed-use districts will collaborative housing be permissable.

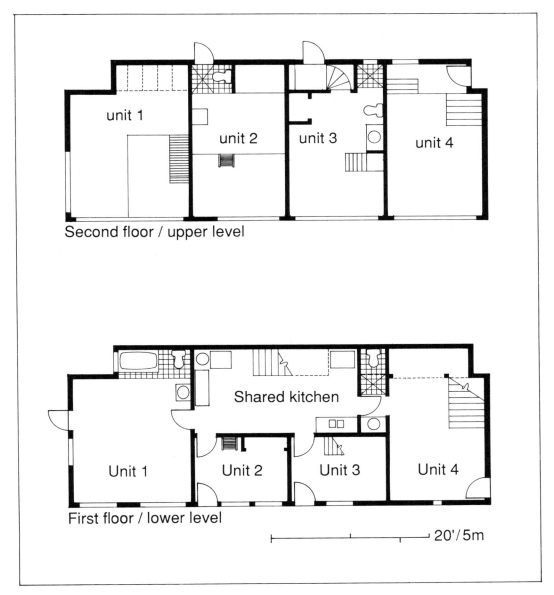

unit 1
unit 2
unit 3
unit 4

Second floor / upper level

Shared kitchen

Unit 1
Unit 2
Unit 3
Unit 4

First floor / lower level

20'/5m

Four large studios with private bathrooms but only one, shared, kitchen allow four households to live in a neighborhood zoned for single-family use. *(Smith & Others Architects)*

Usually, the maximum number of units allowed on a site is determined by counting the number of kitchens. (Originally a house in a single family residential neighborhood had to have only one family.[2]) If five families designed a house where each family had several bedrooms, a bathroom, and a living room, but only used one kitchen together, such a house could be considered a single-family home. But should the families desire to have five separate kitchens in addition to one they shared, the zoning law for a single family neighborhood would prohibit this type of use.

There is no separate designation where cohousing would comply. Although the multi-family district is seen as the place for such developments, other districts, such as garden apartments or two-family residential, may be approved with rezoning or a special-use permit. Exactly where certain types of collaborative housing arrangements can be built is a matter of how the residential zoning categories are interpreted.

Exceptions to the General Plan require a hearing before the city council. Advocates of collaborative housing can approach municipalities in the process of reviewing their General Plan and have them promote it as an appropriate housing alternative that addresses needs not met by conventional single-family houses and apartments. A statement in the General Plan to not discriminate against developments that combine housing with the availability of services, the provision of meals, childcare, and common facilities will help future approval for collaborative developments less difficult to obtain.

In Washington, the CoHo group purchased their 28-acre site knowing that the zoning would need to be changed and approval obtained from the water district for twenty houses, a one- to two-year process. They agreed to take the risk that approval may not be granted and they would have to sell their land. "Hope springs eternal when you're working with bureaucracies," said member Deb Sweet.

With the increased interest in collaborative communities, groups will have to advocate General Plan policies that will support their search for buildable sites.

NOTES

1. For example, from May to October 1990 six families withdrew. Money was the biggest reason, although job commitments and time constraints were also mentioned. The group's original goal of $100 per square foot for the project was at that time estimated 15 percent higher.

2. The concept of family had been held to mean those people related by blood or marriage, but a series of court decisions have stretched the definition to that of a housekeeping unit. This definition has brought many attempts to include roomers, dormitories, and other large-group usage not originally intended by the zoning law. Sometimes an interpretation on the kind of management helps define a household. Boarder and roomer situations, which are not collectively managed, cannot be located in a single-family district, but collective households are allowed since they are collectively managed. Occasionally the courts have allowed the definition of family to permit groups as large as sixty people to live together in a single-family district, although commonly the cases involve organizations geared to the religious or general welfare.

CHAPTER 14

Financing and Ownership Options

When you put down real money that would hurt to lose, you become invested in the process. A dramatic shift occurs—suddenly the group has a life.

Chris Hanson, developer-consultant

Financing has become the critical problem in the production of collaborative housing in the United States. The local government is conspicuously absent in the development of most of the U.S. examples, unlike European models. Lack of government support has required communities to rely on their members' resources through membership fees and money for predevelopment costs. Initially members find themselves shouldering a number of costs without any guarantee of moving in, a very different role from walking through a house and making a down payment.

Members need to understand the various types of financing and the kinds of ownership (tenure) connected to them. They find themselves asking whether a cooperative or condominium makes more sense, and the hunt is on for mortgage financing. The group most likely begins their financial and ownership re-search in confusion and often ends with several members becoming experts.

MEMBERSHIP FEES

Financial commitment to a development occurs in steps. First comes a small membership fee for photocopying and mailings. The next step is a larger nonrefundable fee of perhaps $100–$200 to hire a consultant. Most groups set a monthly fee, usually below $100, which pays for consultants and site analysis. When a site is located, a substantial amount of money for development is required.

A change in membership, as well as in commitment, occurs when money is requested from the group. Those less committed drop out as the amount of money required to maintain membership increases. In some groups where the initial financing comes not from members but from the developer or nonprofit organization, the amount of time members spend at meetings or on tasks becomes significant.

Graduated payments are an effective way of increasing members' commitment. Requesting small sums each month from members and then suddenly a four- or five-figure sum for optioning a site is a more difficult method.

MONEY FOR DEVELOPMENT

Money for development is usually three phased. An initial amount of money is required for predevelopment financing, covering the costs of optioning and surveying a site, preliminary design plans, and possibly hiring a development consultant. The predevelopment financing lays the groundwork for the housing development and helps secure the permanent financing. These preliminary costs are often financed by the members.

The second phase of financing is obtaining the construction loan, which is paid back from the housing sales or mortgage loan when the building is occupied. Lenders expect borrowers to provide some form of equity to become eligible for loans, usually in the form of a down payment between 10% and 25% of the project cost.

The third phase is the mortgage loan. Typically home buyers deal only with this kind of financing. The mortgage lender can be the same or a different source than for the construction loan. A mortgage loan must be committed before a lending source will be inclined to give a construction loan.

Depending on the loan source, the first step in getting financing is to determine the income levels of group members. Bank and real estate agents can provide appropriate prequalifying services and forms. The forms request income information and provide a quick means of determining the amount of loan each member could receive. The maximum mortgage debt service payment, insurance, and property tax equals about 30–33% of household income.

FINANCING OPTIONS

The housing can be financed by the group through individual or blanket loans. A group that cannot qualify for a loan can research other financing possibilities or team up with a nonprofit housing association to obtain federal, state, and city funds (United Way of America). This latter kind of funding typically has various restrictions and regulations.

Entirely Member Financed

Two basic types of loans are available to members: an individual mortgage or a blanket mortgage. The advantages and disadvantages of each type alter with the location, availability, and preference of the members. Individual states may have their own interpretations and requirements for these loans and should be researched.

Blanket mortgages usually provide more affordable housing and allow restrictions on purchasing a unit. Individual mortgages are usually preferred by banks, but resale restrictions are harder to include. Restrictions that do not deal with the purchase price or buyer income are difficult to include under either type of financing.

Individual Mortgage

This is the typical loan for condominium ownership.

Affordability.   This is the traditional mortgage that people obtain for their home, with each household qualifying on its own merits. The responsibility for obtaining the loan is left to the individual, with the option to shop around and find the lowest available interest rate (and lower monthly payments). This is a common type of home ownership, and many lending institutions offer competitive rates. There may also be public programs to help first-time home buyers, such as those from the Federal Housing Administration (FHA). Should interest rates go down after the mortgage is secured, refinancing is not difficult, although there may be a prepayment penalty. Equity sharing may be arranged where investors aid members with down payments.

One of the biggest drawbacks is that individuals who do not qualify do not receive a loan.

Closing costs are on an individual basis, requiring each household to pay separate escrow fees and insurance. Real estate taxes are high because units are assessed as individual homes.

Group Cohesion. The bank, not the group, deals with evictions for delinquent payments. Payment problems by some members will usually not put the entire community at risk (although collecting such member's home owner association fees to operate the building might be difficult).

On the negative side, the community may become less affordable as house prices appreciate. Without additional resale controls, original members who move will require more affluent buyers who can afford the higher monthly payments.

There are some methods to restrict the resale price or to place some conditions of cooperation under individual ownership.[1] Rules drafted by the group to control acceptable buyers or have first right of refusal can be signed, but they must be carefully prepared to hold up in a court of law. Units can be rented indefinitely.

Resale. Resale value may be at market price. (Restrictions may be used with some financing sources.) One of the drawbacks is that the individual household may be responsible for selling the unit, and if a buyer cannot be found, the individual takes a loss in price. (The condominium association could have a first option to purchase and maintain a waiting list of potential members.) If there are resale difficulties and some residents do not keep up their units, everyone can be in trouble.

Blanket Mortgage

This type of mortgage is typical for housing cooperatives, general partnerships, and rental developments.

Affordability. This mortgage covers the whole project. Instead of an individual member's qualifying on his or her income, the project or the group as a whole must qualify. Members who otherwise would not qualify may get in because of the higher income levels of other members. Closing costs are lower because of the need for only one survey and title insurance. Government subsidies may be available, lowering payments. In addition a forty-year amortization schedule, or longer, can be obtained in some situations, and improvements and expansions may be financed through another blanket mortgage. Because the units are not individually owned, the property taxes may be lower. Real estate taxes are lower because they are pro-rated and considered part of a multiunit rental property (not always true for cooperatives).

A drawback is that some lenders, particularly in the West, are not familiar with blanket mortgages. Buyers may find few lending institutions, which may mean a higher rate of interest.

Group Cohesion. Members with low incomes may not have to drop out of the group, and the group might attract members with a wider range of incomes. The drawback is that by taking the qualifications of the group as a whole, the lender places the risk of nonpaying members on the group's shoulders. When a member cannot pay the rent, the other members are responsible. They must cover the rent out of the reserves or eventually evict the person, a situation that can be divisive for the community.

Resale. In stock cooperatives, the transfer value does increase, allowing market-rate prices. A new member must pay his or her share of the blanket mortgage. Due to appreciation, an additional second mortgage, called a share loan, may be required. The assumable first mortgage would be attractive to buyers if interest rates rise, although new buyers would need to obtain two loans.[2]

In limited-equity housing cooperatives the transfer value is restricted. New members can buy a share at an affordable price, but the selling member does not receive a large return.

Other Financing Options

Collaborative housing is not less expensive to build than other kinds of housing. The material and labor costs remain the same whether the housing is developed as a community or for individuals. But by working together as a group, there are possibilities of lowering the costs in some instances. Smaller units clustered together save material costs, as well as road and sewer costs, but these savings may be spent for common facilities, common pedestrian paths, and landscaping. By acting as a developer, the group may save money, but the developer's profit is often offset by operating inefficiencies and compromised decisions from lack of experience or negotiating strength. Buying land together does reduce costs, and in rural areas there has been a substantial savings. In more urban areas, the high demand for buildable sites has made the savings less substantial. Residents who complete parts of the construction work themselves often used the savings to purchase extras rather than substantially lower their unit price. There is a potential for cost savings in these communities, but cohousing communities in Europe financed by individuals have not been substantially cheaper than comparable, slightly larger, traditional housing.

The majority of collaborative dwellings in Europe have lower monthly payments because they are financed, in part or whole, by the government. U.S. groups do not have this option available as easily as Europeans in Denmark, Holland, and Sweden. Nevertheless, there may be limited government grants, loans, and subsidies available for people who cannot obtain their own financing through a blanket or individual mortgage:

Department of Housing and Urban Development: HUD is a source of grants and technical assistance.[3] Aside from senior citizen, handicapped, and rehabilitation programs, it provides loan guarantees instead of direct loans. Rental subsidy programs, FHA insurance programs, and multifamily rental housing are some of the programs available for housing with shared aspects. HUD provides loans for certain limited projects.

Federal Housing Administration: The FHA is a mortgage enhancer. By insuring the lender, the FHA assumes the risk, and projects that ordinarily would be turned down by the lender may get a loan. If there is a default or a foreclosure on the project's mortgage loans, the FHA bails out the lender, not the borrower. It ensures loans for rental housing development, as well as some condominiums and limited-equity cooperatives. The FHA is a division of HUD that insures but does not lend.

Community Development Block Grant: CDBG, a division of HUD, provides funding for a range of community development activities. Priority is given to programs that will benefit low- and moderate-income families.

Federal Home Loan Bank: This agency of the federal government encourages institutions it regulates to meet community credit needs.

Farmers Home Administration Loan Program: Rural housing development can receive subsidies from the FmHA for affordable housing. The direct loan program is for rentals, and there is also a farm workers' housing program. Both programs require all members to be within a certain income range.

National Cooperative Bank: This bank was created to provide financing and technical assistance to cooperatives of all kinds.

Consortiums: A number of lenders operate together under the Community Reinvestment Act (CRA). Lending institutions pool their money through a corporation for loans to the community. By pooling, they reduce their risk and receive community reinvestment credit.

Public and Private Foundations: There are about 25,000 foundations with assets of over $5 billion. Unfortunately, most do not fund land acquisition or construction. They do fund nonprofit organizations interested in promoting affordable housing, they provide seed money for innovative projects, and they fund predevelopment costs.

Convincing public officials hinges on the proposed collaborative housing's making a contribution to the community by meeting a special need and that without public money, the project could not be developed.[4]

TYPES OF OWNERSHIP

No other single decision has as many consequences as choosing the type of ownership for the housing. Equity and financing are closely connected to the type of ownership, but there are many other important issues—affordability, resale and refinancing, liability, development timing, and membership selection. Although one kind of ownership may be appealing from an equity or financing viewpoint, it may have time or refinancing limitations well worth considering. (A comparison of ownership types is found in Appendix B.)

Here we examine some common options. Often the amount of financing that members can obtain and state laws narrow the choice. A discussion among members on limiting resale value will narrow the options too. Researching the remaining options, listening to housing experts, and discussing the pros and cons will help in making the final selection.

Individual Ownership

Individual home ownership is the traditional way of owning a house. Each household individually owns its own home and the land it is on. The dwelling may be sold at market or restricted values. The common legal phrase is *fee-simple estate.*

Common-Interest Ownership

Condominiums: The household owns the dwelling that it occupies plus an undivided share in the common areas, including the land. Residents govern themselves through a homeowners' association and secure individual mortgages.

Planned unit development (PUD): This is a form of condominium where each household owns the land under the building. Common areas, including common land, are owned jointly.

Stock cooperatives: Households form or join a corporation that owns the housing and common areas. The households purchase a share of stock in the corporation and through a lease receive the right to occupy a unit. The share is transferable with the co-op board approval and may be sold at market or restricted value. Households secure an individual or blanket mortgage.

Limited-equity housing cooperatives: These are similar to stock cooperatives except that restrictions must be placed on selling the transfer right. The units cannot be sold at market value but only for the amount of the original share (down payment) plus a maximum increase of 10% a year (Kirkpatrick, Rural Community Assistance Corp.). A blanket mortgage is used here.

Leasing cooperatives: Households join a cooperative corporation that leases the housing from an organization (usually a limited partnership). Generally, the transfer share cannot appreciate. The mortgage is held by the partnership; the co-op holds only a master lease.

Nonprofit Ownership

Nonprofit corporation with management agreement to the tenant association: The residents form a tenant association that signs a management agreement with the nonprofit owner. The management agreement can give the residents some management responsibility, such as choosing new residents and overseeing maintenance. A gradual transition to full ownership for residents is also a possibility.

Nonprofit corporation with lease to the tenant association: The residents form a tenant association that leases the housing from a

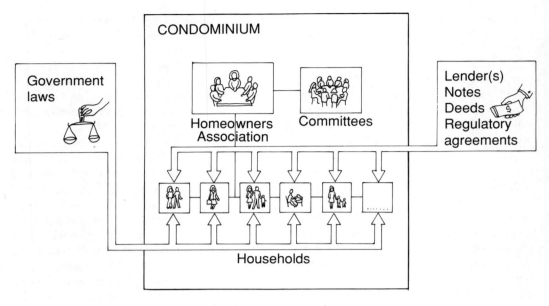

Condominium ownership.

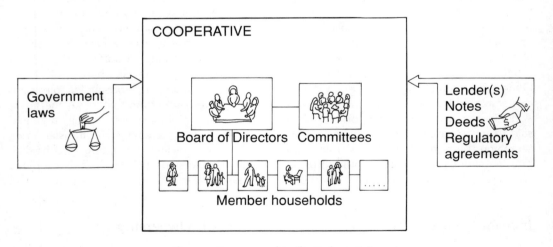

Cooperative ownership (limited equity).

nonprofit owner. The residents can negotiate some management responsibilities, although the nonprofit corporation can regain control of the development quickly if management performance or membership falls below expected levels.

Mutual housing association: Two different kinds of MHAs exist in the United States. One form, popular in Europe, is an association of housing cooperatives. The MHA allows smaller organizations to band together to provide greater services and protection to residents than each could alone. This type of MHA provides both ownership rights and stock in a corporation. Another type of MHA, seen in some student co-ops, takes the form of a rental. Ownership rights are restricted through the lease. This type of MHA does not provide ownership rights and stock in a corporation.

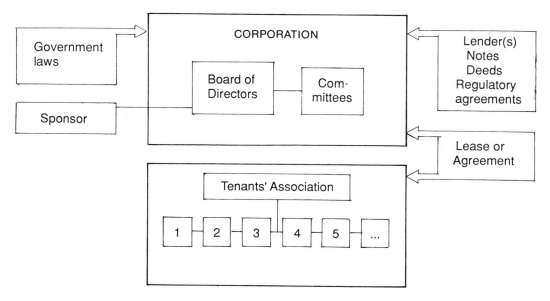

Nonprofit corporation with lease agreement to a tenant association.

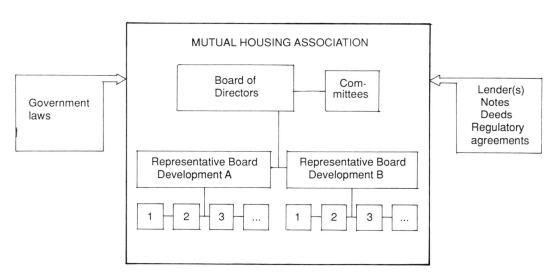

Mutual housing association.

Partnership Ownership

General partnership: The interest is in the partnership, not in the real estate. There is no liability limit, and partners can be held liable for the debts of all other partners.

Tenants in common (a form of general partnership): Tenants have an undivided interest (share) in the real estate. A tenant who leaves can sell at market value. If the tenant cannot receive what he or she feels is a fair price, there is the possibility of forced petition where that tenant can insist on auctioning the property.

Limited partnership: While a limited partner also has limited liability, he or she cannot

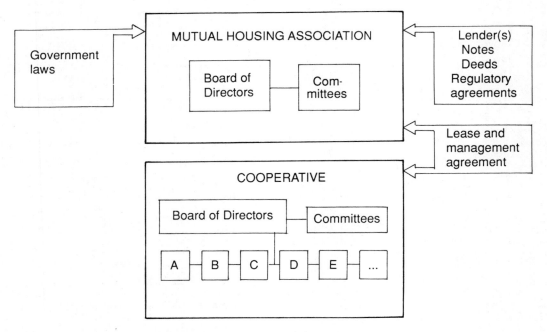

Mutual housing association with lease to cooperative.

participate in the operation of the partnership and does not make decisions If members do participate, they no longer have limited liability.

Partnership with lease to cooperative: A nonprofit organization can become the managing general partner. The residents form either a cooperative or a tenant association and receive a lease from the partnership.

Others

Community land trust: A nonprofit organization holds (owns) the land for the community. Individuals or a cooperative are usually given long-term leases to use the land. The leaseholders own and can sell the homes, and all improvements on the property are subject to the land lease terms. The land trust owns the land; occupants own the improvements.

Rentals: The household has no ownership interest. The rental owner may sell the property at the market value.

A Note on Conversions

The community can be under one kind of ownership and then later be transferred to another kind of ownership. For example, the housing may be developed as rentals and eventually converted to condominiums or a cooperative. The advantages of conversions are that rental developments are easily financed and approved. After a few years, they can be converted, and many of the problems associated with the development of other types of ownership can be postponed or even avoided.

Mixing Tenures

At first glance, it would seem that the ownership form should be an individual decision. If Joe has X amount of dollars, he would pick one kind of ownership, and if Linda has XXX amount of dollars, she could pick another. People often wonder why they cannot have eight units of rental or cooperative ownership

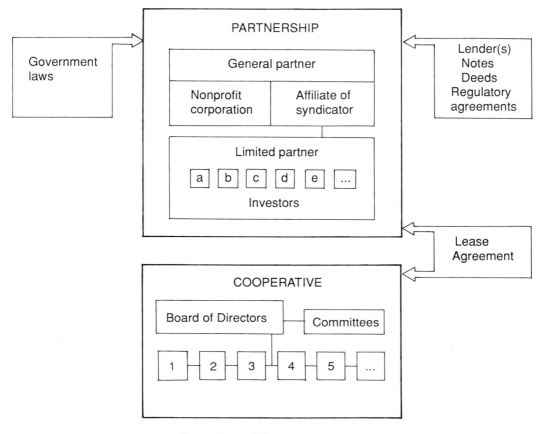

Partnership with lease to cooperative.

and eight units of condominium ownership in one housing development. Legally and financially, such a combination would be complicated.

In the United States, housing developments have not emphasized a mix of incomes. Developments that have below-market-rate financing may encourage an income mix. The Reservoir in Madison mixes low, median, and market-rate residents under the same cooperative ownership. There are few precedents for mixing incomes under different ownerships, but possibilities are enticing. Cooperatives with limited equity and nonprofit rental developments often lack money for extensive amenities, but they do have the benefits of public and government support.

Condominiums have the financial backing for a variety of amenities, but in some places building permits necessary for development are few and restrictions many. A development that combined the two owner structures could reduce the disadvantages of each.

The fear is that in mixing ownerships, the group with less equity invested, such as renters or cooperators, will not be as dedicated, as responsible, or as stable as the owners.[5] The evidence proving this assumption is difficult to find. Looking at traditional condominium ownership for clues may be misleading, for condominium owners are often most uncooperative with each other. Many condo owners rent out their units, and renters have no voting privileges. This is a common problem, and some condominiums operate like rental developments, with more renters than owners. In this respect, perhaps it is not surprising that renters tend to be less interested in and responsible concerning maintenance and management.

Collaboration is assumed to instill a greater desire in people to participate in their community, no matter the ownership type. Nevertheless, some members of collaborative communities, such as in Sunlight, Oregon, have stated their disappointment with the participation of renters. Certain renter groups, such as students and young singles, were felt to be less stable than older renters. The N Street community has gone a step further and helped renters to invest in a home with the hope that they will be more motivated toward working with the community.[6]

Like condominium owners, individuals living in limited-equity cooperatives have, on the whole, demonstrated a disappointing amount of common interest. Looking at these two ownership types gives no clue that members have a greater interest in working together than, say, individual home owners. In many instances, they had less interest (Silverman). At this point there is not a clear answer on how well members under rental, co-op, and condominium ownership collaborate.

If we look at the European examples for clues, there appear to be many different answers. In Denmark, one community contains half condominium owners and half renters (Drejerbanken), and two combine condominiums with limited-equity housing co-ops (Andedammen and Tovstrup Mark). Nevertheless, it is difficult to draw conclusions from these few projects out of the over one hundred built in Denmark.

The Dutch have five projects that mix owners and renters. None of them was planned that way from the beginning, but special funding circumstances required mixing forms. Since the projects were not conceived as different ownerships from the start, agreements were not worked out to the best advantages. In hindsight, the Dutch Collaborative Housing Association has developed the following suggestions (Van Rooijen and Veldkamp):

- Consider the project from the beginning as one whole, with separate dwellings as "apartments" of one building.
- Ensure that all members donate a percentage of their space to the construction of the common spaces and are legally bound to pay for their maintenance.
- In voting, both types of residents should be equally represented.
- Find a way to limit the privileges of home owners, perhaps by tying equity to an index value.
- Draw up a legal document that describes common maintenance, a reserve fund, how residents are selected, and how the dwelling's selling price is determined.
- Help renters move into ownership as their income rises. When an owner leaves, the renter can purchase the home for the index value amount and enjoy the benefits of home ownership.

The answer to whether these suggestions can be translated into the American system of ownership awaits an innovative group.

NOTES

1. For example, second trust deeds have been recorded against the fee title, with a provision that selling above a certain price and/or buyer income will require the second deed to be paid. These restrictive seconds can be used with condominiums, planned unit developments, and single-family residences.
2. Share loans for blanket mortgages may be available through the Federal National Mortgage Association (aka, Fannie Mae), the Federal Home Loan Mortgage Corporation (aka, Freddie Mac), and the National Cooperative Bank (Marcus). Share loans do not apply to limited-equity housing cooperatives.
3. U.S. Department of Housing and Urban Development, *Programs of HUD* (Washington D.C.: Government Printing Office, 1990), lists programs available through HUD for affordable housing.
4. There may be programs that are not focused on an established group. Usually consultants working with community groups or developers approach the government. Residents are chosen during construction or after the housing units are built and an association es-

tablished. A group would need to show that the services being provided are of public benefit.

5. Some of these beliefs are confirmed by statistics. A majority of American households (63.5%) are home owners, and in one year 8.3% of them moved. Renters make up 36.5% of households, and in the same year 37.7% moved. (Statistics are for 1985. U.S. Bureau of the Census *American Housing Survey Series HI-50,* December 1988).

6. Renter turnover is lower if the unit is considered a good deal. In California, for example, about 30% of renters stay less than one year, but for cities with rent control, that figure is much lower. The California Apartment Association commissioned the study of tenant turnover from the California State University at Sacramento.

REFERENCES

Van Rooijen, Herman, and Freerk Veldkamp. 1989. *Centraal Wonen in beeld deel 2.* Utrecht, The Netherlands: Landelijke Vereniging Centraal Wonen.

Kirkpatrick, David H. *Legal Issues in the Development of Housing Cooperatives.* Berkeley: National Economic Development and Law Center

Marcus, Beth. 1985. "Yours, Mine and Ours." *Mortgage Banking Magazine,* July.

Rural Community Assistance Corp. 1981. *Guidebook to Cooperative Adventures.* Sacramento: RCAC.

Silverman, Carol J., and Stephen E. Barton. 1986. "Private Property and Private Government: Tensions between Individualism and Community in Condominiums." Working Paper 451 (December). Berkeley: Institute of Urban and Regional Development, University of California.

United Way of America and Community Information Exchange. 1988. *Raising the Roof: A Sampler of Community Partnerships for Affordable Housing.* Alexandria, Va.: United Way of America.

CHAPTER 15

Design

Intrinsic to this type of design is one significant problem—how to balance the needs and ambitions of the group with the needs and ambitions of individuals.

Ed Weinstein, cohousing architect

The design needs to be divided into small pieces like a jigsaw puzzle—each piece of the design is discussed, arranged, and then reassembled to form a whole design. The task can be difficult and frustrating at times, especially when members hold different opinions that push and pull the pieces into changing shapes. But the process can be exhilarating and exciting because a group-driven design program implies a shift in power, the ability to shape one's own view.

Members begin by discussing the dimensions of the community. The size and density of the development will affect the social interaction among the residents. The number of common areas will affect day-to-day activities. Elements of the site plan, the common house, and the private dwellings are considered: Where do members park? How are common meals served? What kind of windows in each unit?

The design is not a linear process using one proven method. The size of private yards is interconnected with the amount of open space, and reaching a group consensus quickly on such issues cannot be assured.

After numerous hours of discussion, a program of the design decisions is agreed upon by all the members. The architect produces design sketches based on the program, and these are further refined with members in meetings and workshops. After the design drawings are approved, the architect can produce working drawings for construction.

DESIGN STRATEGIES

There is not one proven method to explain what is possible to build and how the common areas and housing work together. The Danes, having a large number of successful examples nearby, can start with field trips. The Dutch are more conceptual, and might begin with an inventory of individual and common activities. In European and American developments, the design process has varied according to the architect's style and pace.

What are effective design strategies? Some architects use few visual images and instead encourage their group to define the relation-

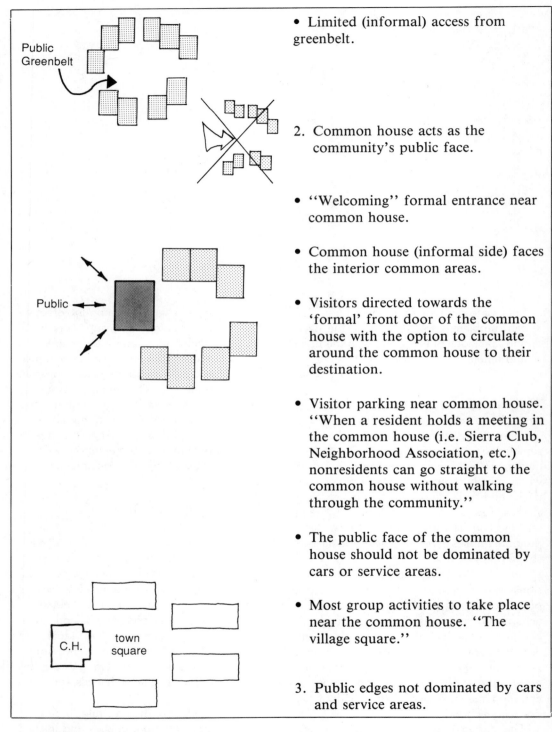

- Limited (informal) access from greenbelt.

2. Common house acts as the community's public face.

- "Welcoming" formal entrance near common house.

- Common house (informal side) faces the interior common areas.

- Visitors directed towards the 'formal' front door of the common house with the option to circulate around the common house to their destination.

- Visitor parking near common house. "When a resident holds a meeting in the common house (i.e. Sierra Club, Neighborhood Association, etc.) nonresidents can go straight to the common house without walking through the community."

- The public face of the common house should not be dominated by cars or service areas.

- Most group activities to take place near the common house. "The village square."

3. Public edges not dominated by cars and service areas.

A page from the design program of Muir Commons, Davis, California, outlining the design concepts. *(Muir Commons with design consultants McCamant and Durrett [redrawn])*

ship of spaces and functions. For example, the Muir Commons design consultants found that the members agreed faster on general concepts than on specific designs. From general principles comes the activities that will occur, and from there an understanding of a place might emerge. Members come up with many conceptual statements—for example, about the garden or the common house—that the architect interprets into a plan. The advantage of this method is that it can result in a clear program; the disadvantage can be that the program remains abstract, allowing a multitude of design solutions.

While this first method explains concepts, another method uses a visual approach, the group is educated through slide shows and tours of places. The Danish architects, Arkitektgruppen in Arhus, began working with a group by first educating the members in architectural elements. Slides from around the world were used to illustrate elements such as a covered street, a tower, and so on. Then the images were sorted out and discussed with the group. A consensus was reached about one kind of element. The architects presented alternative sketches, and one was refined to everyone's satisfaction. The advantage of such a visual method is that the members' limited palette of images is broadened; the disadvantage is that too many images are confusing and that the courtyard or the tile work in the bathroom will, in all probability, not look the same as the image from the Alhambra in Spain.

A third approach emphasizes the designation of functions on a site plan, with areas zoned for private, semiprivate, and common use. The various elements of the plan are placed in the appropriate zones: the housing in the private zone, common spaces along the common zone. This method has been used on the design of multistory housing to create an overall coherent plan. Often in this method a number of elements have already been determined, such as the facade openings and the building structure. This ordered system has the advantage of being easily tied to a budget, and the overall structure can be completed prior to knowing exactly how each infill space will function (Carp, Lukez). The disadvantage can be that limiting the possible choices at the start also limits members search for creative solutions (Krabbendam).

A fourth approach emphasizes questionnaires that are given to members to elicit responses for design issues and details. Questionnaires work best when specific, detailed questions are asked based on previous discussions. The advantage is that results can be tallied quickly and show areas of agreement or disagreement and the range of possible solutions. The disadvantage is that questionnaires narrow the discussion and do not easily address trade-offs, as a question concerning the size and shape of a backyard might not, for example, include the possibility of reducing yards in favor of a play field.

Architects have used models to provide a three-dimensional image of the design that can be viewed from different angles and manipulated. Many people have difficulty imagining a two-dimensional plan and feel more comfortable designing "hands-on" with a model (although they are often found to be too costly and time consuming to construct). A model of the common house is especially useful for understanding the sequence of rooms and limitations of size. Full-scale mock-ups of the finished design allow residents to walk through rooms and try out the kitchen before the project is built.

In Handværkerparken rental cohousing in Denmark, a group of sixteen future residents worked with the architects through the planning and then put together mock-ups at the Full Scale Environmental Design Simulation Laboratory in Copenhagen (Kjaer). In Holland, members of the Delft collaborative community simulated their cluster rooms and kitchens, moving lightweight blocks to create walls and openings. The full-scale mock-ups saved a great deal of discussion time and led to a more efficient design.

These are all good methods for a design process. In truth, a combination of all these methods should be considered. "The trick is to find out what works best with the people

COHO-COMMON HOUSE WORKBOOK
16 February 1990
Page - 21 -

I.   **ENTRY**

    A.   The entrance to the Common House (is, is not necessarily) a place of significant public interaction and display. I would like to have the following as part of this space (circle choices)

        1.   seating
        2.   coat and foul weather gear storage
        3.   mail boxes
        4.   bulletin/message boards
        5.   other (please explain)

    B.   It is necessary for the entrance to be sheltered from the elements but, not necessarily inside and heated. Yes   No

    C.   Once in the entry, I want the following spaces to be close by: (circle choices)

        1.   dining
        2.   lounge
        3.   kitchen
        4.   bathrooms
        5.   crafts room
        6.   exercise room
        7.   office
        8.   other (please explain)

II.   **DINING ROOM**

    A.   The dining room (will, will not) be the primary space in the Common House and, therefore have a feeling of (circle one)

        1.   loftiness and grandeur
        2.   coziness and intimacy

A page from the Common House Workbook of the Coho group, Seattle. *(Coho Group & Bassetti Architects)*

involved and to switch to another method when the group becomes stuck," believes a Danish architect.

ACHIEVING CONSENSUS

Reaching a consensus on the design can be a challenge when twenty, thirty, or more people are involved. "It's not easy to be a person who wants to build a house in this way, nor is it easy to be the architect and design it. Each family has its dream house, and in a way we all must come up with thirty-six answers," said Berit Ziebell of Æblevangen cohousing in Denmark.

In practice it is challenging and time-consuming to complete the design of a collaborative housing scheme. What helps make the process smoother? First, the group needs a clear idea of what they want. Second, a design team familiar with collaborative housing and working with groups needs to be chosen. Third, the group needs to see that regular progress is made. Fourth, and equally important, the group needs to confront actual constraints of budget and time schedules to not "build dream castles in the sky," as one participant described it.

Get a Clear Idea of What the Group Wants

The Muir Commons group was shown several different site plans by their architect. Group member Juli Ingels sees the group's lack of clarity as one reason they could not reach consensus: "His assistant would make drawings and we would pick them apart at meetings. All we could say was, 'that doesn't look exactly like what we had in mind' or 'the paths aren't shaped exactly right.' It was hard for him to fix it without knowing exactly what we had in mind."

A written design program helps the group decide on specific elements of their community and gives the architect a document that forms the basis of the design sketches. Elements in the design program include open space, gardens, and location of common facilities and housing (Appendix C).

The different design techniques, from discussions to questionnaires, help to clarify the community envisioned by members. The Muir Commons group hired design consultants to help them with their programming, and they used a conceptual technique to reach consensus. Group member Brian Dempsey remembers:

We didn't look at visual images. We talked about feelings divorced from sight. For example, we would talk about these kinds of feelings: "I can talk to people as they come by" or "I want a front courtyard." If you design your own house, you can use your personal vision and images. But when you work with thirty people, you have to put it all away. Otherwise you have no idea how many side tracks you can take. Thirty different ideas. We would write everything without pictures. The hard part is consensing [sic]. Chuck and Katie [the designers] could get everyone to agree on something.

Coho group members found they had a number of conflicting ideas on a plan for their large site: Some members wanted to save all the existing trees, some were very interested in views, some wanted to live in clearings and others in the woods. Ideas differed on how spread out the housing should be, and on the number of units built together.

The architects began by sending each household a lengthy questionnaire asking detailed questions about their image of living in the community, such as the distance people were willing to walk from their car to their dwelling. The design team tallied the responses and discussed where there was consensus and near consensus, and which areas had wide gaps in perspective. The architects set up a series of five all-day workshops over several months to focus on one aspect of the design: programming, site, individual houses, common house, and a final summarizing workshop. The first workshop, programming, took members' wish lists from the questionnaire, prioritized them, and translated them into square footages.

"As much work goes into planning and organizing as into the workshop itself. The workshops are designed to meet consensus," said the architect. Group techniques are used, such as brainstorming and dividing into small groups to reach agreement.

The Muir Commons group also held design workshops. They began their common house workshop by stretching large sheets of butcher paper across the wall. Members brainstormed about the kind of spaces they would like. As each of the fifteen people attending added his or her opinion, their ideas were written on the butcher paper for all to see. The ideas and information were then broken into categories, some dealing with aesthetics, some with management issues, some with design.

The next step was to break into subgroups of four to seven individuals by going around the room and counting off. (In this way people who sit together end up in different groups.) The small groups gave each participant a chance to state his or her opinion in an uninhibited way. When the large group reformed, representatives of each small group discussed their group's viewpoint. All the ideas were then gathered and prioritized. Member Chuck Ingels recalls:

We first came up with ideas of what we would like to see in the common house, and then we prioritized them. We broke up into small groups. Each had a cardboard paper with the proportions of the common house and little pieces of paper representing rooms. Well, that's how we decided what we really wanted. We'd take two rooms in our hand and say which came first—the dining room or the extra guest room. We would put down the extra guest room and put in the dining room. We kept doing that with each room until they all got in line. Each representative told their group's priority. And it all came out about even—there were similarities.

Over several weeks, general goals of the common house were discussed to aid in designing rooms. These goals fell under headings such as "general goals," "for kids," "practical goals," and "activities." A mini-design program was compiled for the common house with each room receiving a page. The page was divided into six headings: place, activities, general, relationships, character,

and details. Members discussed the important characteristics and activities for each space until they all agreed. A special subcommittee was formed for difficult rooms, such as the kitchen. The program was then given to the architect.

The Coho group's common house workshop began with a presentation by the architects of three preliminary plans. Each plan reflected differences that had not been resolved from the previous programming workshop, such as guest rooms on the lower or upper level, different service access to the kitchen, a series of alcoves or a larger lounge connected to the dining hall. Members broke up into smaller groups and each of the three architects joined one of the groups. The architects believe the small groups were vital:

The large group can agree or disagree, but in order to resolve problems, to draw or sketch, we could actually get things done in the small groups. Each group came to a comfort level with minor modifications that we could resolve.

No matter the technique, reaching consensus requires compromise and trust among members. Feeling comfortable with group decisions cannot be accomplished by the architect. Over a period of time members learn when to request and when to give in. A Muir Commons member observed:

Once you start, everyone gets the idea, people start prioritizing. People would listen—that is a respect that you would get after a while. I got whatever I want and let Suzie and Sam get what they want. A relationship forms of give and take, and a dialogue happens. There is then the possibility for people to change their minds.

Once consensus had been reached and the group had a clear idea of their requirement, they wrote it down. When differences of opinion resurfaced, the group did not have to rediscuss the issue:

Once we consensed [sic] the whole program, we got out the blocks. Then when someone says "I would like to have this house over here," you can say "No, we all consensed to this program and that's why we can't do that."

PLACE: <u>DINING ROOM</u>

ACTIVITIES	GENERAL	RELATIONSHIPS	CHARACTER	DETAILS

Eating:
-dinners 5-7 nights/
  wk.
-Sat./Sun. brunch
-comfortable seating
  for 80% of residents
  (67 people total,
  more children
  likely).
-overflow capacity of
  100% of residents.
	Flexible: to accomma-
	date different activities
	
	Adjacent space for over-
	flow seating capacity
	-possibly using sittting
	  area.
		Adjacent to:
		-living
		-sitting
		-kitchen
		-direct access to terrace
		
		Not adjacent to:
		-children's room
		-laundry
		-exercise
		-far from messy crafts.
			-homey
			-non-institutional
			-volumned ceiling
			-natural light
				Lighting:
				-drop lights over tables
				-adjustable for other activities
				  (i.e. able to raise for dancing)
				-mostly incandesant
				-zoned: 2 lights per switch
				-dimmer switches
				
				Accoustically well-designed
				
				Display wall for kids' arts

Meeting/lectures
-slideshows
-lectures
-music
 	
Parties
 	
Dancing
 	
Storage:
-extra chairs and
  tables
-moveable platform
  for stage.
	Place to focus:
	-out of circulation
	-temporary stage
	-possible sound system
		Visibility of kids playing
		outside (but not from
		every table)
				Wooden counter to receive
				  dirty dishes at kitchen.
				
				Foors:
				-easy to clean
				-accoustic, quiet
				
				Low-toxic materials
				  (especially glues, vinyl
				  floors, sealed)
				
				Sound stytem:
				-install wiring
				-optimal accoustic location
				
				Phone: accessable to dining.
				
				Tables:
				-various sizes to seat 4-8
				  people
				-movable (non squeak pads)

The common house programming completed by Muir Commons groups with consultants McCamant and Durrett. *(Muir Commons)*

Muir Commons members wrote their agreements into a document twenty pages long, with simple diagrams and short descriptions of goals and design preferences. The architect then had a guide to complete the design. "When he brought us the plan, people could say this may not look like what I wanted, but it fits the needs we wrote down," said member Fred Ransdell.

Choose an Appropriate Design Team

Contrary to popular opinion, the architect's role is not diminished by working with a group. The architect does not become merely a technician or an educator. She or he leads the process forward by staying several steps ahead of the group, with designs for a number of contingencies, and always with an eye to the time schedule and budget. Architects without strong experience in collaborative housing design find many difficulties when working with a multiheaded client whose numbers grow and shrink.

The designer may find that the group takes over and lengthens the process. Chris Hanson, the developer consultant and also a Winslow member observed: "The more power the group claims, the less productive for the architect. The architect then becomes more of a group educator than a designer. The Winslow group claimed a lot of power." In the beginning they did not formalize their design process. One of their former designers said, "We programmed through design and designed through programming. We never nailed it down, and as new members entered we went through dynamic reprogramming." A great deal of time was taken up trying to get a consensus on the elements of the design.

A number of members cited the slow pace and budget overruns as the reason for the group hiring a new design team, Edward Weinstein Associates in June 1990. Weinstein introduced a strict target budget and formalized design process.

Muir Commons members brought in design consultants McCamant and Durrett to aid their architect through the design programming. Typically, in affordable housing schemes, floor plans are often brought in from another project and modified. Such generic plans rarely emphasize community nor do the kitchens, for example, face out to the common area. The need for a unique design prompted the group to hire the design consultants who were then able to help the group reach a consensus on the design program.

Architects with an understanding of collaborative requirements can hear members' desires and translate them into feasible design solutions. They know what aspects to let the group solve, and which to solve themselves. "We presented pluses and minuses and let them go spin. At first we were involved throughout the consensus process," said Coho project architect Lorne McConachie, "but we and the group realized that if we become involved in all their debates our budgets would be eaten alive."

By providing an appropriate design, the architect can help the group reach an agreement. The Coho architect explained:

The group is very process oriented. There is a reluctance to see design before consensus. We are very graphically oriented and we think tools of our design can help you gain consensus. We told them to let us show them site plan options. At first the group was reluctant and unsure what we would bring. But their rising confidence level in us has helped achieve consensus.

Given a number of people with different opinions and desires, tight constraints, and the complexity of the design program, problems will always be encountered during the design. With foresight and planning, reaching consensus can be made easier, and stress on members reduced. But some tension is inherent in the process of reaching group decisions, a tension that helps produce a more competent group and a better community design.

Confront Actual Constraints

Members' expectations for their community must be balanced with the need for a realistic budget and time schedule from the start. Developer Virginia Thigpen found that the Muir Commons budget could easily escalate. The result of the common house workshop was a building of 4,600 square feet with a separate garden tool storage and a car repair shed. This was almost double the 2,500 square feet planned for by the developer. In compromising, the group scaled down the building to 3,668 square feet and chose to give up a planned storage shed.

The time schedule also needed to be stretched for the design of the private dwellings. Thigpen felt that the group had spent many more months than had been allocated on the design programming, and hoped the unit plans would only need some fine tuning "since only three floor plans were possible, and the unit price, size, footprint, and orientation were already set."

Muir Commons members felt strongly that they should be the ones to design their units, especially when the plans they were first shown were not oriented toward collaborative living. So the design of the units began, and the process was further extended when members would bring in their sketches from home or asked friends with design experience to help out.

Thigpen felt that too many choices were allowed the Muir Commons group: "Affordable housing is extremely tight. What is the use of debating a skylight in the bathroom in the design committee or taking a half hour in the general meeting when its not possible because of the budget? And at some stages the decisions are stressful to the unity of the group. Next time I would make more of the decisions prior to involving the group."

If members have different expectations about their roles in the design or the kinds of amenities they can afford, introducing real constraints in mid-process is difficult. Naturally, some members of the group will become attached to a design and resent scaling down the plans. Former Muir Commons member Sandra Cook said, "There was a lot of frustration because the group didn't have the power to create the housing they wanted. It seems like meetings were wasted because the devel-oper would say to us 'you can't have it' or 'you can't do it'."

The developer felt caught between the necessity of cutting back and the wishes of twenty-six households. "It was toughest to reconcile the constraints of our budget with a group programming that implies that people have permission to design their own homes."

Winslow group members began with customized designs of the units. Architect Lynn Perkins, who originally worked with the group said, "We've done it in a more democratic method than necessary. The design would have been simplified if the group early on had made fixed assumptions on the number of one, two, and three bedrooms, and designed generic units. But the group never wanted to make those assumptions."

The architects met with each household to design their own home. When architects Ed Weinstein and Associates took over the design, they found it was not easy to deal with member expectations. "We needed serious standardization and quick delivery," said Ed Weinstein, "but some people want individual attention—a different standard configuration, different windows, a larger footprint. The group collectively has a difficult time recognizing the severity of the budget. The architect stands in the middle, having to respond in favor of the group or the individual, and it's difficult to accommodate both."

Architects and project managers are taking a more aggressive attitude in balancing the desires of members with the constraints of getting a community built: A monthly calendar is sent out to members with dates for decisions marked boldly; pep talks are given about standardization; a small number of prototypes are introduced from the start; and printed sheets are handed out with cost breakdowns of rooms, windows, and doors letting members quickly put a price tag next to their list of desires.

In addition, communication between the architect, consultants, the developer or manager and the group need to be carefully worked out so that conflicting expectations are reduced. Using these and other methods can help reduce the amount of time spent in discussing what is not possible.

See Regular Progress

Nothing is more frustrating for the group than the feeling that they are not moving forward. Architect Dick Metler, working with the Coho group, has found that it is important to have a feeling of progress. They plan their meetings with the group so that there are not too many areas where consensus cannot be reached. "We state exactly what we are trying to achieve, with goals posted on large boards and people can see progress, see where the successes are."

The work set before the group should neither be too much nor too little to do. If too much, people become discouraged and if too little, they lose interest. The group requires a somewhat flexible schedule, updated frequently, since it is difficult to gauge how quickly they can accomplish a task.

Formal meetings between the designers and members to organize group work and discuss unsolved issues help to keep the process on track. The Winslow group meets every other Saturday for four hours with their designer, and in the afternoon the group discusses the design issues raised among themselves. An architectural coordinating team meets with the architect for a couple of hours the following Tuesday to tie up loose ends and prepare for the next phase of work.

Groups working with developers particularly need to be kept informed. The developer often takes over group tasks, such as looking for a site or dealing with city government, and members may not know what has been accomplished. "When they don't see evidence of progress, they start getting antsy and worried," observed developer Thigpen. She has considered writing a regular update for members.

The group is not the only ones who need to see progress. Architect Dick Metler states:

We're used to attacking and moving ahead. The unique thing has been that everyone needed to be comfortable with the design. With traditional clients we understand not everyone will be pleased, and we try to please in most areas. Now we have to achieve total consensus with all. The most difficult part for us has been the slow pace.

ELEMENTS OF THE DESIGN PROGRAM

The ideas of how the group would like to live need to be translated into specific places and square footages. "One of the problems groups have is translating their ideas and visions into hard core data that an architect can pick up and work with," said Coho Project Architect Lorne McConachie. "Rather than spin wheels and dream, focus that vision. . . ."

What are the specific elements that a group must nail down in the design process? Many of the elements that make up the design program are listed below. They are divided for convenience into the overall dimensions and appearance of the community, the site plan, the common space, and private dwellings. In reality, they would not be decided in such a linear fashion, as many elements are interconnected. (A more complete list can be found in Appendix C.)

Dimensions of the Community

A design program begins with how members perceive their community. Collaborative communities come in many sizes, from large communities of more than 200 residents to those of a few households. Their densities also vary over a wide range, as do the common areas members share.

Although many aspects of the design program are decided with an architect, the group can gather preliminary information on their community through questionnaires and discussions. Issues of size and density can be the starting point.

Size

The right size for a collaborative community depends on the community queried. Most

Danes are convinced that twenty to thirty households is right. The Danish architect Jan Gudmand-Høyer (a member of Skråplanet, with thirty-one households) believes that "you cannot run a bigger community and still know everyone well. Behavioral testing has shown that this is the optimal number for working together."[1]

The Dutch believe that communities of twenty households are excessively small. Bob Fris (a member of Hilversumse Meent, with fifty households) states that "fifty families is a golden number. With fifty households we can give a concert for the whole community, but not for twenty. We couldn't keep our bar open three nights a week or have as many cultural evenings. With not too many more, you forget who is who; with fewer dwellings there are fewer possibilities to create common facilities."

The Swedes can show proof of several "right" sizes. Thornblom (Hässelby Hotel, with 190 households), the architect of Stolplyckan, states categorically that about 200 households is the right number: "You have to take the long view. In fifty years, a community of 200 will remain, whereas smaller communities of 10 or 30 families will disappear." Others, such as Karin Palm-Linden (of Slottet, with 16 families), believe that such large housing is alienating and that a smaller number of units is necessary.

The differences in size are connected to cultural biases, to different ownership types, and to the degree of collaboration felt necessary. The Dutch rental projects need more people to make them work. Renters cannot be expected to make the same kinds of commitments as residents in co-ops or condominiums. A percentage will not participate, and therefore a larger pool of residents is required—about forty to fifty households.

In Sweden, a number of midrise collaborative communities have been built with municipal subsidies, resulting in higher residential densities. Through the use of elevators or stairs, a denser population can keep in contact without being spread out. The Swedish system of rental housing allotment, where a potential resident expresses interest in common living but does not necessarily go through a membership screening, requires a more flexible attitude toward cooperation.

Clearly the number of households will determine the level of interaction between members. In general, groups of up to fifteen households will create a more intimate community but one in which more social friction may occur because of the small number of people. Groups of eighteen to thirty-five households provide more choice of association and are small enough to allow members to know each other well. Groups of over thirty-five households can afford a greater number of shared amenities, but their large size means that a certain percentage of households will probably not participate in common dining because of the less intimate nature of the larger group. Subdividing the larger group into clusters of fifteen households or less will create more intimacy, but again, more social problems may occur.[2]

Density and Scale

In traditional site planning, a site is divided into equal parcels, with one home per parcel. In cohousing, the dwellings are typically clustered together at a higher density to create a sense of community and to leave part of the site undeveloped for common use.[3] Housing density is measured by the number of dwellings on an acre of land. The higher the density is, the greater the number of dwellings there are and the closer they are built to each other.

Higher densities can provide cost savings because more people share the costs of the land and the infrastructure. (Clustering houses leaves more land undeveloped.) Another benefit of higher density is that useful outdoor areas can be created through the placement of houses, and a greater number of residents come into contact with each other. There are greater possibilities for reducing energy usage and making use of alternative sources of energy. Another advantage is the mix of resi-

 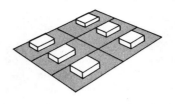

 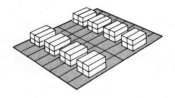

 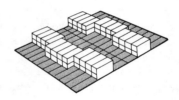

 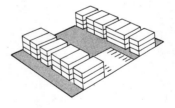

Housing Type	Typical Densities (units/net acres)
Single family Detached	1-12
Duplexes	10-16
Row houses	18-36
Garden apts.	24-36

A key measure of how land is used for housing is density: the number of housing units per acre of land (an acre is 43,560 square feet, about the size of a football field). If an area is developed with homes on lots that are 50 feet wide and 100 feet deep, each home will occupy 5,000 square feet, with eight lots (homes) per acre. One large lot of 2 acres with thirty condominiums on it would have a net density of fifteen units to the acre. *(Greenbelt Alliance, from Room Enough)*

dents. If, for example, 10% of the units are targeted for the elderly, this could mean one elderly unit if a large site is not available. A greater density might result in four or five units for the elderly.

The drawbacks are that higher-density buildings are more difficult to design well, can have noise and privacy problems, and can be more difficult to market to Americans interested in single-family homes. Careful architectural design can mitigate many of these drawbacks.

Dimensions of spaces are an important concern. A common courtyard at 60 feet, 100 feet, or 150 feet will not only differ in dimensions but also in the kind of activities the space is going to encourage. The scale implies many other characteristics, such as seeing or avoiding others, a sense of enclosure or spaciousness, and in many instances the ability of a space to be functional. For example, the kitchen in Stacken, Sweden, does not function at an optimal level because it is too large for the number of people cooking.

Bigger is not always better in designing spaces that feel homelike instead of institutional. The group can educate themselves on scale, as well as design, by noticing the spaces around them, by visiting housing communities, and by simulating sizes to get a sense of their scale.

Amount in Common and Private

The amount of space held privately and in common may be a difficult issue to decide. Each person has a need for privacy, but few people know how much they will require without having lived in the community. To design for the right amount of privacy, the issue needs to be broken down into smaller components, such as: How much fencing is desired? How much back yard space? How much visual privacy from neighbors and children?

Members can divide into subgroups of four or five, discuss the issue, and then present their decision to the entire membership. Similar opinions are grouped and two or three points of view can then be discussed. Deciding on size, amount, and importance of common and private spaces is a good starting point for bringing individual viewpoints together.

The amount of common and private space is often tied to the desired degree of shared chores and activities. Communities that seek a high level of member participation tend to have a larger amount of area in common.

Although the degree of participation is difficult to predict before moving in, it will rise and fall no matter what level is set initially. The design can provide flexibility in the common areas and expansion in the private dwellings for future needs.

The amount of private dwelling square footage designated for common areas averages 10-15% in European cohousing. The average of 10-15% would mean that in a group of twenty households, with each dwelling about 1,000 square feet, the common spaces would be 2,000-3,000 square feet.

The Site Plan

The site plan is a two-dimensional image of the agreements between common and private spaces—where the dwellings are located, the extent of the common spaces, the extent of private land, and the relationships between the dwellings and the common house.

Group agreements are one of a number of influences on the site plan. The plan also derives from the constraints of the site, financial requirements, city codes, the architect's image, and the sponsor's agenda. The group's program in some cases may be the strongest influence; in others it may be weak.

The site plan design can encompass a variety of issues, such as the public edge (join to the neighborhood), circulation (maximize chance encounters), parking, outdoor meeting areas, children's play areas, gardens, art, and dwelling locations and sun access.

The Public Edge

The creation of community need not stop at the borders of the site. The larger neighborhood can be included in many ways and receive more than views of house backs and parking lots. The issue of how enclosed the community should be will determine whether the outside world is embraced or kept at arm's length.

The choice of presenting a public front, quietly blending in, or shutting out the neighborhood will have a major impact on the site plan. The decision will affect the appearance and number of entrances, the location of the car entrances, and the different edges of the site—screened, fenced, or opened depending on noise, sight lines, and human intrusion. Neighbors' detouring through the site can be controlled by entrances that are broad and open, narrowed, or fenced.

The Muir Commons group knew that a child care center and elementary school would be located across the street as part of a larger development, with a large park beyond the school. A greenbelt with bicycle paths would border the site to the east. An apartment complex and single-family homes would also be their neighbors. The members began by discussing whether they wanted clear borders between them and the public or less sense of enclosure. The decision was to have a strong sense of enclosure on the south and west side where there is traffic, and more open on the north and east side toward the neighbors and green belt. The common house would act as the community's public face.

A range of gestures by communities toward the neighborhood are possible: sharing paths, parking, and services such as child care; visually through large windows or framed openings; bordering a neighborhood park or store; and designing compatibly with the surroundings. In Europe, neighbors and strangers alike are welcomed along the public pedestrian path that runs straight through the community of Hilversumse Meent, Holland.

Kilen, in Denmark, has an introverted covered street, yet one side of it opens to a public plaza, while the other end opens to a parking lot shared with another housing complex. In Slottet, Sweden, the open space is jointly used with the home for frail elderly next door. Other communities, such as Sættedammen, choose to be introverted, with only the driveway entrance at the street.

Circulation

Circulation should maximize chance encounters so that residents come into contact with each other regularly. Such meetings create opportunities for discussions, favors, gossip, help, and other neighborly exchanges. Residents who interact during their normal routines experience community on a daily basis.

Having one main circulation route increases the number of times residents will see each other and be seen by others. If there are several routes, residents have the opportunity to come and go unobtrusively.

For one- and two-story dwellings, the circulation is generally contained on one path, with the possibility of ducking out the back. Apartment houses can have a central stairway with one point of circulation or be divided into more points, such as two or three staircases. The circulation points can create clusters of units, such as Stolplyckan in Sweden, where tasks were divided among apartment towers. More circulation points allow greater privacy.

Parking

Designing the circulation system in many communities begins not with pedestrians but with the cars. How deeply the car penetrates into the site is a major issue. In American cohousing being developed, as in Europe, parking is not adjacent to the units but concentrated at the periphery of the site.

One large parking lot at the site's edge has the advantage of a car-free site but is visually unappealing for the street and the rest of the neighborhood. Dividing the parking into several smaller lots has a visual advantage and requires less walking by residents. The disadvantage of spreading the parking is that less of the site is car free and that fewer people walk the same route to their homes.

Since many residents will be arriving at and leaving the parking area each day, the location of the lot can encourage them to walk by common areas located between the dwellings and the parking. Parking next to dwellings does not encourage use of common areas and decreases the safety and usability of such areas.

One deciding factor on locating the parking is the distance residents are prepared to walk from the parking area to their homes. Some groups have drawn the limit at 120 feet (40 meters); others are willing to walk up to 300 feet. One solution has been to separate the two parking spaces required for each household, with one located closer to the dwelling. Some of the parking spaces can have an overhead cover. Another solution is to string smaller parking areas together, creating a bead of parking areas parallel to the dwellings.

It is important to provide the possibility of dropping off groceries from the car, and access by emergency vehicles. Handicapped dwelling units will need to be located nearest the parking facilities. (States have varying handicap ordinances on the maximum distance.)

In addition to household parking, visitor parking spaces are required. Areas for trailers, boats, and junk cars and for washing and working on cars are also appreciated.

The security of cars (and drivers) in parking lots hidden from street and resident views should be considered in higher crime areas. Precautions can include appropriate lighting and a reduction in screening between dwellings and parked cars.

The parking area can be a social spot, with people fixing their cars, members coming and going, and children playing. There are ways of making the parking area more attractive and useful—for example, with plantings or a bench for residents and groceries.

Outdoor Meeting Areas

The outdoor space is an "exterior common house" used for a variety of activities, both common and private. The greater the possibility is for different size gatherings, from several households to all the residents, the more the space will be used.

After discussing many issues of the site plan, the Muir Commons group began talking about specific places on the site. One meeting place they particularly wanted for clear days was a large veranda and terrace in front of the common house. They also discussed "nodes" (courts)—gathering areas between the houses for people to sit and talk. Each node would be oriented to about six to eight houses and located along the main circulation paths, like beads on a string, with the common house in the center. One node is a play area for children, and another a gathering area for several households. Other common places decided on included toddler and children's play areas, natural areas, and the vegetable garden. In addition, the group listed their criteria for parking areas, workshop buildings, an auto repair shop, garden equipment storage, and bicycle and personal storage.

Balancing the many different uses of the outdoor spaces is no small design feat. Children's play spaces, eating areas, quiet reading areas, gardening, and sports may too easily clash when the outdoor space is limited. The outdoor area can be divided into zones of group activities, children's play areas, and more private areas where several households can meet.

The compact site plan of Muir Commons and the more spacious site plan of Winslow cohousing are illustrated on the following two pages.

Muir Commons

220

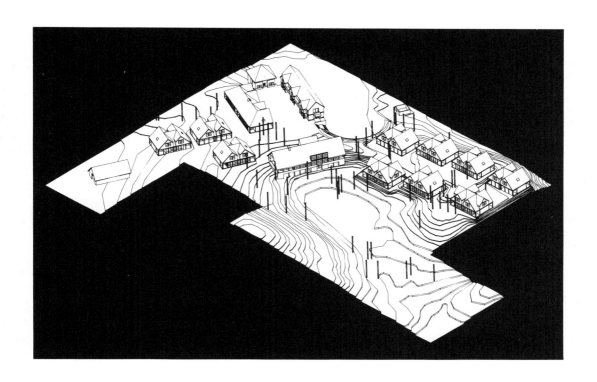

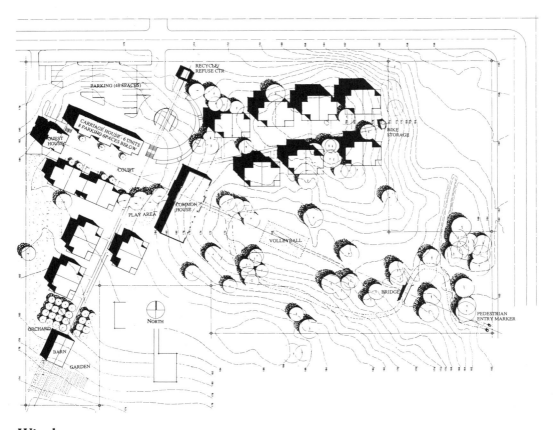

Winslow

Muir Commons, Davis California: overhead view and site plan. The 2.83-acre site for twenty-six households has duplexes, triplexes, and fourplexes grouped near "nodes" or informal meeting areas that are located along one main pedestrian path. Amenities include a central common house, natural areas, an orchard, common garden, and parking at the periphery of the site. *(West Davis Associates and Dean F. Unger Architects)*

Children's Play Areas

Children will play almost anywhere on the site—with all different ages and with children their own age. Play equipment for younger and older children can be separated to avoid conflict. Young children (up to 4 years old) ideally need small playing areas located no more than 50 meters from a dwelling. One or two play areas suffice if parents can keep an eye on the children while working in the home. These younger children enjoy sand play with water nearby, playhouses, small slides, and a paved area for wheeled toys. (A fenced area may be useful for children up to 3 years old.) An overhead covering or trees are useful for warding off heat and rain.

Play structures for older children located in a quiet, isolated, grassy area are not used as frequently as play areas located near where people gather. The outdoor play areas can be divided into a more isolated natural garden, a less isolated play field, and a play structure close to the common house. Wheelchair-accessible play equipment can be included. Teenagers enjoy skateboard areas, which can be noisy.

Winslow cohousing community, Bainbridge Island, Washington: overhead view and site plan. The 5.25-acre site for thirty households has two pedestrian streets that intersect at the community courtyard located in front of the common house. Duplexes are located along these two main axes, and a carriage house screens the parking at the top of the site. Amenities include a common house, guest house, play areas, a barn, orchard, common garden, bike storage, and a recycling center. *(Edward Weinstein Associates, Architects)*

Summer water play in the garden brings children of various ages together. This play area allows some noice privacy for the homes yet is within eyesight of adults. *(Lilian Bolvinkel)*

Play structures for all ages need to have a ground covering to ease falls. They also need to be built to withstand a teenager's play because they will certainly be tempted to use it. Insurance coverage is one factor in choosing play equipment and may need to be considered at an early stage of design. Unauthorized use by neighborhood children should be taken into account.

Common Gardens

Planning and maintaining gardens takes effort and dedication. Garden design begins with discussing the type of gardens desired by the group. There are a number of possibilities:

• Common vegetable garden or private plots
• Herb garden

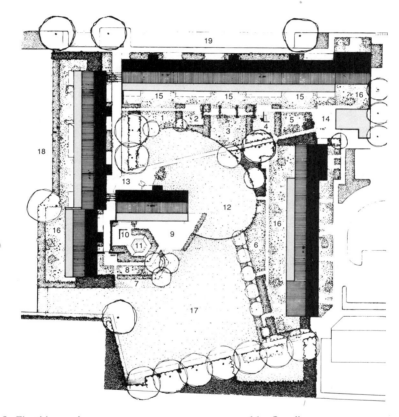

1-8. Flexible gardens
  1. Children's garden
  2. Rabbit and chicken pen
  3. Swings
  4. Sandbox
  5. Picnic tables
  6. Flower garden
  7. Compost area
  8. Botanical garden
  9. Common house patio
  10. Child care play area
  11. Sandbox
  12. Grass oval
  13. Common house square
  14. Bicycle repair area
  15. Cluster garden
  16. Private garden
  17. Municipal green (accessible to public)
  18. Water canal
  19. Parking area off of public street

The common green is divided into a number of outdoor rooms in this Dutch garden design in Wageningen, Holland. *(Kesler, Siemens, van der Vlist)*

- Flower garden
- Natural garden (attracting bugs, butterflies, and birds)
- Grass and sculpture garden
- Children's garden
- Ornamental garden
- Fruit trees
- Trellises and arbors
- Animal areas (dog runs, chicken coops, etc.)

The size of each type of garden can be determined by its use and the number of people available to maintain it. In addition, the location and size of greenhouses, compost bins, fruit drying shed, and a garden tool shed should be determined. The watering system used depends on the size and shape of the garden, the residents' work commitment to it, and seasonal climate.

Not all communities will have a large amount of open space available for gardens, and not all residents want to participate in gardening. Small landscaped areas with appropriate plants can provide greenery in little space with little effort.

The Muir Commons group maximized the garden space on a tight, compact site. Chuck Ingels, an experienced horticulturist and a community gardens enthusiast, was a member of the committee that spent many meetings planning the garden:

While there was a lot of discussion about how best to utilize the limited amount of land, the proximity of a major land grant university and our desire to eat organic food prompted us to include a large 3,700-square-foot vegetable garden, a 6,000-square-foot densely planted orchard with fifty-eight fruit trees, and a natural area of native, drought-tolerant, and edible plant species.

The landscape committee discussed having individual gardens, a single garden, or a combination of the two and decided that a communal garden would promote more social interaction. The nearby University of California provided a grant for establishing the orchard as part of a germplasm repository to increase trees of older fruit varieties.

In some communities, who tends the garden has undergone some adjustments. In Emmen, located in a rural area of Holland, residents found that only a few members tended the communal garden, and they redesigned it with small, private plots. And when a number of residents of Santa Rosa Creek Commons, California, showed little interest in tending the garden, it was decided that only members of the garden committee would pick the produce. Surplus is placed in the utility room for sharing, with members living in odd-numbered apartments entitled to help themselves on odd-numbered days and for even-numbered apartment residents on even-numbered days.

Art

Artists have been included in the shaping of the site plan in some European developments. Funds have been set aside as part of the development costs (Kirstinevang, Denmark) or the group has collected extra money to hire an artist (Kilen, Denmark). Also, artwork has been added after the group has moved in (Wageningen, Holland).

In Denmark's urban neighborhood communities, including art and sculpture has been one of the goals of the development. In Egebjerggård (Oak Mountain Farm), architects and landscape architects worked with artists to enhance the site plan and housing even before construction began. Artists used the themes of nature and natural shapes as a starting point. In the Kirstinevang housing cluster, an oak tree design created with dark-colored bricks appears on the facade. The artist added ceramic oak leaves, enameled in green, to create a three-dimensional effect.

Sculptor Niels Guttormsen has designed two buildings, both overlooking a lake. The first, in the north part of Egebjerggard, is a tower with ground-floor offices and common rooms. The top floor has housing for teenagers and young adults and may include an apartment for a resident artist. The tower is painted in soft pastels, with an enameled blue

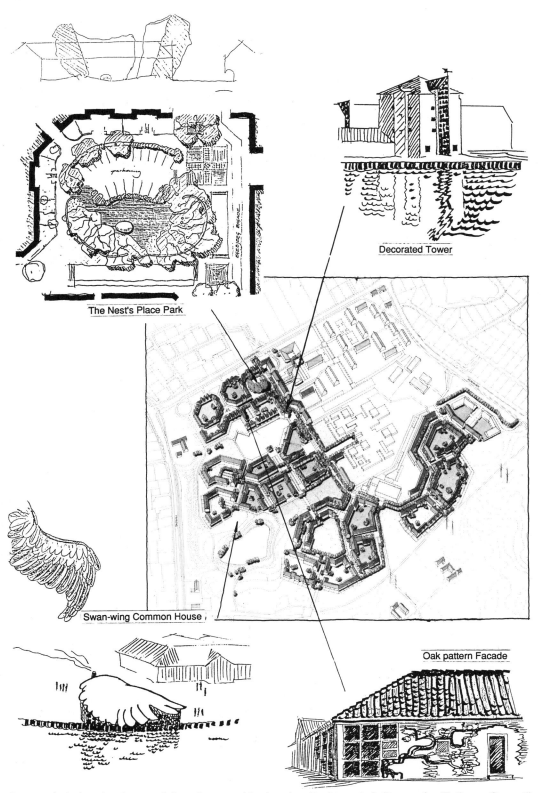

Decorated Tower

The Nest's Place Park

Swan-wing Common House

Oak pattern Facade

Art is included in the design of the urban neighborhood in Egebjerggård, Denmark. *(Ballerup Council)*

tile roof whose tip is crowned with a weather-vane of two bluebirds. He has also designed a common house for Egebjerggard 2 cohousing, at the southwest corner of the community. This common house is sited next to a lake, and the design resembles a swan's wing. (The national bird of Denmark is the swan, and residents hope the man-made lake will become a natural area and bird sanctuary.) Continuing the bird motif, an egg-shaped sculpture is located at the north edge of the development, in Redepladsen Square (the Nest's Place, a plaza built by the Ballerup community with some funds from the Ministry of Culture). The egg conceals an existing transformer, about 3 × 6 feet.

Sun, Light, and Wind

The layout of dwellings requires access to sun, especially for housing incorporating passive solar energy. The sun-loving Danes take great care in this aspect and have charts that provide information on the placement of one- and two-story dwellings for maximum sun exposure (Svensson). Common spaces blocked from sun will not be used as often (except in hot climates), and the same is true for decks and balconies.

Solar access can be a determining factor in how the housing is placed in relationship to the outdoor areas and should be considered early. The location of yards is dependent on solar access, and the effects of later additions to the dwellings can cause shadow lines on neighboring yards.

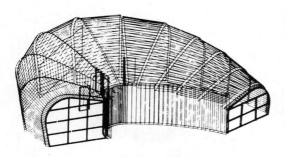

Structural diagram of wing-shaped common house designed by sculptor Niels Guttormsen and architect Jan Gudmand-Høyer.

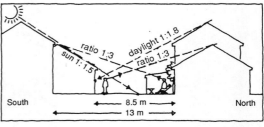

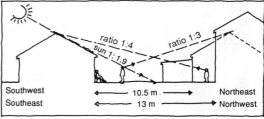

In Holland, the collaborative community of Wageningen is home to two artists, one a ceramicist and the other a printer. Both have their studios in the development and give lessons to the residents. Their artwork decorates the common house, as well as some of the homes. In Stolyplacken, Sweden, the long corridors are decorated with the residents' artwork made in the common art studios, and often there are art shows in the café.

Sun angles used by Danes and Swedes for low-rise housing provide 4–5 hours of sun in the private and common gathering areas, such as living rooms, and 3 hours in other rooms. The amount of sun is also connected to a specific time; for example, in Denmark kitchens need several hours of sun access before 2 P.M., and outdoor areas require 5 hours between 9 A.M. and 5 P.M. *(Svensson)*

Uncomfortable wind speeds also have a deadening effect on private and common outdoor use. Placement of the dwellings can decrease the wind, an especially useful consideration in the winter. Plantings, fences, and other barriers can also reduce wind speeds.

Multistory housing raises other criteria of sun access and wind reduction. Double-loaded corridor buildings and buildings that create an outdoor courtyard need to be carefully considered in this regard. Shading and wind caused by the building can be professionally analyzed.

Passive solar energy should be a design consideration—and is in many cohousing developments, such as Jystrup Savværket. Active solar designs—solar panels and wind generators—have been used in a few projects with mixed success. The high initial cost and upkeep of such equipment have been deterrents.

Common House or Spaces

The common house is the literal and symbolic meeting space of the community. In designing the common house, members decide together on the amount of common space to be built and its uses. Almost all collaborative housing groups have the basic dining hall, kitchen, bathroom, and children's play area as common rooms. Virtually all take the same criteria into account.

The common house, located at the intersection of two pedestrian streets, rises above the housing in Trudeslund, Denmark. *(Vandkunsten Architects)*

Location

The location of the common house or common rooms is one of the main determinants. A central location along well-traveled paths encourages drop-in use. The common rooms and outdoor common areas work in conjunction with each other and are most efficient when they are connected, with an easy transition from one to the other. Mailboxes, shared laundry facilities, and parking areas are all used often by residents. Placed in or near the common house, they will draw residents on a daily basis and encourage them to use the other common facilities as they pass by. Windows onto areas of activity within the common house, such as the kitchen, can also act as magnets for more people to drop in.

At right: In the Winslow common house, the kitchen, dining room, and library are located upstairs; the recreation room, teen room, laundry, and child care are located in the daylight basement. (Guest rooms are in a separate building.) The 6,200-square-foot common house is based on the longhouse, the symbol of community of many Northwest Native American cultures. *(Edward Weinstein Associates, Architects)*

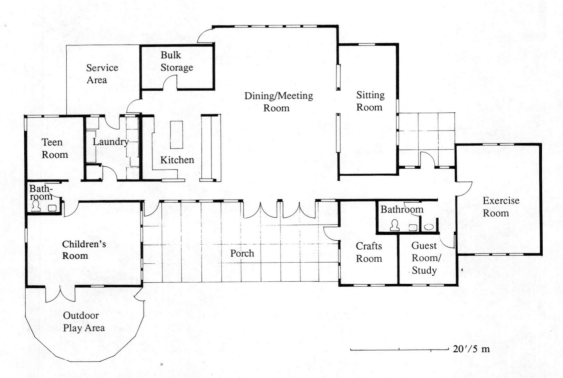

Muir Commons members designed their common house with a large, central dining area; children's play room; and guest, exercise, and craft rooms. The 3,688-square-foot common house has a spacious veranda and front yard that functions as a large gathering area for the community.

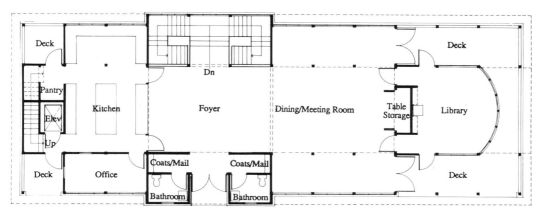

COMMON HOUSE UPPER FLOOR

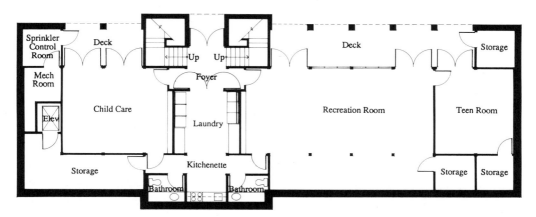

COMMON HOUSE LOWER FLOOR

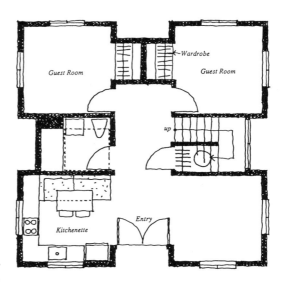

The Winslow guest house, located near the common house, has six rooms and a shared kitchen. These supplementary spaces are useful whenever extra space or privacy away from the household is required. (Edward Weinstein Associates, Architects)

Guest House
Lower Floor Plan   680 s.f.

229

The transparency of the common house provides an easy flow of people and views from outside to inside and vice versa at Sawærket, Denmark. *(Lilian Bolvinkel)*

Common spaces function best when they have some transparency and can sustain a flow of people both inside and outside the space. Residents have the choice of passing alongside and seeing in without committing themselves to staying. Spaces that dead-end require a certain commitment to enter. For example, walking alongside a common sitting area to see who is there is socially easier than entering the room, seeing who is there, and then quickly leaving (Linden).

A visual connection from dwellings to the common house is important as a daily reminder to residents of the common facilities. This is more difficult to accomplish for common spaces in multistory designs, particularly renovations. Some visual connection to common spaces should be assured, whether to the open space, paths, or cluster areas, possibly from just outside the dwelling.

The ideal location for the common house or spaces may not be ideal for the residents living on either side. Concern over noise and privacy is expressed when discussing the location of common facilities. Acoustical insulation, the location of fenestration, level changes, and noise use policies have been used successfully to reduce such problems.[4]

Size

The common spaces supplement the individual dwellings. The square footage available for common use depends on the percentage of area donated by each household from the private dwelling allotment. The amount donated by each household varies from 6% to a high of 50% of the dwelling floor area. Although the average is near 10%, there is a large variation in the amount of common space.

Rooms

A range of different rooms and functions can be found inside the common house. Many more amenities can be imagined for the common house than there is space to realize them. Prioritizing the rooms and functions becomes necessary—a guest room or a hobby room? a larger kitchen or extra storage? Adjacency make a difference in use. Bathrooms should be located near the playroom, the teen room should be more isolated, and the meeting room should be located with public use in mind.

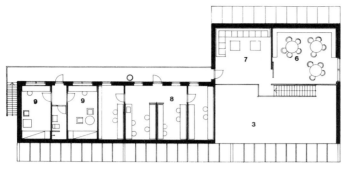

Common spaces in Denmark and Sweden.

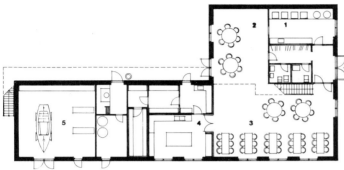

Sun and Wind, Denmark has a separate common house (plan). (SBI)

1. Laundry; 2. playroom; 3. meeting room-dining hall; 4. kitchen; 5. workshop; 6. library; 7. lounge; 8. hobby room; 9. annex-guest room.

Plan of Cat's Head, Sweden, with the main common facilities on one floor of a midrise building. (Herlin)

1. Entrance
2. Dining hall
3. Kitchen
4. Freezer
5. Refrigerator
6. Cold storage
7. Pantry
8. Refrigerated room
9. Living room-fireplace area
10. Laundry
11. Washing machine
12. Pressing
13. Centrifugal drying
14. Wash basin
15. Drying cabinet
16. Dryer
17. Supply storage
18. Bathroom
19. Closet
20. Child's bathroom
21. Staff room
22. Table
23. Children's cubbies or shelves
24. Diaper changing area
25. Deck
26. Railing
27. Stairs
28. Elevator

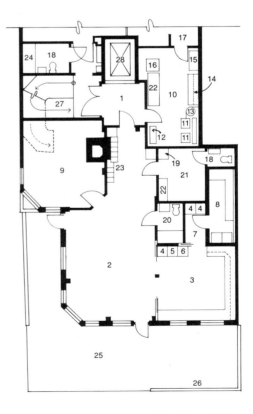

10'/3 m

Common spaces in Holland.

Rensumaheerd, Holland, is a renovation of seventeen large row houses into twenty-seven units, turning sixteen garages into common rooms: café, dining room, kitchen, music room, meeting room, children's play room, guest room, computer room, and a laundry. *(LVCW)*

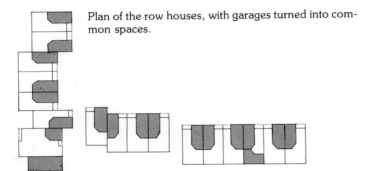

Plan of the row houses, with garages turned into common spaces.

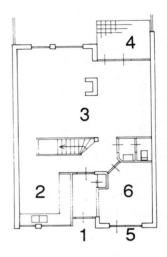

Ground floor plan of a row house.

1. Private dwelling entrance
2. Kitchen
3. Living room
4. Private terrace
5. Common entrance
6. Common room (previously garage)

This playroom was formerly a private garage.

Common Kitchen/Dining Area(s). The most comfortable kitchens and dining halls are the most successful. The reason is that residents choose to cook (and eat) in common because they find it enjoyable.

The stainless steel kitchen of the Swedish cohousing Stacken was installed by kitchen professionals. Large, noisy, and impersonal,

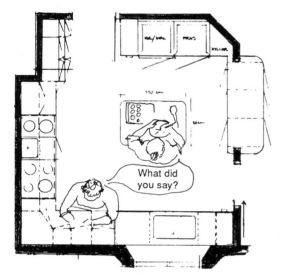

What did you say?

This sketch shows the kitchen in Slottet collaborative housing; it was not built for working together. *(Gunilla Lauters)*

this first kitchen has inspired a reconsideration of common kitchen design. Three Swedish researchers, realizing that common kitchens have different design requirements from restaurant kitchens, began a search for an ideal shared kitchen form (Lauters, Ljungberg, and Linden 1988). The results can be seen in the kitchen design of Rainbow, Sweden, where the stove and sinks are located in the center of the room instead of at the edges. As residents cook or wash dishes, they face one another. Windows on three sides allow passersbys to see who is cooking, and the cooks can see what is going on.

Successful kitchens combine efficiency with coziness; their size is appropriate (Table 15.1). Surfaces are durable, with materials that are not hard or shiny, such as wood. The lighting avoids an institutional brightness. Noisy machines are placed away from the preparation areas so that conversation can be heard. The pantry and other food storage spaces need to be accessible and can be separately keyed to allow delivery people access during the day, when many residents are at work. Walk-in freezers for storage are useful for communities that harvest their food, but smaller cold storage may be more efficient depending on how the dinners are planned.

The kitchen is central to the idea of cohousing, and it should not be isolated. The drama of dinner preparation can be entertain-

Table 15.1 Kitchen and Dining Spaces

Project	No. of Households	Cooking Area[a]		Dining Area	
		sq. ft.	sq. m	sq. ft.	sq. m
Slottet, Sweden	16	160	15	237	22 (+20)[b]
Älvsjö, Sweden	31	312	29	915	85
Rainbow, Sweden	19	258	24	775	72 (+30)[b]
Jernstøberiet, Denmark	21	150	14	775	72
Trudeslund, Denmark	33	237	22	904	84
Purmerend, Holland	7[c]	86	8	183	17
Muir Commons, USA	26	210	20	925	86

Source: Data from Lauters et al., Vedel-Petersen et al.
[a] Excludes pantry.
[b] Extension area.
[c] One of ten clusters with kitchens, together serving seventy-one households.

Rainbow in Lund, Sweden, has a kitchen specifically built for team cooking. This plan of the common areas shows the central location of the kitchen, with windows or openings on all four sides for maximum visibility. A wide central work island allows cooks to work facing each other. A separately keyed pantry area, upper left, allows deliveries during the day when residents are out.

1. Entrance
2. Baby carriage storage
3. Kitchen delivery area
4. Kitchen storage
5. Kitchen
6. Cold storage
   (fruits, vegetables)
7. Refrigerator
8. Freezer
9. Oven
10. Dish washing area
11. Dishwasher
12. Food preparation area
13. Coffeemaker
14. Desk
15. Dining

16. Smoking room
17. Sitting area
18. Open fireplace
19. Patio
20. Playing room
21. Library-music room
    (extra dining areas)
22. Cleaning supplies
23. Photo lab
24. Bathroom
25. Toilet
26. Closet
27. Mini-kitchen
28. Staircase
29. Private dwelling

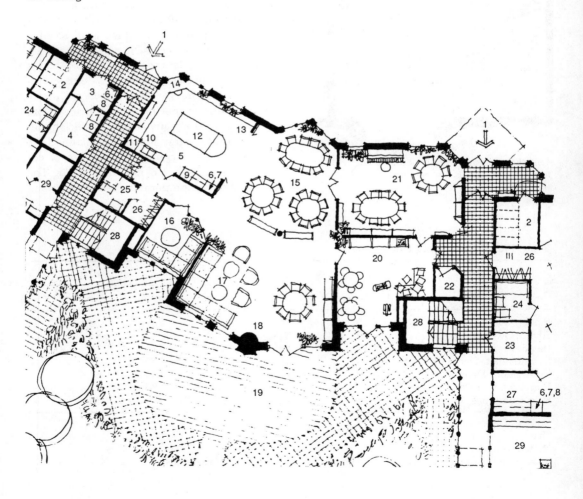

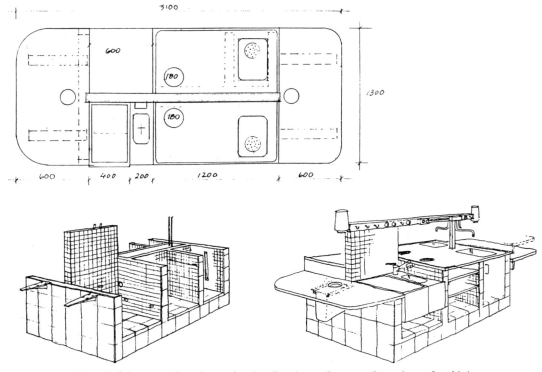

Detail of the central cooking island in Rainbow. (Lauters, Ljungberg, Lindén)

ing and inviting for residents passing by the common spaces. They can be drawn in through windows connecting the kitchen to other spaces. Kitchen location also depends on ease of grocery delivery and garbage pickup. (A kitchen garden of herbs and salad greens may also be a consideration, as well as recycling and composting.)

The connection from kitchen to dining area should be as smooth as from hand to mouth. Dinner can be served from the kitchen, brought out on trolleys, or placed on a counter or separate tables, and in the summer, the dinner must make its way outdoors.

The dining area serves as the weekly gathering area for the residents. The idea is for residents to converse and perhaps linger in each other's company. As they pass the dining hall, a view of the activities inside may draw them in. Once diners are seated, com-

fortable chairs and lighting relax them, and good acoustics allows them to hear each other.

One of the difficulties of dining together is children and their inability to sit quietly for more than ten minutes. Many communities have a playroom near the common dining area. In Rainbow, the central location of the dining room and the proximity of the playroom encourage children to run through the dining area in a wide circle and back again. A very open dining room layout, with many entrances, may not afford enough privacy from children's play, yet a closed dining room and a distant playroom may seem too isolating for young children (McCamant).

Smaller cluster kitchens, with dining for five to fifteen households, have exactly the same issues of noise if there are children, yet cluster kitchens rarely have enough space to include a good play area. They tend to be small and do not benefit from being tucked away, as in Wageningen; they function better in combination with the dining area, as in Purmerend.

Dining rooms need an accessible outdoor eating area that provides shade in summer. The outdoor area can be small and private or large and very public, depending on the location. The ability to join the diners and yet retain some privacy can be desirable.

The dining room is often turned into a multipurpose room for eating, meeting, discussions, dancing, lectures, and parties. A thought to accommodating other functions and storage needs is important.

Meeting Areas.   Over the life of the community, meeting areas have been requested for these age categories in communities of over thirty households: young children (2-6), older children (7-12), teenagers (13-19), adults, and the elderly. Their meeting areas can overlap. The children's areas can be largely outdoor, with an interior playroom that takes into account the different needs of small and older children.

Teen rooms have been very popular in Holland, Denmark, and Sweden. Seen as a den or area to hangout, they work best when they are located away from constant traffic but have a deck, balcony, or window to overlook the action. Teenagers use these rooms for listening to music and partying. The most successful ones have been planned and decorated by the teens themselves. In Emmen, parents did most of the finish and decorating work on the room. After their efforts were trashed "by accident," they gave up, and the teenagers took over. Since then, the room has been well maintained.

Adults enjoy having a coffee room, garden room, or fireplace nook where they can meet to relax and chat. In Stacken, the coffee room has been taken over by teenagers because no other space was available for them, and the adults, especially singles, miss the opportunity to meet. This type of room could be a meeting place for elderly during the day.

Children's Playroom.   The playroom serves a number of functions. During the morning and afternoon, it can be used for informal or formal child care. During and after dinner, the children can play while their parents eat and talk in peace. For child care, the room should be located near a bathroom (and near the kitchen) and have outdoor access. To achieve dinnertime peace, the room cannot be too close to the dining area or so far as to be beyond hearing range of parents.

A more formal child care room is a large undertaking for the community. Cities may have their own guidelines and requirements for such a space depending on the number of children to be accommodated. The common spaces can do double duty in the design of child care by connecting common kitchen, bathrooms, and outdoor areas to one or two large rooms. (Residents have mentioned that the work involved in running the child care was more than they had expected. The number of hours each parent needs to work, plus meetings, maintaining records, and reaching agreements on policies, have worn many parents down.)

The residents of Cat's Head in Sweden rent out their common areas for child care. The benefits are the availability of the facility for the community's children, the ability to meet neighbors whose children also attend, and the money paid can be used for common facilities. The disadvantages are that some of the nearby common areas cannot be used during child care hours because of the noise and that people come in and out of the common house.

Offices and Businesses for Individuals. The notion of locating guest rooms or work space in the common house is a natural extension of sharing leisure space. In Europe, cohousing communities share computers and copiers, as well as desk space.

In several American communities, the common house is used for private business. At Sunlight, several therapists use common house rooms for client sessions. Combining work and leisure spaces in one area has definite drawbacks when business associates or clients wander in and out of the common spaces, if numerous deliveries are required, or if there are other kinds of disruptions in the common spaces. The location of business spaces in relationship to the entrance becomes important. Noise and access within the common house are also important to consider because other residents' use of the common spaces may clash with business interests.

Some of the most successful uses of common house space for individual work have been among artists. In Wageningen, the resident printer and ceramicist make use of such spaces, exchanging free lessons, artwork, and now payments to the community. Their art adorns a number of common spaces and individual dwellings and is a happy addition to the community. (The ceramicist added her touch to the building through the creation of a symbolic wheel of togetherness.)

Combining small multipurpose rooms to be used as either guest rooms or office space has worked well in Jystrup Sawærket, Denmark, and in Sunlight, Oregon.

Professional Services and Special Care Units. Cohousing in Holland, Denmark, and Sweden has considered including groups with special needs into the community. Such communities are usually developed with a nonprofit organization.

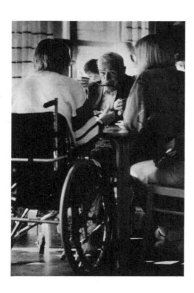

Residents with special needs require not only appropriate design and access but sometimes also special services. In Stolplyckan, Sweden, services include an inexpensive hot lunch provided by a professional cook *(left)* and oral reading of the local newspaper in the library *(below)* for people with poor eyesight. *(Thor Balkhed)*

In Egebjerggård, Denmark, cohousing now being completed will include a health clinic for the elderly and several apartments for youths. In Stolplyckan, units for the frail elderly are mixed among the cohousing dwellings. In Wageningen, Holland, four apartments in the common house are set aside for youths who come from troubled homes. Several residents volunteer to spend time with these teenagers during their residence. A proposed cohousing community in Holland will have a few units for immigrant families to help them adjust to their new country.

In Santa Rosa Creek Commons, in California, the ten low-income units are offered to families in need, including single parents and immigrants. The Reservoir has units for both mentally and physically handicapped residents.

Other possibilities include special nontoxic units for residents with toxic sensitivities and units for the blind and frail elderly.

Laundry. While European cohousing has shared laundry facilities, not all American communities may choose this option because of convenience and resale worries. Shared laundry facilities with as few as two washing machines for over twenty-five households (Sættedammen) work very well. In Denmark, households bring their basket to the common house, where the resident takes out the laundry finished in the washer and places it in the owner's basket or in the dryer and then leaves his or her laundry in the washer. If there is a line, the laundry is left in the basket after being tagged for the kind of wash setting desired, and it will eventually be placed in the washer. In Sweden, the laundry room does not have dryers but drying rooms or cabinets with heated air. Less energy is used, and the clothes, over time, last longer without dryer tumbling. In Holland, the laundry chore is often shared among clusters.

The laundry room is designed with many of the same requirements as any other laundry area, with places to fold clothes, shelves for laundry detergent and measuring cups,

and space to move around. In addition, the laundry benefits from ample windows to allow residents to see others in the common areas, an area for storage of laundry detergent, a wall space for tags, and perhaps a laundry payment system.

Storage. The common areas require a considerable amount of storage area. The dining hall is often used as a meeting room or party space, requiring storage for tables and chairs at a minimum. The kitchen requires food storage. Playrooms with outdoor access may require storage for tricycles, wagons, and plastic swimming pools. Storage needs may include a small office for records, bookkeeping, and keys, cleaning equipment such as vacuums, supplies such as toilet paper and laundry detergent, an area for used clothing, a lost and found spot, a recycling area, and so on. Room can also be provided for a small shop with common items bought in bulk. Other storage, near the entrance or in a separate area, may be needed for bicycles, baby carriages, and winter clothing.

Private Residences

The site plan and common house are clearly in the group's domain, but housing is generally viewed as part of the private realm of the individual. Typically, dream homes pictured by each member must somehow be squeezed into three or four standardized plans. Less space is available and less is needed in the home. Many activities can be accommodated in the common areas—from cooking to exercising. The amount of square footage remaining needs to be carefully designed to function smoothly and give a feeling of spaciousness.

Standardization and Flexibility

The participatory design of dwellings does not mean that each will be unique. The temptation is to customize dwellings, but costs are often too high to allow individualization of all the dwellings. Although the Winslow group began their housing design with customized dwellings, the contractor's estimate was over their budget. They then considered a kit of parts. Households could add extra bedrooms and wings to obtain many different combinations. The contractor, unmoved at this kind of standardization, stated that if the footprint (perimeter) was different, it was a different unit. A new team of designers found a way to keep costs down by designing a basic core whose floor plan included a kitchen-dining room, a living room, a bathroom and stairs leading to bedrooms above. A variety of unit sizes all incorporate this basic core.[5]

Coho members have a similar basic core, with no variation allowed unless at least three members agree to it, and that it not change the footprint of the building. "We went through many generations of plans, with some people wanting to go for the very cheapest house, and others resistant to having just a box on the site," said member Deb Sweet. Their prototypes allow some choices for members—a more expensive or less expensive exterior, a closed or open loft, a slightly larger bedroom, a bigger or smaller bathroom.

Most European collaborative architects design variations of units—roughly one variation for every ten households—that can accommodate some further changes in detail. Many designs with a set number of floor plans provide flexibility within the plan. As the dwelling is squeezed smaller, a reconsideration of the floor plan takes place.

The traditional floor plan—the closed plan—has cooking, dining, and eating in separate rooms. When the freezer, extra storage areas, guest room, hobby room, and garage are cut out of the house, there is a substantial decrease in the area needed for the dwelling. The open plan combines the kitchen, dining area, and living room into one larger room. Many of the Danish cohousing dwellings have an open plan to take advantage of available light, to enlarge spaces that would separately be too small, and to create a more public zone or area. A resident of Skråplanet said, "I loved my open plan when the children were young, and now that they're teenagers, I can't stand it," which sums up the drawbacks of a lack of privacy and little noise separation.

Many variations on the open plan have been designed, such as closing off the living room, dividing the living room from the kitchen by a half level, planning for a wall to redivide the spaces if needed by the household, and even movable walls (Vedel-Peterson et al.). One successful example is Sættedammen, where the post-and-beam construction, combined with ample space, allows the residents to subdivide their dwelling in several ways. In Tinggården, Denmark, unit variation could be achieved by a floor plan that allowed bedrooms to be shifted from one unit to another. The theory was good, but the timing of changes—occurring in both households at the same time—worked against the plan. In Flexibo, also in Denmark, extra units in the back of the dwellings could be used by households when needed, a far better solution that is similar to the inclusion of guest rooms.

In Wageningen, Holland, the problem of varying the units was solved in several ways. Residents can add or remove several walls within some of the apartments so that the same plan can accommodate an open kitchen-dining plan or a less open plan. The apartment layout also has an entrance arrangement that allows the front door to move in front of or behind several rooms located along the hallway. The front door can be located farther down the hallway, with a bathroom and extra rooms in front to be used as a separate living space or as an office. A similar kind of arrangement can be found in Hallehuis studios in Amersfoort, Holland, and in the studio apartments of Purmerend.

Another type of flexibility is to have a variety of unit sizes and floor plans that give residents the opportunity to move within the community through life stages. A new baby can be accommodated by moving to a larger unit, while a divorced person can move to a smaller unit. Since these occurrences are rarely simultaneous, the residents require some patience.

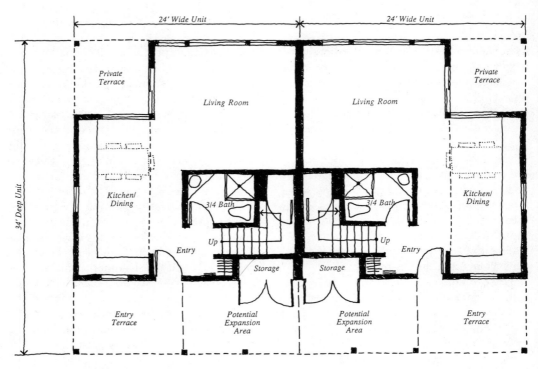

Lower Level Plan
1/4"=1'-0"

Basic Core: Kitchen/Dining
Living
Stair / 3/4 Bath

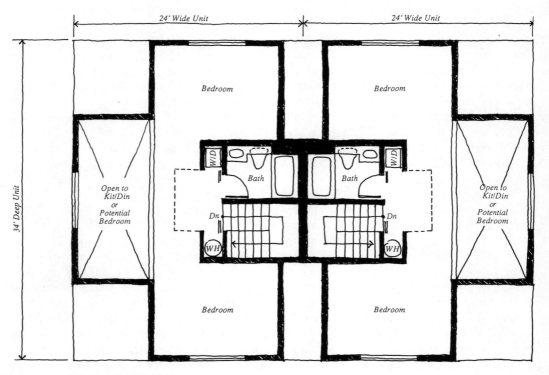

Upper Level Plan
1/4"=1'-0"

Basic Core: Stair/Bath
Potential Bedrooms

In Winslow cohousing, all the dwellings are based on a common utility core *(at left)* around which bedrooms and living rooms are added. Kitchens are located next to the front doors, and living rooms face the private realm to the back. Bedrooms are located first upstairs to the front and back, then downstairs by enclosing the porch, and finally over the kitchen in a dormer to create a four-bedroom unit. A three-bedroom/two-bath unit *(below)* expands the basic core to 1,150 square feet. *(Edward Weinstein Associates, Architects)*

Three-bedroom unit.

LOWER FLOOR

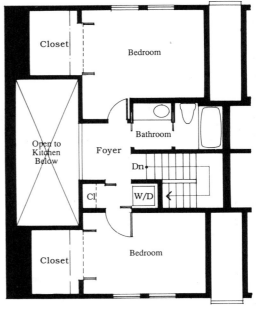

UPPER FLOOR

241

In the ten-story Cat's Head building, Stockholm, each apartment is unique, individually designed with the household, and the plans pieced together by the architect.

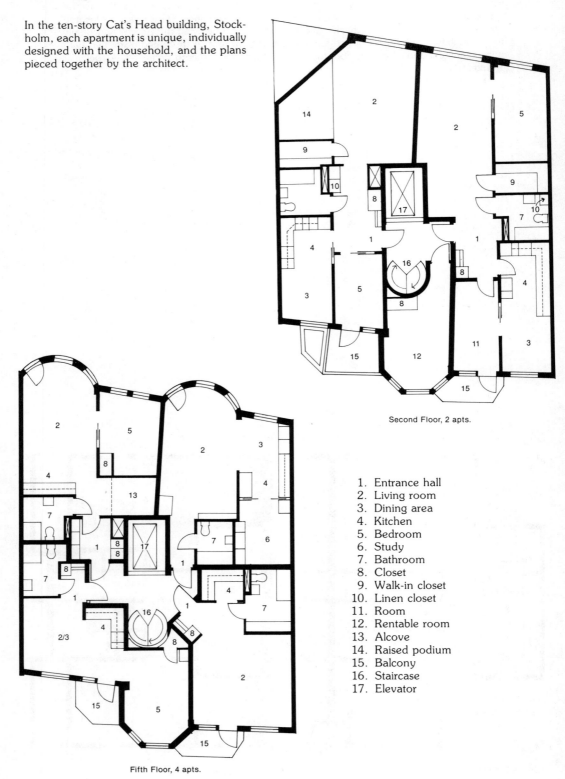

Second Floor, 2 apts.

1. Entrance hall
2. Living room
3. Dining area
4. Kitchen
5. Bedroom
6. Study
7. Bathroom
8. Closet
9. Walk-in closet
10. Linen closet
11. Room
12. Rentable room
13. Alcove
14. Raised podium
15. Balcony
16. Staircase
17. Elevator

Fifth Floor, 4 apts.

In Tinggården, Denmark, seven prototypes make up the seventy-six apartments. *(Vandkunsten)*

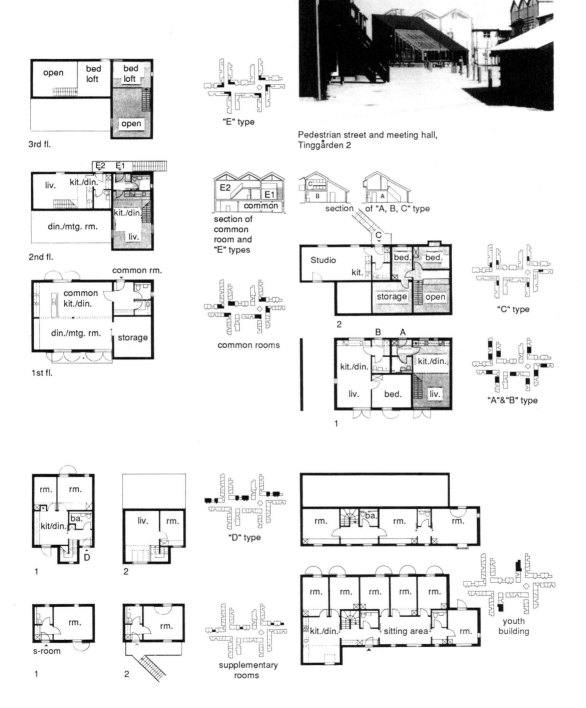

"E" type

3rd fl.

Pedestrian street and meeting hall, Tinggården 2

2nd fl.

section of common room and "E" types

section of "A, B, C" type

common rooms

Studio

"C" type

2

1

"A"&"B" type

common rm.

common kit./din.

din./mtg. rm.

storage

1st fl.

"D" type

s-room

1

2

supplementary rooms

youth building

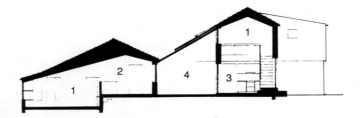

The thirty-five units at Håndværkerparken, designed with open floor plans, vary in size from studio apartments of 26 square meters to five-room apartments at 77 square meters. The one-and-a-half and two-story dwellings are grouped along a covered street.

1. Living-dining room; 2. kitchen; 3. kitchen-family room; 4. covered street.

Cluster floor plans, Wageningen, Holland. The household can enlarge the number of rooms in the apartment depending on the location of the front door and the inclusion of a movable wall; for example, on the third and fourth floors. (LVCW)

Special Needs

Floor plans can also be tailored to special groups, such as frail seniors and handicapped people. These special requirements can be costly and may need to be subsidized by the other households. These residents may need lowered light switches, special bathroom fixtures and layouts, and kitchens designed for wheelchair use. Moreover, making the site accessible for wheelchairs can save costs later of retrofitting when members grow older or a member has limited mobility.

The Winslow group near Seattle plans to include an elevator in its multilevel common house for one of the disabled members. The Muir Commons group has taken special care to make the entire site handicapped accessible for their two wheelchair members.

Zoning

The private dwellings allow visual access to the common areas as well as privacy. The floor plan is zoned into a semipublic area with a window facing the common paths or corridor. Usually this more public area is the kitchen-dining room. The private areas, usually bedrooms and often the living room, are in back, facing out to the private garden.

In multistory collaborative housing, visual access to a central garden can be difficult to provide. Corridors often divide the apartments in two separate directions. The residents of Purmerend faced this design problem; their central hallway would require that half the units face the common garden and the other half face in the opposite direction. The group had a strong preference for all the

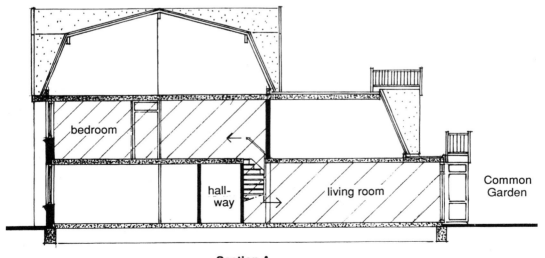

Section A

In Purmerend, Holland, by criss-crossing apartments, each residence has either an upstairs or downstairs view from the living room out to the common garden and bedrooms in the back for privacy. *(Verhoeven)*

Apartment floor plans in Purmerend, Holland.

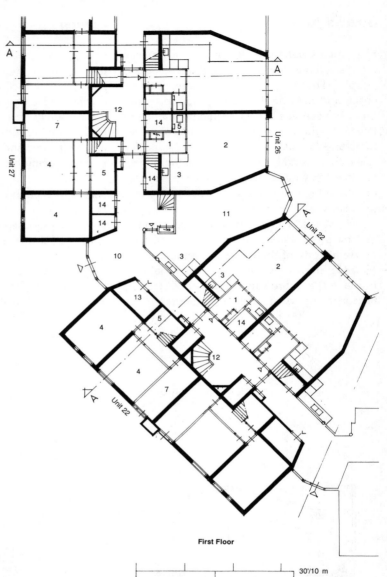

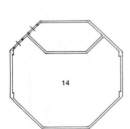

First Floor

30'/10 m

1. Entrance
2. Living-dining room
3. Kitchen
4. Bedroom
5. Bathroom
6. Closet
7. Room with private entrance
8. Connecting balcony
9. Connecting roof terrace
10. Connecting hallway
11. Cluster kitchen-dining area
12. Cluster staircase
13. Cluster bathroom
14. Storage

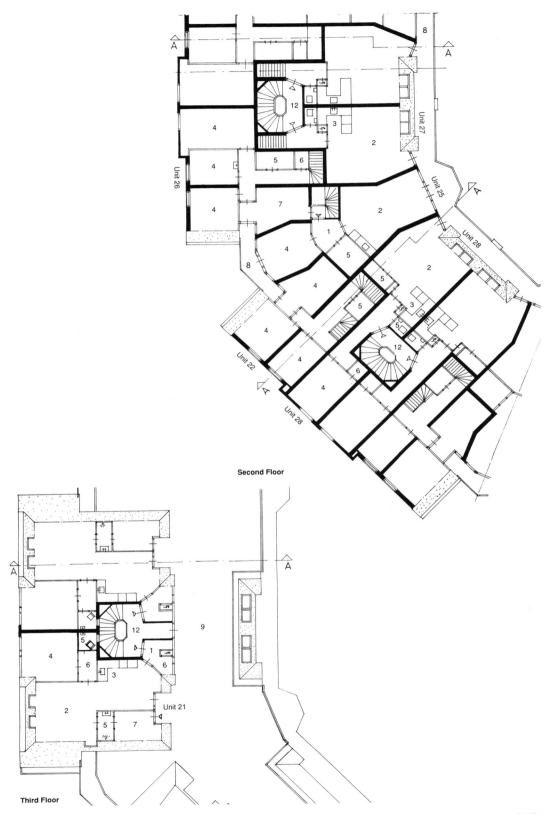

Second Floor

Third Floor

247

units to have visual access to the common garden and that their bedrooms face in the opposite direction for greater noise and visual privacy. The architect's solution was a unique zigzag design that allows all the units to have a garden side and a private side.

Storage

Ample storage rarely seems ample enough. When more storage is required, especially for large items, will the residents build sheds in their yards or place the items in the common house? In Denmark, storage sheds built in private yards facing common outdoor space detract from the overall community appearance and blocked views from the dwelling.

Storage can occur within the house—in large closets, an attic, or a basement. Outside storage can be placed in a separate carport or a storage shed. Storage areas can also be placed in the common house—either in a large room or under separate key in wire compartments. And it can be divided among several places—nearby for seasonal items such as winter clothes and farther away for long-term storage.

Buildings of three or more stories do not lend themselves to expansion, and over time, the press for room squeezes out into the hallway, where bureaus, rows of shoes, and coat racks find a new niche. Lofts, additional storage that can be built in, and ample storage elsewhere can reduce this clutter.

Appliances

In European cohousing, household dishwashers and washing machines are not normally included in the dwellings, but Americans see these appliances as basic amenities. Residents may prefer that the choice be left up to them, with the availability of retrofitting their homes should essential appliances be initially left out. This often turns into a value-type of decision.

DESIGN POSTSCRIPT

Some of the most difficult development problems are not specifically design issues but have to do with difference in values among members. Other conflicts involve the architect, surrounding neighbors, and financing issues.

Conflicts among Members

As the development progresses, decisions become more specific and detailed. At the start, decisions are made without anyone knowing specifically where their home will be. During design development, the stage before working drawings, the locations and sizes of individual residences must be determined. Members decide which of the homes will be theirs, cost differences among the homes, and details about the layout.

Decisions that deal with home and hearth can be among the most difficult to resolve. The individual's rights may be restricted by the group in ways that some members find difficult to accept. Restrictions of time and money require compromises, such as narrowing choices to two floor plans, one heating system, or one exterior house color.

After the design is completed, attention shifts to policy decisions, which raise further difficult issues. By this time, the group has had a number of opportunities to make decisions together. Finding a resolution or compromise, which may have been impossible earlier, is spurred by previous experience and the knowledge that moving in may soon be a reality.

Choosing Homes

"We had a meeting about choosing where on the site we wanted to live. We always dreaded the possibility that we would have to compete among each other for houses," said a member from Muir Commons. The members decided not to choose homes based on who joined the group first but rather through discussion and need. They began by having an all-day meeting at which they divided the site into four sections and had members go to the section they preferred. This process was not fully successful because some members (those without children) wanted a quiet section.

In their second attempt, a large site plan was placed on the wall, and each household indicated their first through fifth choices. A discussion then began, starting with the dwellings the fewest people wanted. If a member's first choice was selected by three or four others, he or she would consider switching to a second or third choice. Eventually a consensus was reached. "In choosing the homes, it was real easy to get attached to one we like. But we felt choosing homes was a bit of a microcosm of our group process. We would look back on it and say it was done in a way that strengthened the group or weakened it. And in the end it definitely strengthened it," said member Jeff Gottesman.

The Winslow group in Seattle went through a similar process in choosing their dwellings. Although their bylaws state that the member with the most seniority can choose first, they decided to save this method as a backup system. "If people joined later, they shouldn't get the worst sites," explained a member.

The choice of a site actually began much earlier by maintaining an egalitarian site design. During the design, colored stickers were given to members, with blue as first choice, to be placed on the sites and houses. The architect Lynn Perkins thus observed:

We found out early which sites and houses weren't in demand. We asked them, "What would it take to *make* you choose it?" Some said more sun; there were other suggestions. So we would redesign and, boom, they would choose over there.

Certain things began to be evident. There were certain units that were better for our wheelchair member, so others tended not to choose it. An artist picked a prime spot with the best light, and no one fought her for it. Give and take—people recognizing each other's specific needs.

Pricing the Units

The common costs of development are usually divided at the time the dwellings are chosen so that members know what their housing choice will cost. In European collaborative communities, there are several methods of dividing costs. One is to proportion the costs according to the amount of the private square footage. For example, two people each pay 10% of the total common costs, but a household with a bigger dwelling pays more of the common costs. Another method is to divide the common costs equally among the households. A third and popular method is a combination of these two systems, with half the common costs divided equally and half by square footage, but it only works well when the units are the same size.

The Winslow group originally decided to use this third method. When they had finished designing their units, they divided the common costs—50% based on the unit size and 50% equally among the households. Member Hanson said, "Once we knew the size of the units, we discovered that the small units could end up paying $150 a square foot and the large ones $75 a square foot, and the small units couldn't afford it." (The price of their site was about one-sixth the price of the development.)

Finding a fair system that all members could accept proved much more complicated than had been anticipated. "Just using construction costs didn't work either, because some sites were more difficult to build on than others but necessary for a holistic plan," said former member-architect Lynn Perkins. The group tried a number of different formulas with the intention that all the houses would fall within a certain square foot range. Their housing design included carriage houses above enclosed parking without back yards. These more apartment-like units blocked the parking-lot view and saved site space. Unfortunately, few members wanted to live in them. "So we kept readjusting the prices," explained the architect, "until you could save

$17,000 by moving into a carriage house." Price adjustments also went to households who moved into the middle unit in a triplex and some units that would be noisier due to their location. In total $150,000 went into rebates, increasing the price of the other dwellings.

In multistory collaborative communities, a similar type of price fixing can be found. Architect Wille Herlin created a matrix of costs for members of Cat's Head in Sweden. The complicated matrix included views, size of units, and many other criteria. A large difference in price was needed for members to choose the lower units without views, a difference much wider than a landlord would impose.

Heating and Natural Resources

A number of collaborative housing groups in the United States have made energy conservation one of their goals. Energy-efficient heating and cooling systems have high initial costs but become cost-effective over time. Architect Bob Small believes the most difficult design decisions are those that are value related: "Is everyone willing to hand carry recycling waste or not have washers and dryers in the units? And the classic—not to have wood-burning fireplaces—to reevaluate the concept of hearth because of environmental damage."

The Muir Commons group in Davis had to decide between a radiant heat system in the floor slab or a central heating and air-conditioning system with ducts. A heated discussion occurred because some members wanted the option of air-conditioning their homes in the hot California summers, while others were adamantly against this kind of "energy waste." The group eventually chose a radiant heating system with the possibility of attaching an air-conditioning unit to a window for those members who wanted it.

Locks and Keys

Surprisingly, locks and keys have been an issue in many collaborative communities.

Opinions vary from keeping common spaces all locked for security to keeping them all open for accessibility. Some parents feel that locking facilities prevents their children from being able to use them alone. Many residents in Stacken, Sweden, felt that it was not fair to deny children access to the crafts and wood shops. Others felt that those kind of spaces need to be locked so that children do not hurt themselves or create a mess. In the Reservoir, Wisconsin, there is also the issue of keeping the cluster common spaces open or locked. These shared areas are right off the entrance, used among four households. A disagreement occurred among several single women, who wanted the entrance door locked for security, and a mother of a young child, who was weary of climbing down to open the door and wanted it to remain unlocked. One solution in Europe is to designate a monitor, who will lock and unlock certain common spaces but clearly not those often used. Another is to use a numbered lock, where children punch in two or three numbers to enter, and the numbers are changed every few months.

Surrounding Neighbors

The group itself is not the only source of different opinions. Neighbors are often suspicious of new developments, especially those that appear different in density or purchase price. Collaborative developments are particularly vulnerable because they are a new housing form. A city council member of a small northern California town, when presented with the idea by an eager cohousing group, called it "communistic." Developments such as a Herbie's in Washington had to fight strong neighborhood opposition because the site plan was not divided into individual lots. Several recently formed cohousing groups are facing neighbors who are supportive, in general, of this new housing concept, but feel strongly it should not be in their own neighborhood.

Fears concerning collaborative developments are also common in Denmark, Holland, and Sweden. In Denmark, neighbors organized to force the Jystrup Sawværket group onto another site in a less prominent location. Neighbors surrounding Stacken, Sweden, expressed surprise that households had their own toilets, not aware that the units were fully independent.

Initially, a number of collaborative communities in Europe were thought to be communes, where promiscuity and drugs reigned, and neighbors fought against their development in their community. As this housing form has become more accepted, opposition has decreased. The group is often strengthened in dealing with outside suspicion and threats to its existence.

Once the development opened, neighbors were invited in and found their worries unjustified. A number of communities hold a yearly event—an open house, a garage sale, or a party—where the neighbors can come in and see for themselves that residents live in a civilized manner. Once the community is established, neighborhood disapproval usually disappears or becomes something to live with, not a threat to the existence of the development.

Neighbors' concern with this new way of living is not limited to the physical form. Collaborative groups can also have a political impact on the community. Residents are organized and can exert an influence at the local level. Members do not often use their influence in local politics because in many instances they do not agree with each other. Generally, little emphasis is placed on common political work in communities. But when they are aroused, especially on environmental and educational concerns, their combined effort can influence the outcome of local issues in small areas. A number of residents of Stolplyckan, Sweden, organized to prevent development on a hill near their community and were successful.

Certain aspects of collaborative living rub against closely held beliefs in American culture that concern social life and morality. Suspicions may be a matter of miscommunications, misuse, or simply the "not in my neighborhood" mentality. Educating the surrounding community and finding opportunities to meet and talk can ease some conflicts. Others may take more time to find resolution.

NOTES

1. He was referring to the theories of British psychiatrist Wilfred Bion, who studied group behavior at Tavistock Institute in Great Britain and developed a theory of group leadership and task completion (Rioch).
2. In Holland, up to fifty households have successfully shared two common houses without dividing the group into clusters and with common houses' accommodating different food preferences.
3. Since the units are clustered, the traditional method of measuring density does not give the best indication of how close residents will live to each other, but it does provide a close approximation of how the community will appear—low housing surrounded by open space, compact four-plex units, or three-story row houses, for example.
4. The group can consider whether some members are willing to live with increased pedestrian traffic in exchange for the convenience of locating next to the common facilities and whether such units could be made more attractive to residents through an increase of space or a decrease in cost.
5. The thirty Winslow units include ten duplexes with two-, three-, and four-bedroom dwellings, a carriage house with two two-bedroom dwellings and four studios with parking below, and four one-bedroom dwellings. All but the carriage house utilize the basic core.

REFERENCES

Carp, John. 1984. "Twenty Years of SAR." In *The Scope of Social Architecture*. New York: Van Nostrand Reinhold.

Kjaer, Bodil. 1988. "Where Dream Houses Come True." *World Monitor* (October), pp. 87–89.

Krabbendam, Flip. 1984. "Participatie en vormgeving, ontwerp en vernieuwing." Plan 10. The Netherlands.

Lauters, Gunilla; Leif Ljungberg, and Karin Palm Lindén. 1988. *Kök För Gemenskap i kolleltivhus och kvarterslokaler*. Stockholm: Byggforskningsrådet.

Lindén, Karin Palm. 1989. "The Physical Structure of the Swedish Collective House—Support or Limit the Inhabitants' Everyday Life." In *Neue Wohnformen in Europa, Berichte des vierten Internationalen Wohnbund-Kongresses in Hamburg*, ed. Joachim Brech, pp. 320-331. Darmstadt, Germany: Wohnbund, Verlag für Wissenschaftliche Publikationen (in English and German).

Lukez, Paul. 1986. *New Concepts in Housing: Supports in The Netherlands*. Cambridge: Massachusetts Institute of Technology, Department of Architecture.

McCamant, Kathryn, and Charles Durrett. 1988. *Cohousing*. Berkeley: Ten Speed Press.

Rioch, Margaret J. 1970. "The Work of Wilfred Bion on Groups." *Psychiatry* **33**(1, Feb.):56-66.

Svensson, Ole. 1988. *Planning of Low-rise Urban Housing Areas*. SBI Report 56. Hørsholm, Denmark: Danish Building Research Institute.

Vedel-Petersen, Finn; Erik B. Jantzen, and Karen Ranten. 1988. *Bofællesskaber*. SBI Report 187. Hørsholm, Denmark: Danish Building Research Institute.

CHAPTER 16

Building

The bidding process begins after the completion of the working drawings by the architect. Either one contractor has worked along with the architect and provides a construction price, or several contractors are invited to give bids, with the lowest awarded the job. The actual cost of the project is now known. If it is too high, the scope of work may need to be trimmed; linoleum may replace wood flooring, decks disappear, and the sauna may be in jeopardy.

Construction eventually begins, requiring coordination and communications among the architect, group, contractor, subcontractors, and financing source. To save on costs, the future residents may decide to do some of the finishing work themselves. This kind of sweat equity needs to be carefully considered in the light of the group's time and the amount of reluctance shown by the financing source. Finally, the project is complete. The celebration begins.

BIDS

The bidding documents, provided by the architect, include the working drawings and the specifications (a written document describing the work and level of finish). The group can choose to be its own general contractor and hire separate workers to do the foundation work, plumbing, electricity, sheetrocking, and so on. In this case, separate bids are requested for each job, a task that requires a large amount of coordinating time. Or the group can hire a general contractor, who will then hire, pay, and coordinate the subcontractors. For a fee, the general contractor reduces the amount of negotiation required of the group or consultant.

A general contractor can be hired through a closed bid, open bid, or negotiated bid process.

In a *closed* bid, a predetermined list of contractors is selected. An invitation to bid is sent to those contractors, and positive responses receive a complete set of working drawings and specifications. A date is set for opening the bids, often two weeks or a month after the bids are sent. The lowest bidder receives the job.

An *open* bid is advertised in the newspaper or through a business exchange to all interested contractors. (To attract bids by minorities, the advertisement can be placed in special newspapers.) The bidding is the same for the closed bid process, although it requires more reproduction and coordination costs. The contractor with the lowest bid receives the job.

The advantage of open bidding is that

more contractors will bid, and perhaps the price will be lower than if only a few contractors provide estimates. The disadvantage is that the lowest-bidding contractor may not be as competent as is hoped. Open bidding is required for HUD financing (Government's Housing and Urban Development Program) and for many city and state financing. (Another requirement is the Davis-Bacon Act, stipulating that the contractor must pay prevailing wages to workers and subcontractors.)

The *negotiated* bid begins before the working drawings are prepared. A set of preliminary plans and specifications is sent to selected contractors with a request for a preliminary bid. The lowest bidder becomes the contractor if he or she agrees not to alter the bid more than 4-5% and to consult with the architect on the final drawings. The group reserves the right not to use the contractor, but they must pay for any time the contractor spends working with the architect (around $5,000-$15,000). The advantages are that the contractor becomes very familiar with the plans and can suggest alternative methods to the architect to lower costs and reduce the number of change orders during construction. The disadvantage is that the architect may not be willing to work with the contractor and that the cost may not be as low as in open bidding.

The Northwest Community Foundation in Seattle recommends the negotiated bid process for cost control. According to developer Chris Hanson, "If the contractor has helped create the budget, that's what it will come in at, or he'll have egg on his face. Competitive bids also work, but unfortunately they can create a negative relationship between the contractor and the architect or developer. In negotiated bids, the contractor is highly motivated to get the job by working with the group."

Groups like Winslow in Seattle have begun working with the contractor soon after the schematic designs have been completed. The contractor and the group sign a letter of understanding (not a contract) to provide a reasonable reassurance that the contractor will get the job. In many instances, the contractor will work without a fee, although the Winslow group agreed to pay for 40 hours of consultation. Since more than a million dollars worth of construction are at stake, the contractor has a strong interest in landing the job and in seeing that the budget remains acceptable. One cohousing architect had this to say about having the contractor on call:

It's been a very fruitful dialogue. Basically he's giving us an idea of where our efforts at standardization are saving money and where they are not. We also try to work with the technology the builder commands. When he's not familiar with our construction technique, we can change it. It's also become a creative entity to get the most innovation for the least amount of costs. The design is experimental enough that you need a relationship with the builder.

The architect may find that the construction documents are more complicated than for typical multifamily construction depending on the amount of customization. Often different households may request different levels of finishes, such as for kitchen cabinets or flooring material.

CONSTRUCTION

Finally the groundbreaking begins. During the construction, the work of the contractor is overseen by the construction supervisor. The architect, both because of his or her knowledge of the drawings and because he or she may have liability exposure, usually takes on the role of construction supervisor. In addition, the group can hire a representative (such as a retired engineer or retired general contractor) on an hourly basis. An agreement should be made with the architect, the bank, and the general contractor concerning hiring a representative. The group's representative will visit the site daily and has an intimate knowledge of construction, whereas the architect visits less often. Daily communication reduces mistakes and allows the group time to evaluate problems and make decisions.

Coordination and communications between the group and the contractor can be handled through one or two members to reduce confusion. Group members have a tendency to visit the site and request special alterations to their dwellings, which can be disruptive for the contractor.

Since the group may require more time than one client to respond to problems, a carefully worked out payment schedule is important. If the contractor expects to be paid by the first of the month, the contractor, architect, representative, and group members can meet on the site to sign the releases at least ten to fifteen days earlier.

SWEAT EQUITY

Construction tasks that can be done by the residents themselves to save costs are called sweat equity. While this is one way to cut the budget, the kinds of jobs that unskilled, busy people can undertake is limited and may require additional liability insurance. Common sweat equity tasks include the following:

Demolition of existing small structures on site
Preparation of the site for construction
Subflooring
Painting
Mounting cupboards
Finishing wood floors
Landscaping
Building play equipment

Of these, interior dwelling work and landscaping are the best choices for sweat equity because they do not hold up the construction if they are not done or done poorly. Many developers and contractors are reluctant to

The skills and cooperation residents learn in doing the work themselves come in useful for future changes and alterations. This skateboard track was originally built by the residents. Eventually the children became tired of it, so this work party is taking it out to make way for another resident-built play structure. *(Thor Balkhed)*

agree to other kinds of sweat equity tasks because of the possibility of holding up the completion date.

The residents themselves can accomplish major construction with the help of a contractor coordinator but such a task can require several years with members' working about 20 hours a week. Careful planning and strong legal contracts that allow nonparticipants to be removed are essential. Sweat equity raises a dilemma that needs to be considered if long-term housing affordability is important. While the first buyers can pay off some of the housing equity with their sweat, the next generation of buyers will need to be of a higher income. For example, the first buyers provide a $5,000 downpayment and work off an additional $5,000. The next buyer will have to come up with a downpayment of $10,000. Under certain types of tenure (such as limited-equity cooperative ownership), there are few ways to compensate people for their sweat equity.

CHAPTER 17

Issues of Community Life

They love each other like brothers—that's why they're fighting.
Comment by a mother during afternoon child care at the common house

After the community is designed, issues about community life become the central focus. How is the community to remain nondivisive and vibrant? What problems will affect the day-to-day life in the community? While

Sættedammen, Denmark. *(Lilian Bolvinkel)*

members can come up with agreements before they move in, issues and conflicts will arise; they are part of living collaboratively.

BEFORE MOVING IN

Before moving in, members attempt to address some issues through policies, bylaws, agreements, and covenants, conditions, and restrictions (CC&Rs). These could include agreements on:

Use

Landscaping
Lighting
Fencing of individual yards and common spaces
Cottage industries
Hobbies (from auto repair to ham radios)
Uses of the common house and liability
Security of common spaces
Allowing renters, subleasing
Maintenance (painting and reroofing)
Additions (individual and common)
Repair funds
Inspection
Rubbish disposal and recycling
Vehicle parking

Meetings

Decision making (voting criteria)
Conduct of meetings
Electing officials and directors
Removal of officials and directors
Committees (decision making, budget)
Election verification
Calling meetings
Annual retreat or evaluation

Behavior

Children
Pets
Noise levels
Work times
Smoking, nudity, alcohol, guns, roommates, and others

Member Responsibilities

Meeting attendence
Amount of required work in the community
Joining a committee
Cooking and cleaning
Conflict resolution

Cooking and Cleaning

Frequency of commitment
Description of duties
Assignment of duties
Children's tasks
Type and kind of food (salt, allergies, alcohol)
Buying/cost
Planning
Work excuses and absenteeism
Nonparticipation
Method of food preparation and sanitation
Use of produce grown on site
Waste

Seller Restrictions*

Community approves new members
Community has first option to buy unit
A ceiling on unit appreciation

Rules on some of these issues are difficult to enforce. Probably the easiest to enforce are those dealing with use that can be written into CC&Rs, deed restrictions that are controlled by a home owners' association. Most of the items listed under "Uses" are not specific to collaborative communities and can be found in every condominium association's CC&Rs. In a condominium, if a member plants a large hedge or paints the house a bright purple, the association can take the offender to court and stand a good chance of winning the case.

Behavior and responsibilities of members are written in a separate home owner's agreement, signed by all the members. A set number of responsibilities can be determined and described. For example, typical responsibilities in Danish cohousing include cooking,

---

*Resale controls can occur in the title, trust deeds, loan agreements, and CC&Rs. Condominium resale controls are not placed in the CC&Rs but in a separate resale agreement.

Participation in community chores is an essential aspect of living collaboratively. Members' willingness to tackle the dirty dishes arises from their own responsibility and interest, and cannot be successfully forced. *(Lilian Bolvinkel)*

duced for members who sign off as having worked a certain number of hours or tasks. Members A and B both pay $100 a month in common fees, but member B is entitled to a 50% return at the end of the month for putting in a set amount of work time. Such a method is not used in the European examples, where some amount of nonparticipation is more or less accepted.

Seller restrictions vary from state to state and among ownership types. Legally these restrictions must be carefully drafted to hold up in a court of law. The more restrictions there are with the same goal, the less inclined a member will be to go to court since the battle will be long and costly. Therefore, including three or four restrictions adds legal friction. Consult with a housing adviser or lawyer for exact wording on restrictions.

Some, such as the Winslow group, initially wanted as few restrictions as possible on home owners. "We believe that to have a community, you need a basic trust and respect for each other," explained several members. Although there will always be residents who think this way, be forewarned. Restrictions do not change the basic trust and respect between members. Assume that residents will get along well, but write restrictions so that in the event of a failure there will be a document to point to and say "but we agreed beforehand." Hopefully these restrictions will never need to be used because of the basic trust between residents. "Everyone has the desire for a lot of personal freedom, but somehow it's got to be balanced within the context of the group being strong," believes member Paul Seif of Muir Commons. To find that balance can take many long discussions.

cleaning up after a meal, and cleaning the common house. All of these tasks can be done once a month as part of a work crew. In addition, members are expected to attend a general meeting and serve on a committee once a month. Without special contingencies written by a lawyer, there is little legal recourse if a member chooses not to participate in these requirements. It is difficult to force a resident to cook a common dinner, join a committee, or work 8 hours in the garden. Under certain rental and leasing cooperative agreements, however, a member's lease may not be renewed if that member shows uncooperative behavior, such as not attending monthly meetings.

There are other possibilities of ensuring some equality between a member who works and one who does not. Depending on the type of ownership, the monthly fee can be re-

CONFLICT AND EMPOWERMENT

After moving in, residents can expect a certain amount of tension between members as part of living collaboratively. "I enjoy living here," said Marianne, a cohousing resident. "I have someone to be happy with and someone to be mad at. It's not only my husband and children I always wait for." Some of the

pressure is taken off the immediate household by having nearby neighbors and friends. But more is expected from these members of the community and more time is spent with them.

That almost all collaborative communities find a way of living with conflicts of values speaks to their ability to reconcile divergent viewpoints. To many members, this is the heart of creating a real community, where diverse people learn to live with one another.

Types of Conflict

The conflicts that typically arise in collaborative communities are strikingly similar in the United States, Denmark, Holland, and Sweden. They generally fall into five categories:

1. Miscommunications
2. Territoriality[1]
3. Personality
4. Expectations from collaboration
5. Values (morals and beliefs)

These kinds of conflict can occur among neighbors in other types of housing, but in collaborative living there is a much greater involvement in day-to-day decisions among residents. Along with greater intimacy and equality of power comes a greater potential for conflict among members.

Miscommunications

Conflicts that involve miscommunications appear to be the easiest to resolve. These kinds of problems are often solved by rules, notes, or other attempts at organization. They can, however, mask other, deeper conflicts that make such attempts at organization fairly ineffective. These often fall into the other four categories.

Territoriality

Residents in collaborative communities use the common areas as an extension of their own private spaces. They find, though, that the line is fuzzy on how the common area is used for private purposes. Common areas belong to everyone, yet residents feel a certain sense of personal ownership and responsibility toward the space. Should children be allowed to climb the fruit tree? Can a private heat pump that creates noise be installed outdoors? Can a family paint the house red?

In Sunlight, Oregon, a resident who delighted in rhododendrons began to plant them in the common areas. (The community owns 7 acres of common land.) He bought and planted them himself and tended them faithfully. The delight of the other residents, however, slowly diminished as more and more rhododendrons appeared. Some residents began to complain that the natural landscape was being altered. The gardener pointed out the beautification of the area. A meeting resulted, and a plan to get the approval of the community before planting was decided, but this member did not follow the spirit of the agreement.

Claiming common space as private territory is more likely in densely built developments. For example, the community of Purmerend, Holland, has a very actively used common green shared by seventy households. The households are divided into ten clusters. (The private outdoor area for households is, in some cases, a planting strip 3 by 5 feet.) A corner cluster that had less room than the others took over part of the common outdoor area for its private use. Other clusters felt they should have the same rights and made plans for taking over a share of the common area. Some residents opposed the idea; others were for it. An overall garden plan is now being decided. This is a territoriality conflict that could have been obviated if the architect or landscape architect had provided more outdoor area or a careful landscaping of the existing area to include a hierarchy of uses. Not only was private and common outdoor space required, but an in-between size was needed for small groups to gather.

In communities that have private residences and common areas all under one roof, territoriality issues can be greater be-

In Stolplyckan, Sweden, the initiative that this small group of residents took to create a deck from the common land directly outside their apartment tower was decried by some other residents as "undemocratic" and "privitization" when the community as a whole was not asked beforehand. *(Thor Balkhed)*

cause the common area is right outside the front door.

Personality

Residents do not share equal talents or inclinations. When a problem is discussed, one resident says, "Let's do it!" and another says, "Let's think about this a bit more." These residents are two opposites that can be found in every community.

One of the unwritten responsibilities of members is to speak out, not easy for some residents. Almost as a common is the outspoken resident. In Stacken, Sweden, a few people dominated the common meetings. "We would go from a meeting which we thought was a wonderful meeting, where lots of problems were solved, and afterwards we heard people say that was an impossible meeting—nothing had been done, no real

questions have been raised," recalls the architect. "They were angry because those people who found it easy to talk, like me and some others, had been saying a lot of things while they had not been talking themselves." Little notes would appear with opposing viewpoints that would stir people up during the week. To address this problem, small committees were formed where people felt at ease talking about the issues.

In Sunlight, Oregon, as in other communities, there are those who are confrontational about differences and those who avoid speaking about them. "If you don't put out negative stuff, it builds up in you, but if you put it out in a big dump, that person becomes offended. Some people feel like it's very important to do that—but I don't think it works well," said Barbara Church. "We haven't developed a useful way to say when we are unhappy about things. So far no one has come up with a great solution."

Expectations from Collaboration

Personality differences are expected in any group of people. More difficult to accept is the variation in attitude toward collaboration, from the idealistic to indifference. A certain idealism is required to start a core group, to push for funding, and to convince the municipality about such a housing idea, knowing that any tangible result will be several years away at best. The role of members will change of necessity. Once moved in, members become involved in the day-to-day requirements and seem to lose sight of loftier goals. The idealistic individual will find many disappointments.

Paul Groenendaal is an ex-member of a collaborative community he helped to start in Holland. When the community started, Paul had political ideas in mind, and he feels that by being polarized about the "little things," the big things he hoped would come out of the group never did:

I was too idealistic for that way of living. I wanted too much. Every week there were discussions with the group about the kitchen, the cooking, cleaning the house, financial things, and so on and so on, and talk and talk. But they are not real problems to speak about, I think. Then you have to speak about politics, things out of the house. The small problems were blown up to elephants, clean or cleaner—for one clean, for another cleaner. Big things—like people outside, the earth, the town, the milieu, the nature, the military, the bombs, philosophy of life—these are problems. By talking about the little things, the real things in life have no role.

Ideology appears in every cohousing community. In Jystrup Sawærket, Denmark, two couples felt very strongly that not enough was done in common. They believed, for example, that the community could do more to live in an environmentally responsible way and that residents should spend more time within the community. The two couples eventually moved out.

Members who hope for a feeling of "one big family" are particularly irked by members who are perceived to do less than their share. The "free-loaders" who appear to some other residents as shirking their duty seem particularly to irritate those who had high expectations of members. Since residents cooperate for the good of the community and the benefits come to all, it is difficult to "make" people work. Berit Ziebell, a resident of Æblevangen cohousing in Denmark, noted, "In the beginning we were more organized, and said, 'You have to do this and this,' but then people didn't choose to work. At first we were hard and thought, 'That one's lazy,' but now we realize people have their own reasons. . . . We have learned to be tolerant and find ways of agreeing."

A certain level of tolerance is exercised concerning role expectations, but there are members who cross that wide line of tolerance not by their lack of work but because of some behavior other residents find socially disruptive. Although various social agencies (as well as some residents) had high hopes for the healing powers of living collaboratively and felt this was the appropriate place for dysfunctional people, this has not proved to be the case. Such people often caused a disruption in the community. Lars Ågren said of an alcoholic who moved into Stacken, "It's not a problem the community can solve. It's a process. First they destroy the life of the people in the house, then they destroy their own possibilities in the house, and then it's finally very clear that they can't live in the house, and they move."

Values (Morals and Beliefs)

Conflicting values manifest themselves in a number of areas but are rarely directly addressed. One large issue is between those who believe in rules and those who believe that rules stifle community, creativity, and daily life. Conflicts over children often are a clashing of these opposing values between parents. Those who believe in rules and discipline have a hard time dealing with those who do not, and vice versa. In Santa Rosa Creek Commons, California, the way children behave is an ongoing issue, one that is never solved. In Stacken, the children who paid little attention to rules are now teenagers. A Stacken resident believes:

Some of the teenage girls are very aggressive persons and a bit negative. I think it's from their parents. They tell people to go to hell. When we talk at the meetings, their parents think it's not so bad—that perhaps we've done something before that made them angry at us. These parents just talk around the issues and can't see the problem. No discipline. The children notice that their parents support them, so they never stop saying these things. They could do anything, and they don't tell them to stop."

Density appears to be associated with more problems concerning children (Marcus). In Stacken, there is a high percentage of children and a small amount of private outdoor area provided by balconies. In the less dense Danish developments, however, issues revolving around children also appear difficult to resolve.

In Sættedammen, Denmark, residents had strong ideological beliefs about child care and the participation of parents in child care. After some time, the parent child care system ended, in part because of the difficulties of taking time off work, in part from a feeling that some parents were not "good enough" at this task. A person was then hired for the job, but not everyone was satisfied with this arrangement. "We have a number of teachers among ourselves, and we have an ongoing discussion whether professionals are better for the children or taking care of them ourselves. We thought one way and then the other." A while ago, needing a short-term solution, they asked the older children to watch the younger ones. "It turned out absolutely wonderful. The big kids [14 and 15 year old] have grown up with the little ones, and they aren't so pedagogical. They say: 'You do that!' and the little ones are very happy to do it."

Cleanliness is another issue that seems to arise often. "If I clean the place ten times, I'm much better than someone who cleans five times. They think it's a cleaning problem, but if you live with a man and always argue about cleaning, you can be sure it's not a cleaning problem," said an ex-member of a Swedish community. Residents who live in multiunit

housing and share hallways mention this issue much more often than those who live in low-rise dwellings.

Diversity and Members' Conflicts

Of the five types of conflicts, the ones that concern the basis of collaboration—role expectations and differences of values—are hardest to resolve and have a more divisive effect. The likelihood of these types of conflicts occurring increases with the size of the group, number of different backgrounds, and life stages of residents.

Certainly, diversity of members is one ingredient in conflicts between members. Yet communities of all like-minded people are considered undesirable in collaborative housing, where the goal is to create a diverse community.

Is there a proper balance? Collaborative housing developments have varying degrees of member diversity. In Denmark, Holland, and Sweden, as well as in the United States, communities under condominium or cooperative ownership tend to have members of similar age and backgrounds. Publicly funded rentals or those that have units at restricted prices are more diverse, reflecting different priorities in creating a community.

Members of Santa Rosa Creek Commons strongly believe that a mix of ages, incomes, and cultures is what makes a "real community."[2] The American communities that are most diverse are rentals or limit equity (limit resale profit).[3] They tend to be located in urban areas, near services such as shopping and child care, the dwellings are either apartments or multiplex housing, and the monthly payments are low. Communities in the suburbs or outside town, with single-family homes and several acres of open space, are not as diverse. The high housing cost, the residents' dependence on cars, and distances from jobs limit the kind of people who can move in. Most of these communities are not diverse in age, race, or class.[4] Often the ages of the home owners are similar, and the community ages along with the members.

The issue of conflicts between members in the more diverse communities, such as the Commons, is treated differently than in many home owner collaborative communities, such as Sunlight. The Commons has many pages of clearly written rules and an ongoing education program on living cooperatively, as well as a formal conflict-resolution procedure. A great deal of time and commitment are required to maintain a cooperative spirit. Sunlight, in contrast, has few rules. Member Stephanie Sussman states that rules are "not an issue": "There is an underlying understanding that people need to be respectful of others. There are a few people who would like to see more rules, but they're so few that it wouldn't fly." Residents at Sunlight do have conflicts, but they are resolved informally.

In Europe, the rental collaborative developments have the most diversity (singles, single parents, various ages and incomes). They tend to have more conflicts and less participation than developments owned by the residents. The causes—limited involvement in the development, higher densities, a weak membership selection process, larger number of households, or other factors—have not yet been carefully studied.[5]

Member-Community Conflicts

Members of collaborative communities want to have the best of both worlds: they want to belong to the local community and at the same time be unhindered—"to live like an insect, free in the world," as one member described it. Community provides many benefits but requires time, effort, and learning to live with others.

Development of a collaborative community can take from about one to four years, and meetings occur at least once a month. For about six to twelve months during the design stage, members can count on meeting a minimum of three times a month, and usually more (from 12 to 40 hours a month). Once they move in, residents spend 8-40 hours a month working to organize the community in the first six months. The larger amount of time is in developments where residents do the finishing work on the common house and landscaping. Once the development is on its feet, residents are usually expected to contribute about 6-8 hours of work each month. Members' time, commitment, and responsibility are a facet of every collaborative community, although they vary from development to development. No development is without requirements.

"Families must not only now have careers and children but also community," said Birte Sorenson (Savværket, Denmark). Members often commute longer distances because of their community location, rearrange their schedules to include cooking or cooperative child care, spend time at meetings, and maintain some level of sociability. Conflicts between their personal requirements and those of the community do clash. Some members find there is less time (and inclination) to see friends outside the community. Others have a difficult time juggling work, family, and community.[6]

A certain amount of individual sovereignty is also restricted by the needs and requirements of the community. Pets are one example of member rights' often running against community desires. The community as a whole can decide that dogs and cats are not permitted, but individual members feel pet ownership is their right. In Stacken, Sweden, several children born in the community were allergic to animals. Although keeping dogs and cats was forbidden, people kept them anyway. In Tradit, a collaborative community in Sweden (near Stacken), animals (particularly cats because they defecate in the children's sandbox) are a big issue. One cat owner explained:

I have to go out with the cat and follow her around for an hour and clean up after her. I *have* to do this. There are many small children, so people can understand their requirements, but there are only three cat owners, so their needs are overruled. I for one don't think children should eat sand. Now I feel I'm told what to do, and I don't like it.

Other communities, such as Jystrup Savværket, are very relaxed about cats and tolerate their use of the children's sandboxes but are more particular about how much time members spend in the community.

On the whole, most communities are easygoing about completing tasks and attending meetings. "We believe those who do their jobs just have the most fun," said a Bryn Gweled member.

The amount of time and energy devoted to community changes over time. Members in collaborative communities are not always outgoing, or social, or contributing to the common good. They cannot sustain a high level of community participation continuously. There is a rhythm, albeit irregular, in residents' being more and less communal. People get together, ideas are discussed, projects accomplished; then the pendulum swings the other way, and people see less of each other and few projects are accomplished until another swing begins.

CONFLICT RESOLUTION
AND EMPOWERMENT

Of course there are problems in living in a group like this. This is not a utopia; we are not here to be free of conflicts. You invite conflicts with a will to solving things. In living apart from your neighbors, there is little or no ability to have conflicts. To me this is a more active way of living. (Bob Fris, of Hilversumse Meent, Holland)

The role of conflicts in collaborative housing is complex although largely beneficial. Conflict allows differences to be aired, adjusts norms and relationships within the group, and helps to establish cohesion.[7] Overcoming problems together also gives residents a sense of accomplishment. Particularly important is that conflict can bring about change, and living collaboratively requires changes in attitudes and habits. "In our life, in our brains, we have to have something to work on," explained a resident. "These things we can't get through; this is in some way the meat of our daily life."

Conflicts in collaborative communities differ from those that occur in a neighborhood. Most collaborative conflicts have to come to a

resolution; otherwise the community feeling slowly disappears, and people spend more time behind closed doors. To find a solution, discussions and a certain amount of compromising is the favored method. In this way, conflicts can often lead to a stronger sense of community.

Not all conflicts are necessarily resolved. Some conflicts are composed of a diversity of mutually contradictory elements and cannot find resolution. Instead residents ignore the situation, try to compromise, or avoid the source of conflict. Although some communities have a formal conflict-resolution process, it is not always successful. In the Commons, conflict resolution could not solve problems arising from cultural and life-style differences.[8] To expect all residents in a community to get along as friends is unrealistic.

Common evening meals and other activities help greatly in bridging differences and

Common dining provides a setting where differences can be discussed and often are appreciated. *(Lilian Bolvinkel)*

misunderstandings that can lead to conflict. Residents can spend time together in a non-threatening way, perhaps chatting over a cup of coffee after dinner. The frequency of such meetings adds to their impact. Differences of values and personalities can be appreciated or at least understood and tolerated more easily. A Swedish collaborative housing resident commented, "I know their personalities and how they will react. She [her next-door neighbor] can be impatient, but you know that; you know what to expect."

As people get to know each other well, the number of conflicts often drops. Alice McCarter of Sunlight, in Oregon, says:

As people know each other's personal patterns, it gives them more leeway in conflicts. If I know someone blows up and cools off, and comes back with a reasonable head, I'm not going to react to the blow-up. That kind of getting to know people relieves conflict. But . . . I may not be his friend.

Another resident tells of her initial belief that people in communities had to live in harmony: "We were a little skeptical and hesitant. What if you didn't agree and didn't get along? Well, we found that you just didn't agree and didn't get along, and that was acceptable."

From what the residents say, one gets the sense that they have been empowered through living in collaborative housing. Many have learned new communication skills to deal with conflict or learned a tolerance of living with conflict. Resident Birgitta Sundelin says:

Living here, I have become more open. I can talk about conflict now. I think it's very good because everyone has the same difficulties, in a way. Nothing new. I nearly got a shock when I first moved in here. People talking about problems. And then the women—they talked about their family relationships so frankly. Oh dear me—that they talk about the family in that way. But it's helped some of the couples who live here. You get so much from talking to others. And you can get along better with your husband; I think so.

Community living is not static. Residents want to live this way because they find value in relationships that involve them. Living collaboratively alters residents. A member of Sunlight calls this

a much saner way to live. I'm *not* a real outgoing gregarious type of person. The community gives me a chance to know others, where before, at first brush, I would discard them. But the community by its very nature continually teaches me that if I hang around long enough to get to know someone, there's a lot there to be found. . . . I'm a manager of a large organization and it's taught me people skills. It really has empowered me.

A number of residents living in collaborative communities have been motivated beyond the areas of the project. By living in a community, they realize the many possibilities that exist for cooperation. For example, residents in Stolplyckan banded together to stop development of a nearby park.

Many communities have gone beyond their initial vision—some changing their shared meals from three times a week to every day. In the Danish community of Trudeslund, most of the residents have bought a vacation home together. Members of Hallehuis in the Netherlands share a car, and in Hilversumse Meent, they share computers. Members also become more involved in the larger neighborhood. Through daily social contact, issues are shared and talked over, and more instead of fewer residents are inspired to local action.[9]

The first generation of children has already grown up in this way of life, and most parents agree it makes for a different kind of child. Adults, too, have begun to grow old together. The first generation living in collaborative housing realizes that as their lives change, so can their community. As the children grow, parents start thinking. In Sunlight, some of the members are talking about perhaps beginning a new community on a flat piece of land, more appropriate for older people. In the Danish community of Æblevangen, resident Berit Ziebell says that the members have started thinking together about their future and a new sense of community:

We don't all agree on what we see far ahead of us. We had a weekend where we talked and set

The children have a common meal together at Jystrup Savværket, Denmark. *(Lilian Bolvinkel)*

goals. Were we going to become one big family and put our accounts all together, or will we stay the way we are? We talked. Should we buy a farm where we could withdraw when we are old or buy a house in the city for the children? We are many families who don't think the same, and it's good we don't have the same feelings and meanings. Yet we know we don't want to be exactly the way we are.

NOTES

1. Territoriality is a pattern of behavior associated with the ownership or occupation of a place or geographic area by an individual or group and may involve personalization and defense against intrusions (Holahan).
2. This is not to say that all members in the Reservoir and in the Commons find these types of communities their ideal. A former member of the Commons feels that such a human mix results in too much diversity and too much conflict. She believes that "there is more than enough cultural differences between any thirty people from the same background."
3. Regardless of whether the community is diverse, all were developed by a fairly homogeneous core group with similar views. In order to survive, beginning groups cannot handle too much diversity of methods or goals. Santa Rosa Creek Commons was developed by a core group of very like-minded members. Once the development and construction was completed, a larger and more diverse membership was incorporated into the existing group. When a nonprofit association develops the housing, such as in the Reservoir in Wisconsin, the groundwork is laid out by professionals. After construction, members are chosen. To overcome the lack of homogeneity among diverse members, a strong leader is required. The director or coordinator of the nonprofit association is such a leader and establishes rules that are followed by members to obtain the housing.
4. This is not because of overt discrimination. In each case, the community has stated its interest in a diverse population. But housing prices have proved to be an effective barrier for the less privileged. The long process of development is another deterrent toward diversity. Those with less dedication, time, and resources eventually drop out, seeking more immediate solutions to their housing problems. Size is another factor. Communities developed by the residents under condominium ownership are usually small—between five and twenty-five households. If 10% of the

units are targeted for low income, that could mean one or two units. Communities attract more or less diversity. Collaborative communities have to go out of their way to attract people different from the core group, a situation parallel with the Danes: "We've found that people don't want to buy into this community unless they have some strong sympathy with this way of living," explained an American collaborator. Although the United States has a diverse population and there is a great housing demand, this does not mean that a diversity of people will necessarily rush to join collaborative housing groups.

5. No matter the tenure, few European communities have a diversity of class, because blue-collar workers have not been strongly attracted to the collaborative concept. Only a handful of elderly can be found in the newer projects, although as the communities age, the number of elderly increases. (Swedish service houses are the exception.)

6. It is debatable whether residents save time living in collaborative communities. Although no long-term study has been completed, the general belief is that time is spent differently. Less time may be spent in running personal chores and more time spent at meetings or socializing. The quality of time, though, would not be equal. Socializing, for example, is preferred to waiting in line at the grocery counter.

7. Researchers have found that conflict helps to establish unity (Coser) and change. The interactionist philosophy, as encapsulated by S. Robbins, states, "Survival can result only when an organization is able to adapt to constant changes in the environment. Adaptation is possible only through change, and change is stimulated by conflict.

8. The effectiveness of conflict resolution appears higher among conflicts of miscommunication and lower among disputes that involve values because they are harder to alter (Robbins).

9. The kind of strength and empowerment that arises from experiencing collective work is not necessarily an idealistic glow of community. A sense of empowerment can be on an individual level or appear in opposition to community—for example, learning building skills and choosing to construct a higher fence around one's garden. The residents of the Danish collaborative communities have a greater than average disposition to sue their architect, even if he or she is a member, because of roof leaks and other problems.

REFERENCES

Coser, Lewis A. 1956. *The Functions of Social Conflict*. Glencoe, Ill.: Free Press.

Holahan, Charles, J. 1982. *Environmental Psychology*. New York: Random House.

Marcus, Clair Cooper. 1986. *Housing as If People Mattered*. Berkeley: University of California Press.

Robbins, Stephen P. 1978. " 'Conflict Management' and 'Conflict Resolution' Are Not Synonymous Terms." *California Management Review* **21**:69.

New Housing Terms

Collaborative Housing (Cohousing) Common areas and facilities—with rooms for shared cooking and dining—combined with private self-contained housing units (including private bathrooms and kitchens). Social and supportive services, such as child and elder care, may be included. An intergenerational mix of residents govern and maintain the housing, with an emphasis on community.

Collective Member- or worker-owned enterprise with three or more people who make decisions democratically.

Commune A community alternative to modern society where new forms of living are tried, such as a reorganization of the family. Popularized in the 1960s as unstructured, often rural retreats.

Congregate Housing Support services such as cooking and cleaning are available from a staff to help residents, often impaired or elderly. Living units are small; some have private baths or partial kitchens. Also in the same building are common spaces for group activities and meals. This type of housing is usually developed and owned by private or public agencies.

Cooperative Housing Private self-contained units with shared ownership of certain common elements, such as the site. Members do not own their units individually; instead they have one membership in the cooperative. A board of directors, made up of members, manages the cooperative. Generally membership is open, although there are cooperatives for specific groups, such as students.

Intentional Community Formed by groups of people who share a commitment to some common purpose (such as personal and social change), often to a transcendental value. Housing, work, and income may be shared or held individually.

Kibbutz A family-oriented type of intentional community developed in Israel where land, housing, and income are held jointly. Members work together on a rotational basis and share meals, child care, and other aspects of daily life.

Service Housing Small flats or hotel-like rooms serviced by a central kitchen with hired staff.

Shared Housing Several people renting or buying housing together. Each person has a private room and shares the rest of the house. Shared housing is subleased or owned by a private or public agency; home sharing implies residential ownership or rental.

A Comparison
of Ownership Types

FEE SIMPLE VERSUS CONDOMINIUM

Condominium ownership is very similar to fee simple (traditional home ownership) except that it provides a legal structure for owning common spaces and for common governance. Fee simple has no built-in mechanism for common interests. Both forms have the same tax advantages and similar individual financing, insurance requirements, and personal liability. Condominium ownership has shared liability of the common areas. Condominiums are governed by a homeowners' association, which decides on rules, collects fees to maintain common areas and the reserve funds, and puts limits on individual rights to alter the unit. Fee simple is free of such limitations.

Very few collaborative communities have been formed under fee-simple ownership. The N Street community is an exception. The main difficulty is that home owners cannot be required to attend meetings or pay for common expenditures. The community depends on the voluntary goodwill of each home owner, which may decrease as home owners move and new owners move in.

Under both of these ownership types, if the housing becomes highly desirable, the value will increase, and only wealthier buyers can afford the housing. Rules by the condominium association to control resale, acceptable buyers or have first right of refusal must be carefully drafted to hold up in a court of law. Such rules may be included but are ordinarily unacceptable when the condominium is sold at market value, except in some subsidized condominiums.

CONDOMINIUMS VERSUS STOCK COOPERATIVES

All other things being equal, cooperatives provide a better mechanism for controlling membership and group participation because the corporation, not individuals, owns the units. A co-op structure provides for strict bylaws, interviewing of new members, and the right of first refusal to the group before a sale.

But all other things are not equal, and there are disadvantages of stock cooperatives in states where they are considered unusual. The main disadvantage is that few banks will provide loans to "unusual ownerships"; therefore interest rates may be higher among the few banks that do, resulting in higher monthly payments. The same can be said for refinancing the building, which may be difficult. In addition low-down-payment government loans may be available to help qualifying individuals obtain housing—but only under certain types of ownership. The resale of the unit is another point to consider. Buyers turning to real estate agents may find them hesitant to recommend an unfamiliar form of ownership. Collaborative housing requires more responsibilities and commitments from members than other developments, and an unusual form of ownership may create further doubt in a buyer's mind.

LIMITED-EQUITY HOUSING COOPERATIVES VERSUS CONDOMINIUMS

The main advantage of limited-equity housing cooperatives (LEHCs) is that they provide permanent affordability. A cap is placed on the amount of profit gained from selling a house. An LEHC is particularly useful for first-time home buyers or for people who otherwise could not qualify for a home loan. The initial share purchase price (down payment) is low, the average monthly cost is low, and the tax benefits may be the same as for traditional home ownership.

The main advantage of condominiums over limited-equity ownership is that members do build up their investment if the units appreciate. An affordable unit for the original owner is sold at a profit, becoming less affordable for the next buyer. Therefore, the down payment and monthly costs rise over time.

In condominiums (and stock cooperatives) both down payment and monthly mortgage payments may appreciate, whereas in an LEHC, only the share value (down payment) appreciates, usually specified under state law. Assume a community with a building that costs $100,000, with a $10,000 down payment (and a $90,000 loan), that has appreciated 10% in one year. Under condominium ownership, the owner has made $10,000 on the original investment (100%). Under LEHC, the owner has made $1,000 on the original investment (10%).

Depending on the state regulations, development of LEHCs can take longer than condominiums. Financing sources for cooperatives may be very limited, and refinancing may be even more difficult and expensive. Government subsidies and loans could potentially lower monthly payments but involve red tape and delays. There is also the possibility that members with more money may drop out because of lower appreciation potential, and the group as a whole would have a lesser chance to qualify for cooperative financing.

In many states, condominium development may be easier to accomplish. Subsidies depend on the income group and restrictions for maintaining that group.

Cooperatives are a much better vehicle for ensuring membership selection and control. For example, the number of renters and their length of tenure can be controlled in an LEHC. Under condominium ownership, renters may become a large portion of the residents. There is little precedence under either ownership for guaranteeing that members participate in common activities.

Sample Design Program

The Public Edge

Creating a recognizable form
Sense of openness or enclosure
Type and number of entrances
Location of car entrances
Linking with the neighborhood
Barriers along busy edges
Areas to be screened

Circulation

Car access on site
Location of main entrances
Location of main parking
Type of circulation paths (centralized, decentralized)
Possibility of vehicle access
Handicapped access

Outdoor Areas

Garden
Wild areas
Semiprivate areas
Gathering areas for small groups

Location of Buildings

Solar access
Group activities

Children's play areas, noisy activities
Quiet zones
No homes feel isolated
Some homes in lower traffic areas
Visual access from homes to common house
Layout promotes single community
Parking close to buildings
Feeling of privacy between units
Cluster homes

Privacy

Private side to houses
Semiprivate outdoor area

Private Dwellings

Desired house location
Distribution of house types
Acoustics and light
Types of extensions
Open or closed floor plan
Size of rooms
Number of stories
Activities that can be moved to common house
Preferred flooring
Formal or informal entrance
Separate entrances for bedrooms
Bathrooms (number, type of ventilation)
Laundry hookups
Storage locations

Source: Muir Commons.

Location of deck or balcony
Size of rear yard
Roofing materials
Facade claddings
Finishing (sweat equity)
Energy considerations
Type of heating system
Ceiling heights
Options (fireplace, air-conditioning, vaulted ceilings, etc.)
Type of front door
Bedroom location
Soundproofing

Common House or Spaces

Types of spaces
Acoustic considerations
Lighting
Flooring
Size of tables

Kitchen size
Pantry
Delivery entrance
Garbage access and removal
Recycling
Number of entrances
Soundproof room
Storage (common and private)
Number of bathrooms
Use by guests
Dance or gym floor
Handicapped access
Emergency preparation storage (for earthquakes, storms, etc.)
Options (wood stove, fireplace, entertainment center, coffee bar, etc.)
Exercise
Work spaces
Electrical current
Garage

Membership Agreement

Muir Commons (MC) welcomes and encourages diversity of membership in race, religion, sex, and age; with the understanding that the purpose of MC is to foster strong community involvement of the residents.

1. MEMBERSHIP

1.1.1 Membership in the Muir Commons group (MCg) is by household, with each member household having one vote. The following guidelines assume that involvement in the group is a reflection of commitment, and that those committed to living in the MCg should be the ones to make the decisions which will affect their community.

1.1.2 Continuous status is defined as the period of time during which membership status has not changed.

1.2 *Voting members* have full and equal rights in the MCg.

1.2.1 *Active voting membership:* to achieve and maintain voting membership a household must:

A) Sign the group's statement of intent.

B) Pay membership dues and any other fees agreed to by the group, as specified in the procedures governing membership dues and fees.

C) Attend 3 meetings per month, of which at least one must be a general meeting. The other two meeting requirements may be met by attending a general meeting, working groups or performing working group tasks.

D) Accept and assent to decisions already reached by the group.

1.2.2 Date of membership shall be the date of the first meeting of the three meetings a household attended which resulted in continuous voting member status, as defined in section 1.1.2. After becoming an active voting member, failure by a household to meet these requirements in any month, including failure to respond to a delinquency notice within 10 days by paying any overdue membership dues or fees, will result in the household's changing from voting member to non-voting member status.

1.2.3 *Membership during an absence.* A voting member may maintain active and continuous membership status during an absence by notifying the membership secretary of the intended period of absence. His/her vote will be considered an abstention during this period unless a proxy vote has been received.

Source: Muir Commons.

1.3 *Non-voting membership.* A household may become a non-voting member by paying and maintaining membership dues. Non-voting members may attend general and working group meetings and will receive mailings. Failure to pay membership dues will result in the household's losing membership in the MCg.

1.3.1 Date of membership will be the date of first dues-paying which resulted in the household's continuous non-voting membership status. Voting members whose status changes to non-voting will carry with them the date of membership as defined in section 1.2.2.

2. DECISION MAKING

2.1.1 Our intention in decision making is to build a consensus among all voting members or quorum for every decision.

2.1.2 Decisions shall be reached only at General Meetings, except design decisions, which may be reached at Design Meetings.

2.2 If we cannot accomplish consensus after reasonable discussion in two meetings, a member may call for a vote. A motion to have a vote must be seconded and carried by a simple majority of those present.

2.3 A quorum consists of 2/3 of current voting members.

2.4 A draft proposal shall be published in the newsletter or distributed to all voting members before being discussed at a general meeting to reflect upon and to propose changes.

2.5 A vote may be taken only if a quorum exists, and a proposal must be passed by 2/3 of the *entire* voting membership.

2.6 If a 2/3 vote is not reached a decision may be held over until the next general meeting. To meet a deadline a special meeting may be called for the vote. In this case, the standard quorum still applies but the advance notice requirement is suspended.

2.7 If a voting member cannot attend a meeting, s/he may extend a proxy vote by contacting two voting members or by sending a written statement explaining h/her position.

If a proxy has been extended, the member shall be considered present for purposes of reaching a quorum.

2.8.1 A verbal vote will be taken by a reading of the current voting member list and recorded by the membership secretary.

2.8.2 In special circumstances, the vote will be anonymous and tallied by two voting members.

2.9.1 Design Meeting agendas shall be set by the Design Committee and communicated to all members via newsletter, General Meeting announcements, or telephone to those absent from the General Meeting.

2.9.2 Design decisions made at Design Meetings shall be made in accordance with the above principles of quorum, consensus, etc.

2.9.3 All design decisions shall be reported at the next General Meeting. New input, questions, and dissent will be taken by a Design Committee member, and a decision may be reconsidered at the next Design Meeting.

3. ORGANIZATIONAL STRUCTURE

3.1.1 The committees and appointed task-persons necessary for the MCg will come out of the *voting membership.*

3.1.2 Participation in the committees and tasks is done voluntarily and can be discontinued by notifying other committee members and finding a replacement, or giving proper notice to the MCg general membership.

3.1.3 Committees and task-persons will report to the general membership. They cannot make final decisions unless specifically directed by the voting membership.

3.2 Coordinating Committee

A) The coordinating committee includes one representative from each working group listed below and two representatives from the voting membership at large.

B) A 3-month commitment to this committee is necessary to ensure efficiency.

C) The commitment will start mid-month with a system of staggered participation to ensure continuity (e.g., two 3-month terms and two 2-month terms).

D) Terms may be served consecutively by a member or rotated.

E) This committee needs to be very flexible. It meets 2-3 days prior to each general meeting in addition to other times as needed.

3.2.1   Tasks of the Coordinating Committee

A) Liaison with WDA & M&D [the developer and design consultants].

B) General MCg correspondence with the public, contractors, etc.

C) Compiles monthly calendar.

D) Prioritizes issues and tasks.

E) Sets agenda for general meetings with input from committees, task-persons, working groups, and voting members.

F) Designates facilitators and minutes takers.

G) Coordinates tasks as needed.

3.3   Working Groups

3.3.1   Design

Subgroups: landscape, playground (more as needed).

3.3.2   Finance/Legal

Subgroups: Bylaws, insurance (more as needed).

3.3.3   Group Process

A) Oversees the direction the group is taking and its efficiency.

B) Makes sure everyone is heard.

C) Keeps the group focused.

D) Makes recommendations to MCg as needed.

E) Develops programming process.

F) Fields grievances.

3.3.4   Communications and Records

A) Is responsible for compiling, editing and sending the semi-monthly newsletter and other mailings to members.

B) Files minutes and reports.

C) Maintains mailing list and phone tree.

D) Compiles newcomer orientation packets.

E) Condenses minutes for the newsletter when necessary.

3.4   Tasks

3.4.1   Membership secretary

A) Maintains voting membership records.

B) Compiles attendance (from minutes).

C) Keeps track of the waiting list.

D) Arranges newcomer orientations and gives out newcomer packets.

3.4.2   Treasurer

A) Collects membership dues and fees agreed to by the group.

B) Sends warnings for overdue dues and fees.

C) Pays MCg bills.

3.4.3   Child care

A) Will be considered as equal to attendance at meeting of same date.

3.4.4   Minutes takers

4. WAITING LIST

4.1   The goal of the waiting list is to create an equitable method of determining which households, at any point, will be guaranteed the opportunity of buying or renting a house in MCg and in what order additional households will be extended that opportunity as houses become available. This method rewards active participation.

4.2   The following criteria shall be considered (in the order listed) for position on the waiting list:

A) Continuous voting members by date of membership, as defined in section 1.2.2.

B) Continuous non-voting members by date of membership, as defined in section 1.3.1.

4.2.5   House selection

A.   Voting member house selection.

When a house becomes available it will be made known to the general membership immediately by phone tree and in the next newsletter. All interested voting members must contact the Waiting list Coordinator (WLC) as soon as possible and a meeting date will be set for these parties by the WLC within two weeks. At this meeting the participants will work out among themselves whatever house exchanges are necessary.

B. Waiting list for non-voting members. Whatever house is available from the above process is to be offered to the member at the top of the waiting list. The household has a maximum of 2 weeks to decide to become a Voting member and accept the available house; knowing that this will allow participation in process A. If the household decides not to become a Voting Member then the second household gets the choice and so on. Where there is a tie for eligibility for Voting membership the relevant parties must meet and decide which household becomes a VM. If an impasse results, a method of random selection will be used and supervised by the Waiting List Coordinator.

4.3 The list shall not be construed to determine the choice of houses within the group of households who buy houses in MCg.

WINSLOW COHOUSING GROUP

Disclosure Statement

I/we have attended three regular business meetings of the Winslow Cohousing Group (WCG) and have received copies of the following records and documents of WCG:

> *Articles of Association*
> *Bylaws*
> *Amended Bylaws*
> *Principles of Consensus Decision-Making*
> *Cost of Membership*
> *Mortgage Qualification Assistance Sheet*
> *Cooperative vs. Condominium Ownership*
> *Estimated Proforma of Development Cost*
> *List of Participating Members*

I/we have been informed of the following records of WCG available for inspection on request:

> *Architects' resumes and work histories*
> *Contract with Architects*
> *Development consultants' resumes and work histories*
> *Contract with Development consultants*
> *Minutes of general meetings*

I/we have read or examined the above and am/are satisfied that WCG has fully disclosed to me/us all the factors regarding the risk of becoming a member active in the management of and contributing to the capitalization of WCG.

I/we also recognize that, should I/we need to withdraw any contribution made to the capital of WCG, such withdrawal may not be possible before a loan is obtained for construction of the project or WCG is dissolved and the property sold.

Signed on _____ , 1989, at _____ , Washington.

_____

_____

Danish, Dutch, and Swedish Collaborative Communities

DANISH COMMUNITIES

Zealland

Name	Location
Åbakken	Strøby
Æblevangen	Målov
Allergi-Fællesskab	Vanløsey
Andedammen	Birkerød
Bakken	Humlebæk
Blikfanget	Birkerød
Blok 12	Farum
Elleslettegard	Vedbæk
Fælleden	Holbæk
Farum	Farum
Fuglsang park	Farum
Hestøbvænge 2	Birkerød
Højtofte	Holte
Ibsgården	Roskilde
Jernstøberiet	Roskilde
Jystrup Savværk	Jystrup
Kæphøj	Roskilde
Karolinelund	Hundested
Bondebjerget 1-4	Odense
Drejerbanken	Vissenbjerg
Gyndbjerg	Bjert
Højby	Morud
Villestofte	Odense

Jutland

Name	Location
A70 Tovstrup Mark	Sporup
Abakken	Abakken, Stroby
Ådalen I & II	Randers
Almennytt. Bofællesskab	Skive
Andelsboliger Med Landbr.	Viby J
Anderlsbyen I Skive	Skive
Asgård	Skive
Askebakken	Nørre Sundby
Blåhøj	Arhus
Bofaelleded	Beder
Bofaellesskab 83	Århus
Drivhuset	Randers
Engesvang	Silkeborg
Fladengrund	Esbjerg
Frugthaven	Skørping
Gjesingnord	Esbjerg
Kilen	Valby
Klinteby	Fakse Ladeplads
Lerbjerg Lod	Hillerød
Margrethehåb	Roskilde
Nørgård Plantage	Værløse
Økologisk Landsbysamfund	Hundested

Name	Location	Name	Location
Otium	Birkerød	Solfang	Fredericia
Sættedammen	Hillerød	Sonden Ud	Beder
Skråplanet	Ballerup	Stautrup 2 & 3	Risskov
Slagslunde	Stenløse	Thorshammer	Skive
Sneglebo	Roskile	Tingstedet	Herning
Stanvsbåndet	Farum	Toustrup Mark	Sporup
Stejlepladsen	Holbæk	True Byvej 23	Mundelstrup
Stokken	Jyderup	Uldalen	Nørre Sundby
Tinggården	Herfølge	Vadestedet	Ry
Tornevangs	Birkerød	Væksthuset	Skødstrup
Trudeslund	Birkerød	Valmuen	Hjortshøj
Tubberup Vænge	Herlev	Vejgård Bymidte	Ålborg
Våningsstedgård	Karlslunde	Vestenvinden	Ribe
		Vidjekær	Skanderborg
		Vildrosen	Beder

The Island of Fyn

Name	Location
Blangstedgård	Odense
BOF	Odense
Grønmosegård	Skødstup
Grusgraven	Hinnerup
Gug	Ålborg
Gyldenmuld	Skanderborg
Gyndbjerg	Bjert
Håndværkerparken	Højbjerg
Hjarup	Haderslev
Højvang	Vester Tværvei
Jerngården	Århus
Kamillelunden	Hjortshøj
Kirkebakken	Beder
Klokkehøjen	Risskov
Kolbøtten	Åbenrå
Lille Grundet	Vejle
Lynghoved	Ry
Mejdal 1 & 2	Holsterbro
Midgården	Beder
Milepælen	Beder
Møllegården	Mårslet
Nonbo Hede	Viborg
Nova	Horsens
Overdrevet	Hinnerup
Regnbuen	Fredericia
Snåstrup Mølle	Brabrand
Sol og Vind	Beder

For further information contact:

Lansforeningen af Bofællesskaber
Hans S. Andersen
Trudeslund 2
3460 Birkerød
Denmark

Lansforeningen af Bofællesskaber
Hans Jørgen Petersen
Skelagervej 431
8200 Århus N
Denmark

Danish Building Research Institute
Cohousing Information
Postboks 119
DK-2970 Hørsholm
Denmark

DUTCH COMMUNITIES

Name	Location
Amstelveen	Amstelveen
Anna Bijnshof	Oestgeest
Arnhem	Arnhem
Aurijn	Hoorn
Banier	Rotterdam
Beuk	Rotterdam

Name	Location
Bijvanck	Buizen
Breda	Breda
Cayenne	Nieuwegein
Delft	Delft
Drielandenhuis	Haarlem
Emmen	Emmen
Gerestraat	Leiden
Heemskerk	Heemskerk
Heerd	Groningen
Hestia	Lelystad
Het Woonschap	Westervoort
Het Punt	Wageningen
Het Hallehuis	Amersfoort
Hilversumse Meent	Hilversum
Hofstede	Doetinchem
Jozefhuis	Hoorn
Kerkrade	Kerkrade
Klopvaart	Utrecht
Lelystad	Lelystad
Lismortel	Eindhoven
Maasniel	Roermond
Meenthe	Tilburg
Mienskiplik Wenjen	Sneek
Nieuwegein	Nieuwegein
Opaalstraat	Nijmegen
Pionier	Vlaardingen
Regenboog	Alkmaar
Rensumaheerd	Groningen
Rups	Alkmaar
Spijkenisse	Spijkenisse
't Vierschaar	Apeldoorn
't Oud Armenhuis	Leeuwarden
't Houtwijk	Den Haag
Uithoorn	Uithoorn
Vught	Vught
Wezwa	Utrecht
Winihoes	Groningen
Witte boom	Den haag
Woongroep de wierden	Almere
Woonkollektief Purmerend	Purmerend
Zaandam	Zaandam
Zevenkamp	Rotterdam
Zoetermeer	Zoetermeer
Zwartehandspoort	Leidne
Zwolle	Zwolle

For further information contact:

Landelijek Vereniging Centraal Wonen (LVCW)
Grenadadreef 1-J
3563 HE Utrecht
The Netherlands

SWEDISH COMMUNITIES

Stockholm Area

Name	District
Flygtrafiken	Skarpnäck
Fristad	Spänga
Hässelby familjehotell	Vällingby
Katthuvudet	Södermalm
Kupan	Alvsjö
Orion	Fruängen
Prästgärdshagen	Alvsjö
Rio	Gärdet
Södra Station	Sodermalm
Stacken	Göteborg
Svärdet	Södermalm
Taljan	Gröndal
Trekanten	Liljeholmen
Vildkornet	Hässelby Villastad

Outside Stockholm

Name	Location
Arken	Uppsala
Blenda	Uppsala
Blomstret	Gåvle
Fabriken	Jönköping
Fortuna	Helsingborg
Fullt hus	Buddinge
Lergöken	Södertälje
Nålmakaren	Eskilstuna
Oxbacken	Västerås
Prästgärdsmarken	Väsby
Regnbågen	Lund
Slottet	Lund
Södervärn	Malmö

Name	*Location*	For further information contact:
Solbringen	Karlskoga	"Kollektivhus Nu!"
Stacken	Göteborg	% Axel Ruhe
Stolplyckan	Linköping	Kollektivhuset Stacken
Trädet	Göteborg	Teleskopgatan 2
Tunnan	Borås	S-41518 Göteborg
Yxan 3	Landskrona	Sweden

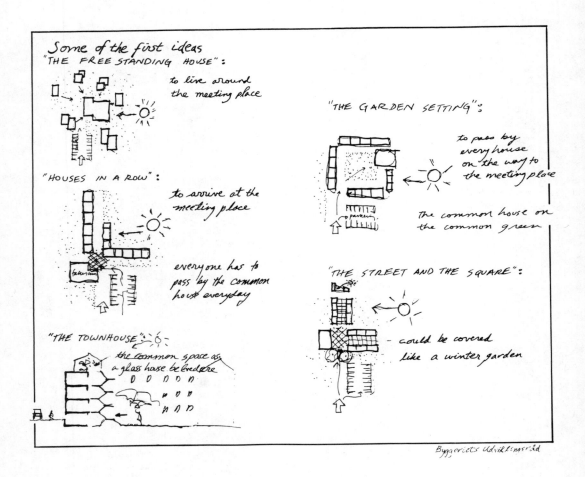

Some of the first ideas

"THE FREE STANDING HOUSE":

to live around
the meeting place

"HOUSES IN A ROW":

to arrive at the
meeting place

everyone has to
pass by the common
house everyday

"THE TOWNHOUSE":

the common space as
a glass house be lived here

"THE GARDEN SETTING":

to pass by
every house
on the way to
the meeting place

The common house on
the common green

"THE STREET AND THE SQUARE":

- could be covered
like a winter garden

Byggeriets Udviklingsråd

APPENDIX F

Diagrams of Communities

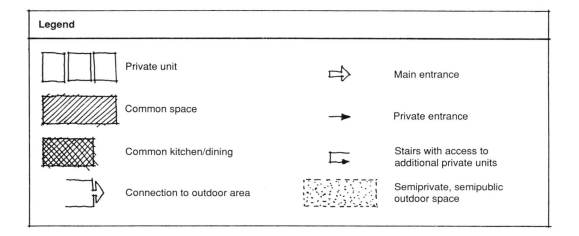

Legend

Private unit		Main entrance	
Common space		Private entrance	
Common kitchen/dining		Stairs with access to additional private units	
Connection to outdoor area		Semiprivate, semipublic outdoor space	

The illustrations of Tinggården, Sawærket, Hilversumse Meent, Het Hallehuis, Stacken, and Stolplyckan are from Jürgen Schuh, 1989, *Kollektives Wohnen, Eine ver-* *gleichende Untersuchung in — und Ausländischer Beispiele*, Gesamthochschule Kassel, Germany: Fachbereich Architekture.

DENMARK

Sættedammen, Denmark

City: Hillerød
Built: 1972
Units: 27
Architects: Teo Bjerg and
 Palle Dyreborg
Ownership: Condominium

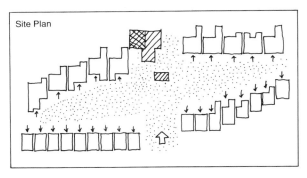

Site Plan

Tinggården, Denmark

City: Herfølge
Built: 1 during 1977/1979
      2 during 1983/1984
  (built in phases)
Units: 1 has 79, plus
  16 supplementary rooms
    2 has 76, plus
  14 supplementary rooms
Architects: Tegnestuen Vandkunsten
  and Karsten Vibild
Ownership: Nonprofit rental

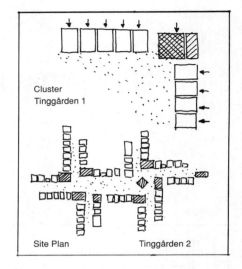

Savværket, Denmark

City: Jystrup
Built: 1984
Units: 21
Architect: Tegnestuen Vandkunsten
Ownership: Cooperative

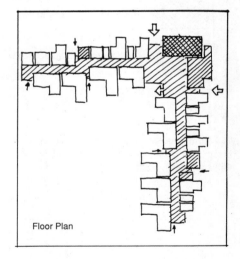

Kilen, Denmark

City: Østerhøj
Built: 1989
Units: 21
Architects: Colon & Gudmand-Høyer
Ownership: Cooperative

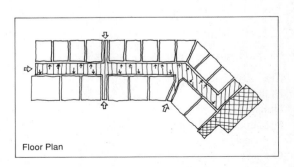

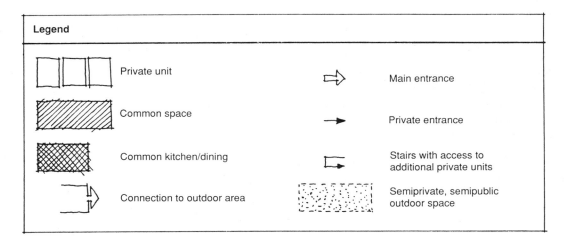

Legend

Private unit

Common space

Common kitchen/dining

Connection to outdoor area

Main entrance

Private entrance

Stairs with access to additional private units

Semiprivate, semipublic outdoor space

HOLLAND

Het Hallehuis, Holland

City: Amersfoort
Built: 1984
Units: 31 studios and
     22 rooms
Architect: Dolf Floors
Ownership: Nonprofit rental

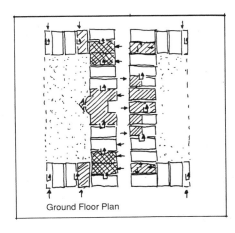

Ground Floor Plan

Hilversumse Meent, Holland

City: Hilversum
Built: 1977
Units: 50
Architects: Leo de Jonge and
     Pieter Weeda
Ownership: Nonprofit rental

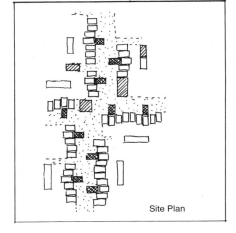

Site Plan

Het Punt, Holland

City: Wageningen
Built: 1985
Units: 56
Architects: Hellinga/Treffers and
   Polgár
Ownership: Nonprofit rental

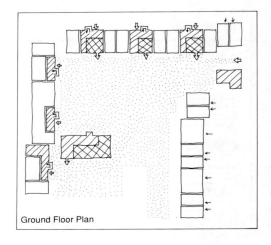

Ground Floor Plan

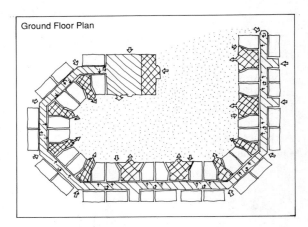

Ground Floor Plan

Purmerend, Holland

City: Purmerend
Built: 1985
Units: 71
Architect: Jan Verhoeven
Ownership: Nonprofit rental

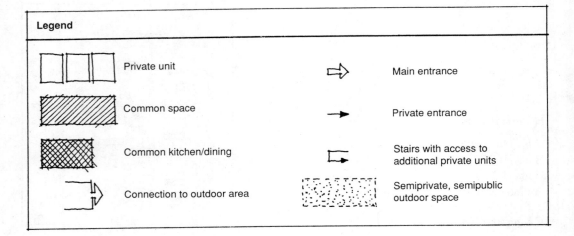

Legend

Private unit	Main entrance
Common space	Private entrance
Common kitchen/dining	Stairs with access to additional private units
Connection to outdoor area	Semiprivate, semipublic outdoor space

SWEDEN

Stacken, Sweden

City: Gothenburg
   (Göteborg-Bergsjörn)
Built: 1980
Units: 33
Architect: Lars Ågren
Ownership: Nonprofit rental

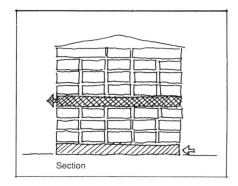

Section

Trädet, Sweden

City: Gothenburg
   (Göteborg-Kortedala)
Built: 1985
Units: 38
Architect: Clæsson Carlsson
   Arkitekter AB
Ownership: Nonprofit rental

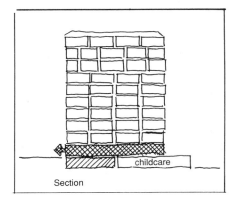

Section

Katthuvudet, Sweden

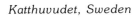

City: Stockholm
Built: 1986
Units: 26
Architects: Ville Herlin
Ownership: Cooperative

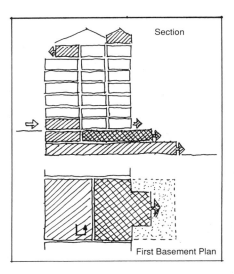

Section

First Basement Plan

Stolplyckan Service House, Sweden

City: Linköping
Built: 1980
Units: 184
Architects: Höjer and Ljungquist
Ownership: Nonprofit rental

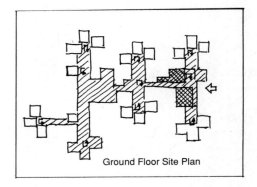

Ground Floor Site Plan

Legend

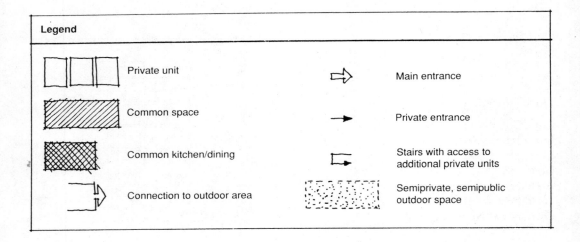

Private unit	Main entrance
Common space	Private entrance
Common kitchen/dining	Stairs with access to additional private units
Connection to outdoor area	Semiprivate, semipublic outdoor space

UNITED STATES

Sunlight, U.S.

City: Portland, Oregon
Built: 1978/1979
  (built in phases)
Units: 15
Architects: Church & Maslen
Ownership: Condominium

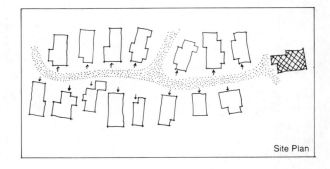

Site Plan

Santa Rosa Creek Commons, U.S.

City: Santa Rosa, California
Built: 1982
Units: 27
Architects: Jacobsen, Silverstein
  and Winslow
Ownership: Limited equity
  cooperative

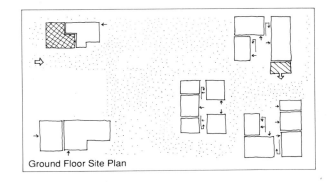

Ground Floor Site Plan

The Reservoir, U.S.

City: Madison, Wisconsin
Built: 1988
Units: 28
Architect: Design Coalition
Ownership: Leasing Cooperative

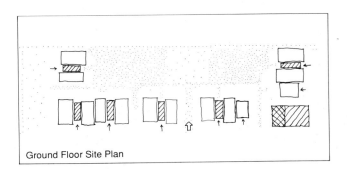

Ground Floor Site Plan

Muir Commons, U.S.

City: Davis, California
Built: 1991
Units: 26
Architect: Dean F. Unger
Ownership: Condominium

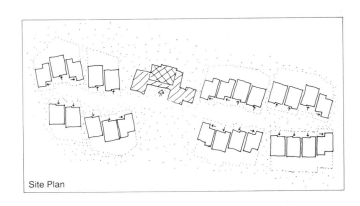

Site Plan

Glossary

Appraisal The market value of a property as estimated by a professional appraiser.

Appreciation The rise of a property's value; often caused by inflation or demand and not attributed to property improvements.

Assessment (Operating) Proportionate share of the annual budgeted cost to maintain the common areas and to maintain sufficient reserves to assure financial stability.

Building Code Ordinances adopted by city or state to regulate health, safety, and welfare through control of design, construction, use, and occupancy.

Child Care Caring for small children while the parent(s) are otherwise occupied.

Cluster Housing Housing grouped into a clustered pattern.

Common Area (Space) Usually all of a development that is not specifically delineated and described as dwelling units or space for private use.

Common Expenses Sums assessed against the residents for repair or replacement of common amenities and facilities, maintenance, administration, and other agreed-upon expenses.

Community A group of people living close to one another and sharing certain common ideas, interests, or backgrounds.

Condominium A form of ownership in a multiunit development in which separate units are owned by individual owners, with joint ownership of common areas.

Congregate Housing A housing development, usually for the elderly, with a central dining facility that provides meals and with small living units, some or all without kitchens. Developed and managed by a sponsor.

Construction Loan A loan to finance construction. A completed building requires permanent financing.

Consultant A professional retained to assist in the development of a project.

Contractor A builder who is hired to construct, usually from an architect's drawings. A general contractor hires subcontractors, who work on the various components of the construction project.

Cooperative Housing Housing owned mutually by residents through purchasing a share in the co-op corporation. The residents pay rent on their separate unit, which is their share of the mortgage payments, maintenance, and utilities. In a limited-equity co-op, the purchase price is kept low, through re-sale restrictions and the units remain affordable over time.

Cost per Square Foot   The development price divided by the total floor area.

Day Care   A place set aside with facilities and equipment for watching and caring for small children. See *Child care.*

Density   The average number of housing units per acre of land. The higher the density, the greater the number of units.

Department of Housing and Urban Development (HUD)   A federal department that provides assistance for developing housing and communities.

Detached House   A house for a single family not attached to any other house—for example, a suburban home.

Developer   A for-profit or nonprofit investor or agency who provides the necessary organization and financing for the housing development process.

Displacement   Rehabilitation efforts by a higher-income group that render a neighborhood unaffordable to the previous residents, typically a lower-income group.

Down Payment   Money paid to a purchaser by a buyer to secure the purchase.

Dwelling Unit   A living space with cooking facilities occupied by only one household.

Equity   Increase in value of ownership interest in the unit as the owner reduces debt by paying the mortgage; often calculated as the market value minus the existing loans.

Fair Market Value   The highest price that can be obtained for a property on the market.

Floor Area   The total floor area measured to the outside of exterior walls.

Home Owners' Association   An association of home owners that governs the use and maintenance of the common property.

Inclusionary Zoning   Requiring a percentage of affordable units in a new residential development of a certain size.

Infill   Available land in an already developed area or neighborhood.

Land Trust   A trust set up to preserve land for a certain purpose—either as sites for affordable housing or open space—usually with the intention not to sell.

Lien   A claim recorded against a property as security for payment of a debt.

Limited-Equity Cooperative Housing   See *Cooperative housing.*

Live/Work   A space used in part for residential purposes and in part for nonresidential purposes, such as a business or artistic enterprise.

Low Income   Families or individuals who do not exceed 80% of the median income in an area, as determined by the Department of Housing and Urban Development.

Moderate Income   Families or individuals whose income ranges from 80% to 120% of the median income for an area, as determined by the Department of Housing and Urban Development.

Nonconforming Use   A type of use for a development that does not conform to the regulations.

Nonprofit Organization   A type of corporation that is organized for a not-for-profit purpose and cannot earn profits for the benefit of a particular shareholder.

Open Space   Areas that are left natural rather than built up.

Partnership   A type of ownership in which two or more people share the benefits and the risks.

Planned Unit Development (PUD)   A type of zoning in which there is flexibility to cluster housing units, include commercial development, and create common open space in one subdivision.

Pre-development Loans   A loan that finances land acquisition, the site plans and soil tests, the preliminary architectural designs, and fees prior to building.

Public Housing Affordable housing units available to low-income families who cannot afford market rate housing.

PUD *See Planned unit development.*

Rehabilitation Restoring deteriorated buildings to like-new conditions; can involve remodeling, use conversion, and structural and other improvements.

Row House or Townhouse Dwelling units attached in a row vertically, each with a private entrance.

Rural Development Housing built in the open country or within a town outside an urban area.

Section An architectural drawing showing a cross-section through a building, as though it was sliced in half vertically by a knife.

Section 8 Housing A Department of Housing and Urban Development program that provides housing assistance payments by making up the difference between the resident's payment and the cost of the unit.

Site Plan A bird's-eye view of a property showing the placement of buildings, the landscaping, and site improvements, such as roads.

Subdivision A parcel of land divided into lots, usually fifty or more.

Subsidy Lowering the cost of housing through grants from the government or from other funding sources.

Suburb An area outside the central city with lower-density housing development.

Undivided Interest The joint ownership of common areas in which the individual percentages are known but are not applied to separate the areas physically.

Urban Area A metropolitan area with a population of 200,000 or more.

Zoning Division of land into districts or zones with particular land uses permitted.

Index